MALCOM IS MISSING

MALCOM IS MISSING

A TRUE STORY OF MURDER AND A DAUGHTER'S QUEST FOR JUSTICE IN MEXICO

BY ROBERT OSBORNE

RMB

First Edition

For information on purchasing bulk quantities of this book, or to obtain media excerpts or invite the author to speak at an event, please visit rmbooks.com and select the "Contact" tab.

RMB | Rocky Mountain Books Ltd.
rmbooks.com
@rm_books
facebook.com/rmbooks

Cataloguing data available from Library and Archives Canada
ISBN 9781771607377 (softcover)
ISBN 9781771607384 (electronic)

Editor: Peter Midgley

Printed and bound in Canada

We would like to take this opportunity to acknowledge the Traditional Territories upon which we live and work. In Calgary, Alberta, we acknowledge the Niitsítapi (Blackfoot) and the people of the Treaty 7 region in Southern Alberta, which includes the Siksika, the Piikuni, the Kainai, the Tsuut'ina, and the Stoney Nakoda First Nations, including Chiniki, Bearpaw, and Wesley First Nations. The City of Calgary is also home to Métis Nation of Alberta, Region III. In Victoria, British Columbia, we acknowledge the Traditional Territories of the Lkwungen (Esquimalt and Songhees), Malahat, Pacheedaht, Scia'new, T'Sou-ke, and W̱SÁNEĆ (Pauquachin, Tsartlip, Tsawout, Tseycum) peoples.

We acknowledge the financial support of the Government of Canada through the Canada Book Fund and the Canada Council for the Arts, and of the province of British Columbia through the British Columbia Arts Council and the Book Publishing Tax Credit.

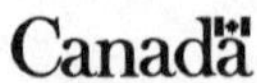

CONTENTS

ACKNOWLEDGEMENTS

I have to admit right up front that I have a love/hate relationship with Mexico. I love the art, the music, the food and, most especially, the people. I consider Mexico City to be one of the most dynamic places in the world to visit. But balancing that out, I can't be blind to the massive amount of corruption and crime that is endemic to the country – particularly in its justice system. I've done more than half a dozen documentaries on Canadians whose lives have gone off the rails as a result of a corrupt justice system in Mexico. Needless to say, that tempers my enthusiasm for the country, but it doesn't totally undermine all the facets I truly love. When people ask me if I'll go back and visit, I always say yes, but I keep my eyes wide open to what could happen and I take every precaution to prevent it.

Having gotten that off my chest, now I'd like to thank the dozens of people who went out of their way to help with this book and the documentary that came before it. A few deserve a special note of thanks. And those thanks have to start with Brooke Mullins and her two daughters. If they had not been willing to let us into their lives neither the documentary nor this book would have gotten off the ground. And letting us into their lives meant a great deal of sacrifice: I was on the phone to Brooke nearly every day for more than a year, checking out details, asking her to provide documents, and working with her to double-check every fact. We had Brooke engaged in filming activities for weeks. That occupied an enormous amount of her time – time she was unable to spend with her daughters. I am very aware of that sacrifice and I can't tell them how grateful I am for all they gave.

I also think Brooke's former partner, Zab Vanderhyden, deserves a special mention. He stood by Brooke for many years during this ordeal and was there to help out during the documentary at a moment's notice, despite the fact that he was trying to keep his restaurant alive during the COVID pandemic. A second note of thanks for his wonderful food. He gave me a whole new appreciation for kale.

I think our fixer in Mexico, Gabriel Cosio, also deserves a special shout-out. Gabriel is a working journalist in that country and anyone who can read a headline knows what that can mean. He risks his life on a regular basis to get his work done. Gabriel was there for us as a constant support for any aspect of the project that took place in Mexico, whether it was acting as our fixer when we were filming, translating complex legal documents for me during research, or just being an ear to bend when I needed an opinion.

Kate Crawford and her two children also deserve a nod of thanks for their help throughout the process. Robb Stasyshyn and Patti Kerr likewise deserve mention for their support, as do both my wife, Jari, and my daughter Alexa for their unfailing support for both projects – my talented wife was the co-producer, writer, and director of the documentary.

And, finally, I'd like to thank the many people in Mexico who helped out on both of these projects, often at some risk to their own safety. They never seemed to hesitate to step forward and offer us assistance. Thank you.

PROLOGUE

Puerto Vallarta could never be described as a quiet city. Not by me. It seems to be on the move almost 24 hours a day. And along the main routes the traffic is brutal. The last time I was there filming, I began to dread the daily commutes between our hotel near the airport and the downtown – about ten kilometres that sometimes took up to 45 minutes. And nowhere is that constant bustle more apparent than in what is called the Romantic District. For those who have never been to Puerto Vallarta, a little context. Of course, the Romantic District is the oldest part of the city – one that still features some cobblestone streets and a couple of very nice old colonial-era buildings. The cathedral in particular is rather nice. It's a relatively recent structure – from the 1940s – but its red-brick walls tower over the surrounding streets and the onion-shaped dome on the top of the tallest spire is quite dramatic – angels holding up a crown. I've also always kind of liked the boardwalk along the beach. But then again, I'm a sucker for a walk along the ocean. As for the rest of the Romantic District, I think it can be summed up in a couple of words: loud and bright. About ten square blocks of the old part of the city that have morphed into a slice of what might be called the more garish side of Mexican culture. Kind of what a ride might look like at an Orlando theme park called "Mexican World." Think of a cliché and you'll find it down there – up to and including sombreros and brightly coloured blankets. Go down there any time of day and it's always hopping with activity. The nighttime takes on an even more surreal look. The area blossoms with countless bars, nightclubs, souvenir shops, pharmacies, and restaurants, all set against a backdrop of neon signs – flashing reds and greens and intense purples scattered along the streets. It's not unusual to see someone standing on the sidewalk offering rides on a donkey. Signs for a myriad of prescription drugs (available across the counter) abound – erectile dysfunction drugs, sedatives, pain killers, antibiotics, steroids…you name it and you can probably get it down there. The stores sell an assortment of cheap trinkets – lots of Day of the Dead souvenirs. The sound is a little overwhelming as well – a constant din of traffic noise. The drivers are not the least bit shy about using their horns. And coming from every bar and restaurant, a blast of music, with each place seeming to compete with the other for dominance.

The area is packed with tourists, night and day. And, truth be told, they all seem to be enjoying themselves. Interestingly, I've observed there are a number of subspecies of tourists in Puerto Vallarta. There is a strong contingent of gay men and women who love the city. According to the website, Gay Puerto Vallarta Travel Guide, the city is known as the San Francisco of Mexico and was "Gay Travel Approved" by the site in 2017. The site says,

> Zona Romantica the city's Castro district. Packed with dance clubs, more than 20 gay-friendly bars, saunas, gay boat tours, cabarets, a gay beach, a gay bar hopping tour, and a thriving arts and culture scene, it's the official gayborhood in Puerto Vallarta. If you're looking for your time in Puerto Vallarta to be gay-centric, you never have to leave Zona Romantica.[1]

But Puerto Vallarta has a much more cosmopolitan mix than just gay people. There's also the "all-inclusive" set. Tourists from cruise ships who are in the city for a day or others who are at a resort for a week or two. They all wander around in their uniform cargo shorts and T-shirts (for men) and sundresses (for women). Look for the bright red burned flesh to pick them out of the crowd. Then there are the expats: American and Canadian men and women who've moved down here either permanently or who come for six months of the year to avoid the winters up north. It's harder to spot this group. They spend a lot of time down here so they tend to blend in – nice tans, reasonable clothing, and often they won't be hanging around in the more touristy areas; you'll find them at out-of-the-way bespoke bars and cafés they've adopted over the years. One of the give-aways for expats is either an older woman with a much younger Mexican man or an older man squiring a young woman around. That's what Malcom Madsen was. He was an expat who lived here for a good chunk of the year. He was also a 68-year-old man who'd met a young woman down in Puerto Vallarta and had built a life around her: they shared a house, Malcom picked up all the bills, and Marcela Acosta Ramos provided company. Malcom had been her lover and benefactor for several years.

On the night of October 27, 2018, Malcom and Marcela were out on the town celebrating her birthday early, since she was turning 44 in four days' time. Marcela wouldn't be in town on her birthday, so Malcom wanted to make this evening special. They planned to have dinner on the beach at their favourite restaurant, the Blue Shrimp, and then drinks at one of their favourite clubs, Andales. Marcela dressed well for the evening, putting on a frilly pink taffeta dress and high heels. Malcom, whose normal wardrobe didn't extend far beyond shorts and T-shirts, also went for something a little dressier. He wore a blue short-sleeved dress shirt and loose-fitting black slacks. They also both wanted to enjoy a few margaritas throughout the evening, so rather than take Malcom's van, Marcela decided to call an Uber. Oddly, according to Malcom's daughter, Brooke, he didn't call the car service himself, as he usually did. Instead, "Martín, Marcela's brother, paid for an Uber to pick them up to go out that night." Brooke was never sure what, if anything, that little gesture meant. Maybe it was just Martín being considerate towards Malcom and his sister. Maybe it meant Martín had other plans for the van.

The Blue Shrimp has a kind of Gilligan's Island feel to it (for a more contemporary comparison, you might think about the set of the tribal councils on *Survivor*). The outside looks as if it would fit better on some Polynesian island. The interior features lofty thatched ceilings held up by large bare wooden logs and beams. There's a nautical theme to the place and it's filled with tchotchkes of various kinds – a dugout canoe with a mermaid sitting in it; life-sized sharks and reef fish hang from the ceiling; a stuffed pelican sits in one corner, overlooking the whole restaurant. Part of the restaurant spills out on to the adjacent beach. If you choose to dine al fresco and you're eating there at sunset, I'm told you stand an excellent chance of seeing a spectacular lighting display over the ocean. Apparently, the food is excellent. It's a favourite of the expat community in Puerto Vallarta and as the name suggests, they specialize in seafood, particularly shrimp.

It's possible to be very specific about what time Marcela and Malcom arrived at the Blue Shrimp. Their cell phone records show the two were at home until around 9 p.m. They arrived at the Blue Shrimp around 9:30 p.m., and they were there for approximately two hours. According to Marcela, Malcom hit the booze pretty hard (though his friends say he was never much of a drinker). Oddly, there were no witnesses who placed the two of them at the restaurant, even though they knew the manager and some of the staff well, so we can't be sure about what condition Malcom was in when he left. Their next stop that evening was their favourite bar and we know a great deal of what happened there.

About a two-minute walk from the Blue Shrimp is another popular expat stop in the Romantic District, Andales Restaurant and Bar. This isn't one of those quiet spots. It fits with the ambience of the rest of the Romantic District – loud and bright. It spills out on to the sidewalk that runs past the bar so there's just as much activity outside as inside. And remember that donkey I mentioned earlier? Well, Andales actually does have a man with a donkey standing outside the place as part of the attraction. The place is usually filled with regulars. Marcela and Malcom arrived at 11:20 p.m. How do we know that? Because we have access to the footage from the security cameras inside the bar. The footage has a time stamp on one corner, so it's possible to know what happened, and when, at this bar with unerring accuracy.

The place was packed, but Marcela and Malcom soon found a table, coincidentally (luckily?) situated right under one of the cameras. They ordered a couple of tourist-size margaritas and settled down for the evening. On the footage, they don't seem to be chatting very much – they just sit there sipping on their drinks. At one point Malcom leaves for the bathroom. When he comes back, he seems to have scratched his head and he keeps tamping at it with a Kleenex. Marcela also goes to the washroom at some point. They don't stay long. Just over an hour later, the two are seen walking out the door. They walk over to a taxi stand and get into one. Marcela has clearly asked for their drinks to go, since she's carrying two take-out cups. They exit the camera screen at 12:29 a.m. on Sunday, October 28, 2018.

And that is the last time Malcom Madsen is ever seen.

Virtually everyone involved in this story agrees on those basic facts about the evening. Not much debate is possible when there's actual video footage. But accounts about what happened afterwards and why and how Malcom disappeared are as varied as the people who relay the stories, as varied as the people who are engaged in the story. If you believe Marcela, she and Malcom took a taxi home and went to bed. Malcom left for his tree house the next day and was never seen again. But if you believe Brooke, then what happened after Andales was a twisted story of greed and murder – one in which her father was kidnapped and his body dismembered and hidden so that no trace of him has ever been found. Brooke has been trying to prove her version of events is the true version and she's spent the years since her father's death working virtually full-time to do that. Without any training, she set about investigating the disappearance of her father and trying to convince, cajole, and sometimes browbeat one of the most corrupt judicial systems on the planet into listening to her, examining what she found, and acting on that information.

This is her story.

CHAPTER ONE

MISSING

Finding this story was really a matter of chance, with perhaps a dash of journalistic instinct. In the summer of 2020, I was in Vancouver spending a little time scuba diving and visiting friends. One morning I opened up the local paper and buried in the middle was a couple of paragraphs that told a vague story about a woman from Port Hope, Ontario, trying to find her missing father. It gave her name – Brooke Mullins – but few details. But something about the story resonated. During a long career as a journalist, I've found that stories that get buried by one news organization can often turn out to be the most intriguing. So I went online and found Brooke's Facebook (now Meta) page, *Justice for Malcom*. While scrolling through the posts, I became more and more interested in her story. Here was a woman who had decided to virtually single-handedly take on the Mexican justice system – in my experience a notoriously corrupt system that often seemed more interested in making money from bribes than dispensing justice. This had the potential to be a great story. The next day I had the first of many long conversations with Brooke. By the end of that first conversation, my partner Jari and I were convinced this was an excellent idea for a documentary. We arranged to meet with Brooke once we returned to Toronto.

So, on a warm September morning, Jari and I got in our car and headed for Port Hope. We were both looking forward to finally meeting Brooke. But I was also a little curious about the town. Port Hope may be best known as the location where the Canadian government is engaged in a massive cleanup of low-level radioactive waste left from a radium and uranium refinery operated by a Crown corporation called Eldorado Nuclear.

Some reports say it left some two million cubic metres of contaminated soil. The government has long argued that the waste presents no risk to the health of the community, but many don't buy that argument and so, bit by bit, contaminated soil is being scraped up and disposed of. The ultimate goal is to leave Port Hope completely free of the problem, but there's no firm timeline to accomplish this goal. An hour east of Toronto, I pulled off the freeway into Port Hope. It's not much to look at when you first exit the highway – some gas stations, a chain hotel, and a couple of the usual fast-food joints that are endemic to every town in Canada. Since we were early, we decided we would take a look at the downtown. As I drove in, the place started to look a whole lot nicer: a lot of beautiful old red-brick houses on quiet tree-lined streets. But it was the downtown that really charmed me. Like a snapshot from a tourist brochure put out by the Ontario government. It was classic small-town Ontario. A lovely main street sided by neat-looking two- and three-storey buildings, with the bottom storey given over to a number of boutique stores – bookshops, antique stores, and a lot of nice-looking cafés and restaurants. The buildings probably dated back to the late 1800s or early 1900s. There is a fast-flowing river that cuts through the east end of downtown and to my delight, when I peeked over the railing, I noticed the stream was churning with migrating salmon. The banks were lined with fishers casting into the mass of fish who seemed oblivious to the hooks, working intently to navigate the series of waterfalls they had to overcome to get upstream. We walked up one side of the main street and down the other, looking in the windows of the stores. A couple of side streets branched off from the main drag – equally rustic and similarly populated with charming shops. Port Hope was an unexpected, delightful discovery. A place where I could conceivably spend some time. If the documentary went ahead, I'd hopefully be spending quite a bit of time in town.

It was time to meet Brooke. Her home is a well-kept Victorian structure – a large red-brick house dating back to the 1800s (I would guess) on a large property. I knocked on the door and Brooke answered. She is a tall, willowy blonde with a shock of long curly hair and penetrating blue eyes. She has a warm smile and was stylishly dressed and well coiffured (something I would learn was the norm for Brooke). Critics have dismissed Brooke as being what one of my friends calls a "trustafarian" – that is, someone who comes from money and who has never faced any hard realities in life. And, certainly, Brooke does spend time socializing with friends who seem equally well-heeled, her children go to private school, and she drives an expensive car and lives in a beautiful house. But if that was as far as your analysis of Brooke went, you would be missing the mark considerably. Beneath that well-presented surface lies a woman with a penetrating intelligence, a steel backbone, and an unwavering determination. She has the focus of a heat-seeking missile when she sets her mind to something. She is fiercely protective and loving towards her two girls and prides herself on her unwavering loyalty to her friends and family. Once I got to know Brooke, I realized those initial superficial impressions meant very little in terms of what kind of a person she really was. She has at her core all the qualities that would be essential when it came time for her to take on one of the most corrupt and indifferent justice systems in the world. There's another defining quality that drives Brooke – a need to connect with her father, a need to be recognized by him as someone special. That need was denied to her when she was young and cruelly taken away from her just as she and her father were really starting to connect when she was an adult. It's a loss she keenly feels.

To understand how that need arose in Brooke, I think it's necessary to know a little bit about Malcom. I'll take a deeper dive into him later but for now, a few highlights. Some might call Malcom Madsen a free spirit. Others might be less charitable. Slender and with a shock of curly brown hair, he'd spent much of his life experimenting with different philosophies, lifestyles, and creative endeavours. At one point he'd even moved to New Mexico to follow the pathway of the Genesis Alliance, a group whose beliefs include the idea that humans were the product of aliens seeding humankind throughout the universe. He flirted with other fringe ideas and various international conspiracy theories throughout his life. None of those beliefs affected Brooke, but Malcom also seemed to have a hard time settling down to a family life. He came from what might be described as a "moneyed" family. That didn't mean Malcom lived in the lap of luxury; quite the contrary, he always worked for a living. He spent most of his career selling commercial real estate. In his mid-20s, he'd met Brooke's mother, Dale. The two had a brief relationship that resulted in one child, Brooke. But Malcom left the family and Brooke was raised by her mother. Malcom, she says, was an inconsistent father throughout her childhood:

> I wanted his attention, his adoration, so badly. A lot of the time he wasn't there and he wouldn't be there to pick me up when he said he would be and I'd wait at the window for him. I had to work through that during this as well, to kind of reflect on our relationship. We've had some intense moments and it's been a bumpy relationship at times.

It was this kind of emotional baggage that Brooke says gave her very mixed feelings about her father and any relationship she might have with him. She says she believes Malcom always loved her, "but as a child, you just feel unwanted at times. I guess it all comes down to I always felt that I wasn't enough or I was a bit of a disappointment, which many, many people out there can relate to, I'm sure." As Brooke matured, her relationship with her father began to change. He seemed better suited to relating to his daughter as an adult. Brooke in turn began to understand what made her father the way he was. "He grew up in Jamaica," she told me during that first visit to Port Hope. "As a little boy he was a wild child, running around, trapping animals and insects and looking at them. He really loved nature. He was forced to move back to Canada, where he was put into a very strict schooling and I think that was really hard for him." Brooke thinks Malcom spent much of his life chasing the freedom he'd known as a child. He wouldn't find it again until well into his 60s. Brooke's interpretation of Malcom's choices could be described as generous, but one that is typical of Brooke. She is not a person to speak harshly of others. Ultimately, as her father returned to her life, she began to find some room for reconciliation: "I mean, we're all products of our own childhood and I think his childhood made it harder for him to parent or want to be a parent. But I'm sure he knew I loved him. I stood in my kitchen and said, 'Dad, I love you,' and he had wept."

When Brooke's mother passed away in 2007, Malcom became more engaged with Brooke and her family. She believed he was particularly fond of his role as a grandfather after Brooke's two children were born in 2006 and 2010. Brooke's long-time partner at the time, Zab Vanderhyden, says Malcom changed after the kids were born. Though Zab says Malcom was never a touchy-feely kind of guy who showed his emotions, "I think that grounded him a bit, to have grandchildren. I think he was really proud of Brooke. Maybe he didn't say it all the time, but I think he was really proud of her. She carried herself really well and I think he's proud of how she carried herself." Slowly but surely, Brooke and her father were starting to rebuild their relationship. That continued even after the summer of 2011 when once again Malcom moved away. Only, this time he wasn't running from his family or seeking some religious ideal; this time, it was a simple matter of choosing to become a snowbird.

When Malcom turned 61, he decided he'd had enough of working in real estate and living through Canadian winters. He'd been living in a small community north of Toronto called Sutton and after he retired, he pulled up stakes and moved down to Puerto Vallarta in Mexico. Brooke says he had a nice routine going, spending half the year in Canada and half the year in Mexico and Puerto Vallarta. Mostly, he would go down in late September and, aside from returning for Christmas, spend most of the winter there. Initially, he rented a room in a funky hotel called Posada de Roger, but eventually he started to make some moves to create a more permanent home for himself. He started by buying a tree house. As Brooke explains,

> Los Chonchos is a small community; I think there's about 25–30 *palapas* – they're tree houses on stilts – and it's about 45 minutes from Puerto Vallarta. You take a water taxi and it's quite a boat ride. There's no dock at Los Chonchos; you jump in the water with all your gear and everyone's really helpful there and they come down and carry your stuff to your *palapas*. So everyone's just living in these open, stilted, airy, really rustic little tree houses and it was his favourite place in the world.

Los Chonchos is a unique community. At least it's not like any place I've ever seen before. In the first place, it's isolated. There is no road in. There is a path that leads to a road about an hour's walk east through the jungle. And there's a small seaside village about 45 minutes' walk along a trail south of Los Chonchos. But other than those two tenuous connections, it's about as isolated as you'll find in Mexico. During a brief visit we spent there while filming, I had a chance to experience that remoteness. Stars that stretched out in an uninterrupted swath covered the unlit night sky. The only noise we heard was the gentle crash of the waves and the sounds emanating from the forest – a lot of buzzing of insects.

Now when you hear the phrase "tree house," you may be thinking of some kind of rustic platform – possibly boards nailed crudely between branches, with a rudimentary railing and some kind of tarp to keep the rain off. Think again, because that's not Los Chonchos. It's more along the lines of what might be described as "glamping." When you first come ashore at Los Chonchos, all you see are the thatched roofs sticking up here and there in the dense jungle canopy. As you get in among the trees, you begin to see what these structures really entail: thatched luxury cabins built on stilts high up in the forest canopy. There are about a dozen of these tree houses and they're well spaced out – you mostly can't see one from the other. The layout of the tree houses varies, but most often they include a massive deck – Malcom's was about 20 square metres – with comfortable rattan and wooden furniture arrayed tastefully over a terracotta tile floor and looking out over the ocean. They all have large, well-stocked kitchens with all the amenities – fridge, stove, sink with running hot and cold water. Many have multiple bedrooms, complete with queen-size beds covered with mosquito netting. All of them have well-appointed bathrooms with hot water and flushing toilets. Most are tastefully painted or have natural tropical wood posts. The floor plan is open, with one room separated by screens or partial walls. They all have unobstructed views of the Pacific Ocean that are definitely worth whatever money the owners might have laid out for them. Sitting on the balcony, it's not uncommon to see humpback whales and schools of large rays passing by. They are a slice of luxury in the middle of the jungle.

Malcom loved to fish and used to go down almost daily and catch large reef fish. A cook-up on the beach over an open fire would follow, with cold beer to accompany the treat. Brooke thinks Malcom found his spiritual centre when he found Los Chonchos. He certainly loved his tree house and whatever time he spent in Mexico was now mostly spent there as opposed to in the city of Puerto Vallarta itself. The tree houses at Los Chonchos do have some small drawbacks. First of all, you can't own the land. You have to lease it from a local Mexican owner. Mexico has some fairly ridged guidelines about foreigners owning coastal land, so the community at Los Chonchos has all banded together and it leases the land collectively. The fees are modest – a few thousand a year – and the lack of ownership has never been a problem according to the residents I spoke with. Malcom had no problem with the arrangement, no reason to believe that the status quo wouldn't continue for the remainder of his life. The second drawback is that you have to pack in all your food and whatever other supplies you need, for however long you're going to stay there. If you want to eat, you pack it in. If you need toothpaste or soap or toilet paper or whatever, you pack it in. If you run out, you face an hour-long boat trip and a 45-minute taxi ride into Puerto Vallarta to renew your supplies.

Los Chonchos also lacks a few amenities. Electricity is provided by solar panels and can be a little inconsistent. The community has cell phone service, but it's sporadic and you often have to climb up the mountainside to get a clear signal. These days, they have Wi-Fi, but it can be spotty. Having said that, the minor inconveniences that people put up with to stay in these cabins in the trees are nothing compared to the solitude and tranquility the location offers. Malcom loved to stay there. It didn't matter what he was doing, he just loved the atmosphere. In fact, according to his friend Robb, he found a lot to do. He worked on his jewellery – Malcom had always been a very talented silversmith. His subjects were often drawn from his surroundings at Los Chonchos, particularly the insects he was so fascinated with. He was also forever tinkering with his own tree house, making sure that everything was working just the way he wanted it; creating new inventions to make his life a little more interesting. And, of course, he also spent time fishing. Some of the few pictures that exist of Malcom show him with his catch of the day.

While Los Chonchos was where Malcom loved to be, it wasn't his only residence in Mexico. After he'd leased the tree house, he also purchased a large five-bedroom house in Puerto Vallarta. That was where he stayed with his live-in girlfriend, Marcela, a local woman who Malcom met in 2012. She was considerably younger than he was – Malcom was 68 when he went missing and Marcela was days shy of 44. Marcela was not what I would describe as an attractive person. While she was physically in good shape when the two met, she always seemed to be dressed in clothing that was too tight. In her pictures, she often wore too much makeup. Some of Malcom's friends described her as cheap-looking. She also seemed to always have a very hard expression on her face – one that might have indicated Marcela had led a tough life. In one email between Marcela and Malcom, she explains that her family had property in the "pink zone" in Puerto Vallarta, which is the area in which prostitutes work. This has led some people to suggest that perhaps Marcela had made her living as a prostitute before she met Malcom, but I've not found a shred of proof to support that.

What I am sure of is that she spoke virtually no English, though she claimed to understand a lot. Her emails to Malcom were written in English, but I have a feeling they were the product of Google Translate. I say that because having used Google Translate constantly during the years I worked on this project I became familiar with how it distorts translations, with verb tenses not agreeing, words that seem out of context, and phrases that are too literal. That's what Marcela's emails read like.

Malcom and Marcela had met through a mutual friend. Robb Stasyshyn remembers the meeting well: "We probably were just out on the town in Puerto Vallarta and Malcom asked a friend of ours, John, 'Do you know any women?' Malcom gave him his email address and they would send photos and everything. And then one day we were going out and he happened to be meeting Marcela that evening."

Within a few years, Malcom and Marcela had moved in together. They didn't marry, but Malcom was clearly interested in a serious relationship and seemed to be in love with her. In one Christmas email in 2012, Malcom wrote, "Good morning my love, Merry Christmas … I am a very fortunate man with love in my life. And you are the icing on top. I thank the powers around me for bringing you into my life. I love you so very much." And if Marcela's emails are to be taken at face value, then she was quite enamoured with him: "Hello sweetheart mine … I just want to tell you that I love you more than my life, I think about you all the time and I miss you … I love you." Malcom was serious enough about the relationship that he bought a house for Marcela and her family and allowed them to live there without charge. That's a serious commitment by any measure. Malcom also used the house as his base of operations when he was in town.

According to Brooke, prior to meeting Malcom, Marcela, her two adult sons, and her mother and father had all been living in a one-bedroom apartment. Now they had a five-bedroom, five-bathroom house. The move to a middle-class neighbourhood was a significant upgrade.

Brooke was not overly fond of Marcela. For a start, the age difference bothered her. "My dad has had lots of partners throughout my life," she told me. "He and my mother have been separated since I was born, so he's had girlfriends. I've never had an issue. But when he told me that she was quite a lot younger than him and then when it came out that she was only three years older than me, it bothered me, definitely." She also had some questions about why her dad had begun a relationship with Marcela in the first place: "He had made it clear that there was definitely a bit of a language barrier, so I really couldn't see... I just put two and two together. I didn't like what either of them were looking for in the relationship." For Brooke, Marcela's motivation was clear – she was looking for someone to take care of her financially. Robb didn't buy Marcela's assertions of love for a New York minute, either. "At first," he said,

> she seemed like a nice person and everything, but then I was invited to the house. I went to the house and I just, you know... She would always have her hands on you and was always flirting with you and would joke with Malcom while she's flirting with me or somebody else and it made it very uncomfortable.

Zab Vanderhyden, Brooke's former partner, is a striking character who has stood by her throughout this ordeal. He's an extremely talented chef with a deft touch around spices and an ability to spin up gourmet dishes in the blink of an eye. He certainly doesn't look like my idea of a chef. He's a powerfully built man. At one point I asked him if he was a bodybuilder and he laughed me off, telling me "I just like to work out." Originally from Guyana, his family immigrated to Canada when he was 6 years old in 1960. They settled in Toronto. That's where Zab went to school and ultimately decided to become a chef. He attended George Brown College and graduated with a degree in culinary management. He's spent most of his life working in quality restaurants around the world – head chef at a Ritz Carleton in Toronto and the Westbury Hotel in Liverpool. In 1991 he decided to launch his own restaurant in Ottawa. Since then, he's launched three more, with the latest incarnation, Craft Food House, opening in Cobourg, Ontario, in 2017. It's been quite a success for him, and when I ate there, I could taste immediately why that was the case. I had his butter chicken kale salad for lunch one afternoon and it was amazing. I don't like kale, but I wolfed that salad down to the last scrapings.

Zab speaks candidly about what's on his mind, and he was even more blunt about what Malcom might have been looking for with Marcela: "Maybe it was the sex." After that initial comment, he expanded a bit more: "I think he liked having her around. It wasn't a relationship, it looked like she was a caregiver." He laughed at his own description. "I don't know how to put that... she cooked for him, she cleaned for him... I don't know how you call that, but that's what I thought."

Brooke says that, from the very beginning, Marcela went out of her way to be unfriendly to her. She thinks Marcela's attitude may have stemmed from the fact that she felt insecure around her and felt threatened that Brooke was in competition for Malcom's attention. It's also possible Marcela worried that Brooke would work against her and Malcom's relationship and she would end up on the street again. Brooke remembers vividly the first time she met with Marcela in Puerto Vallarta. Brooke had flown down to spend some time with Malcom and he wanted her to meet Marcela, so they met for dinner one evening. Brooke and Malcom arrived at the restaurant first. Marcela made an entrance shortly afterwards:

> She circled and she sat right across from me and as she sat down, instead of looking at me, she surveyed the space around me. She looked around and then finally her eyes fell on me and it was very clear to me she was letting me know that I was of no consequence to her, that I wasn't even worthy of her attention.

Brooke explains that the evening went downhill from there and when they finally parted, she and Marcela were barely on speaking terms. She was also barely on speaking terms with Malcom in the days following that episode. According to Brooke, Malcom had not been oblivious to the tension between the two women:

> We didn't speak until the next morning when he came to get me at my room and I don't even know if I said anything. I think he just looked at me and he could see how upset I was about the night before. I'm not sure that we actually spoke about it at that point. Over the years, we've had many a moment where I've said something and he always shut me down.

That first meeting set the tone for the relationship between the three of them. Marcela became the proverbial elephant in the room between Brooke and her father. Ultimately, Malcom decided there was only one way to handle the dynamic. "My father and I went to Denmark to visit family," Brooke recalls, "and he said to me at one point, 'I don't talk to you about her and I don't talk to her about you.'" That uneasy relationship lasted for years.

In the fall of 2018, Malcom was once again making plans to head down to Mexico for the winter. He planned to spend a few days in Puerto Vallarta catching up with friends and seeing Marcela, and then head out to the tree house at Los Chonchos to open it up for the season. Brooke saw him just before he left:

> My father went down, I believe it was October 13, 2018, and we

had sort of an agreement, a rule between us that he always called me from the airport because he had a few hours to kill, so I spoke to him on the phone the morning that he flew. He was in a very good mood. He was excited to go down and get out to his tree house.

In addition to promising to call Brooke once he'd reached Mexico, Malcom had also made plans to meet up with his good friend Robb Stasyshyn, a US expat who also owned a cabin at Los Chonchos and acted as a kind of overseer for the owners. On first encounter you might think Robb was a former "biker type" – someone who spent a lot of his life living on the rougher side of things. He's a solidly built man with long, dark hair tied back in a ponytail and a pepper-coloured, straggly beard. He's another person who speaks his mind without any hesitation. But once again, if you thought of Robb as a biker type, you couldn't be more wrong. He's an affable bear of a man with a profound sense of generosity and an abiding curiosity about life. When the crew and I dropped by his house in upstate New York, it took a concerted effort to actually get down to work. The house was like walking into a scene conceived by Hans Christian Andersen: playful fairytale-like objects were scattered among the surrounding trees and covered the exterior of the house – carved dragons, gnomes, and small animals were all stashed away in little nooks. Capping off the whole effect were dozens of wind chimes of various sizes hung in the trees. Depending on how the multitude of wind eddies swirled, a whole different symphony of sound was created. The whole area felt like it belonged in the world of Snow White or Rapunzel rather than upstate New York.

Stepping into that world and shaking Robb's hand was truly a pleasure – I liked him right from the start. Malcom and Robb met up when Malcom bought his place at Los Chonchos. As Robb remembers,

I spoke to him on the phone because I had one of my houses for

> sale in Los Chonchos and he decided to buy it... okay, well, we need to get a contract signed and take care of that. And he was coming down to pick up a used vehicle and he goes, "I'll stop at your house on my way back to Canada." So that's when I met him and immediately when I met him, I was like, "This guy's really cool." We hit it off. We spent a couple hours at my house, [then he] got in his new used car and drove back to Canada.

Since that first meeting, Robb and Malcom had spent a lot of time together at Los Chonchos and had become fast friends. When possible, they liked to meet up on the way down to Mexico and travel out to Los Chonchos together.

In 2018 Malcom had gone down ahead of Robb, but they had agreed Malcom would come back to Puerto Vallarta and help Robb travel out:

> We would talk every couple days when Malcom got to Mexico. He was going to pick me up at the airport. He knew when I was coming. He told me what he was doing – that he was going out to Los Chonchos a week, maybe two weeks, early to get the place opened up, come back to Vallarta, pick me up at the airport and then that following Sunday, he was heading out to stay out there.

But, oddly, just a few days before Robb was going to jump on the plane and head down, there was silence from Malcom. "Prior to me arriving, all of a sudden, no communication. So, it's like, *Hmm, I wonder what happened?* He must have gone out to Los Chonchos. Sometimes phones don't work out there – sometimes nothing works out there," Robb says.

But when the silence stretched out to several days, it began to bother Robb that he couldn't connect with Malcom. He says it just wasn't like Malcom to stay out of contact for that long, and the cell phone service might have been spotty at Los Chonchos but usually it came back on after a few hours. Robb decided to reach out to Brooke, who was the only person he knew from Malcom's family. He asked his long-time partner, Patti Kerr, to see if Brooke knew where her father was. She was the one who kept in touch with Brooke, so it was natural for Robb to ask her to reach out. She had met Malcom shortly after Robb, and her recollection of him squares with what other people have said about him:

> I remember when Robb first met Malcom, one of the things he said to me was "You're going to love this guy, he's perfect for Los Chonchos." And I went down there and I met him. He and Brooke were down there together, and I met him and I thought this guy is amazing. He's brilliant, he's fascinating. I always used to say he's part Einstein and part Peter Pan because you would have a conversation with him, and he could literally talk about anything. He was incredibly intelligent. But then he also had this childlike wonder about him... You never, ever saw anybody who had such a fascination with nature but especially insects and arachnids. He was just an amazing soul. Fascinating, fascinating. I adored him.

So when Robb told her he had not heard from Malcom, she agreed that they needed to talk to Brooke. At this point, in early November 2018, Brooke was not the least concerned about her father's whereabouts. It wasn't that unusual for him to arrive at Los Chonchos and lose cell service or just become engrossed in hanging out there and forget about the outside world. But it was a little disconcerting for her to receive a message from Patti. "She found me on Facebook," Brooke remembers, "and she messaged me that Robb had been trying to reach my dad, that he was supposed to meet my dad at the airport and drive him in, and that they were going to go out to Los Chonchos together the following day."

Patti recalls that Brooke got back to her right away and told her he was at Los Chonchos. "Then she said, 'Has nobody seen him?'" Brooke says she remembers "making the bed with Zab in the evening and mentioning it and I remember him saying, 'Are you not worried that your dad hasn't been reached?' And it's weird because I almost felt like I stepped outside of myself. I just remember I felt like I was standing outside of myself as I said, 'No, I'm sure he's okay, he probably just doesn't have his internet.'"

Patti asked Robb to check once again to make sure Malcom was not holed up at Los Chonchos. Robb decided the best way to settle the matter was to ask his friend, Ruben Urtiz, the manager/caretaker for the properties at Los Chonchos, to walk over and check to see if Malcom was there. Ruben lives in El Tuito, about 45 minutes' walk east of Los Chonchos, and since Robb is one of the managers on the owners' side, he talks to Ruben all the time and asks him to check on things at Los Chonchos. If a big storm is coming in, he'll walk over and make sure all the tree houses are closed up and ready for the rain and wind. When Robb asked him to please check and see if Malcom made it there, Ruben said he was going to Los Chonchos that Sunday or Monday. After he'd been, he called Robb back and told him Malcom's place was still closed up. No one had been there.

The next check that Robb thought about making was with Marcela. To do that he dispatched Malcom's go-to guy in Puerto Vallarta, the taxi driver, Jesus Romero. A young, slight, energetic kind of person, Jesus is a guy who gets things done. Need a part for a pump? Ask Jesus. Looking for a place to rent? Ask Jesus. Need someone to look after your condo? Call Jesus. Need a contact who can help you with some government paperwork? Talk to Jesus. There really doesn't seem to be any job he's not capable of executing. When I was in Puerto Vallarta filming the documentary, *Malcom is Missing*, we hired Jesus as our driver. He did everything, including taking care of any nosey or greedy police officials who came snooping around. He translated, he drove, he acted as our liaison with people in locations. He was amazing. If we needed to film inside a restaurant, Jesus would just tell us to hold up for a minute and shortly afterwards he'd be back telling us, "No problem."

Malcom found Jesus to be much the same and he depended on him for every little fix-it job he was working on. So, naturally, when Robb needed some local intelligence, he called Jesus. Jesus remembers the conversation well, as my interviews with him show: "Rob call me. 'Do you know where is Malcom because he's not here. He said he's gonna come Sunday.' And I told him, 'No, he don't call me this time.' And so he told me to go and ask Marcela, ask in the house." Jesus says he drove over and knocked on the door of Malcom's house. Marcela answered, but according to Jesus, she wasn't very welcoming: "When I get there, I call her at the door and she coming out and she take her face out only and she's makeup and she got a nice dress. When I come in, she put another big T-shirt and she's like, 'I don't know where is my husband, he take a taxi from here.'"

But Marcela's story didn't add up for Jesus for a couple of reasons. Supposedly, Malcom had called a taxi on the afternoon of Sunday, October 28, and had gone to Los Chonchos. But first of all, Jesus was Malcom's regular driver. If Malcom needed to get to the airport, he called Jesus. If he had some running around the city to do, he called Jesus. When he went down to the dock to take a water taxi down to Los Chonchos, he always called Jesus. It didn't make sense that for this occasion only Malcom would call any old taxi to come and get him. But there was another reason a red flag went up in Jesus's mind. Marcela couldn't recall any details about the taxi that picked Malcom up. So Jesus had a suggestion:

> I told her, oh, easy. You have cameras. Malcom paid to install cameras. And she say, "No, the cameras is not working now. They are just... we broke something." That's what she say. It's not working now. And I tell her, oh, so, at what time he take the taxi because the neighbours have cameras. And she say, no, nobody have cameras, I already asked them and they say it's not working too.

Having every camera in the neighbourhood fail at the same time seemed to be an unlikely coincidence to Jesus. He decided there was something wrong with the story Marcela was telling him, so when she invited him into the house, he nervously declined. "She said, 'Come in, come in.' And I said, no, I'm okay here. I'm going to call Robb and tell him he's missing and she say, 'Oh, okay. So, if you know something, let me know.' That's the last time I talked to her."

At this point, Robb had exhausted his ability to search for Malcom from his home in upstate New York, but he did know two valuable facts: Malcom was not at Los Chonchos and had not been there recently, and Marcela was telling a story that didn't seem to hold up very well. He decided he had to contact Brooke and let her know what was going on. Brooke says she was at a lunch with a girlfriend when the call came in: "I got a call from Patti and I went outside to take it, and they told me my father had been searched for at Los Chonchos, by the staff, and he was not there. And I knew in that moment my dad was missing and I had a complete meltdown."

CHAPTER TWO

THE FIRST TRIP

Malcom disappeared on Sunday, October 28, 2018. It took a few days for friends and family to realize he was missing. But once Brooke understood something was wrong, she decided she had to fly down to Puerto Vallarta and immediately start looking for her father. She booked a flight for November 4. Zab wasn't able to join her right away, but he promised to come down within a few days. Once there, she would meet up with Jesus and Robb and an old friend of Malcom's, April Aboud, who flew in from where she lived in Costa Rica. The plan – somewhat hastily thrown together and based on the assumption that some wrongdoing had occurred – was to try and find Malcom and either rescue him or pay any ransom demand that was on the table to get him back. They soon found out the plan was easier conceived than executed. Puerto Vallarta can be a tough town if you're not a tourist.

Puerto Vallarta has a checkered past, with a precolonial history that stretches back to 580 BCE. But Hernán Cortés wiped out the local Indigenous population in 1524 and after that the area lay dormant for some time. There are some suggestions that Banderas Bay provided refuge for pirates during the 17th and 18th centuries and became a convenient layover for Spanish galleons. But the town really began to be settled in the early 19th century, when it was initially called El Carrizal or Las Peñas. Spanish settlers began to move in to farm the rich agricultural lands of the Ameca Valley. It also had some prominence as a mining centre. In the early part of the 20th century, it changed its name to Puerto Vallarta. Shortly afterwards it began to go through a period of serious turbulence. Twice, revolutionaries used the town as the centre for "La Cristiada" – the fight against a repressive federal government in Mexico City. But after those unsuccessful revolutions the town lapsed back into its sleepy former ways, mostly growing fruit for export to America.

Then Puerto Vallarta was "discovered." Not by the conquistadors this time, but by American travellers: in the '40s and '50s it became a retreat for artists, many of whom came there to escape the madness of America during the McCarthy era and form a little expat community in a part of town known as Gringo Gulch. Director John Huston put the place on the map in the 1960s with his film *Night of the Iguanas*. When his two stars, Elizabeth Taylor and Richard Burton, decided to spend some very public time arguing on the beaches, the city's fate was sealed. Suddenly, Americans knew all about the sleepy little town and they began to flock there – first by the hundreds, then by the thousands. Notoriety came at a real cost. By the turn of the millennium, Puerto Vallarta had a façade instead of a soul, one constructed for the amusement of the tourists from America and Canada. The massive towers of chain hotels stretched endlessly along the waterfront. The few gaps between resorts were already filled with construction cranes when I first dropped into the town in 2008 – new hotels seemed to be going up as fast as they could be built. The narrow streets of the town were filled with tourists. Every sidewalk café was jammed with sunburnt people, all of them guzzling beer or margaritas and ordering baskets of warm, deep-fried corn chips with spicy salsa and guacamole. The craft market, a fixture along a couple of streets at the south end of town, was usually jam-packed. People took great delight in bargaining for the brightly painted baubles. Why wouldn't they? They were on holiday, they had money to spend, and they were in a warm and inexpensive vacation town. Puerto Vallarta was booming. What little was left of its soul – the odd building featuring some exquisite examples of colonial architecture – was now merely a backdrop for photographs.

By 2008 the city still had a sizable expat community. I'd run across it the first time I was filming down there: a news feature on a Canadian expat who'd gotten into a world of hurt with the Mexican authorities. Brenda Martin (more details on her case later) had been living down there for a number of years when she'd been arbitrarily arrested by Mexican police and charged with fraud. There was virtually no evidence to support the charge. We went to talk to her friends and found quite a large community of Americans and Canadians who lived in the city full time. It seemed that a modest pension could be stretched quite a bit when you lived in Mexico. For a few thousand dollars a month, you could rent a nice little house and have a cook and cleaner come in part-time. Food was relatively inexpensive and you couldn't beat the weather. That's changed a bit these days as prices have risen, but the basic math still works out. Compared to Canadian or American living costs, Puerto Vallarta is a deal. Malcom was part of that expat community, which had grown considerably since 2008. Now the expats had businesses, homes – whole areas where they dominated the neighbourhood.

Brooke knew the place well – at least she knew the tourist and expat side of the town. She'd been down to Puerto Vallarta multiple times. Like Malcom, she'd even considered moving there eventually when she retired. So naturally Brooke thought her familiarity with the city would give her an advantage when searching for Malcom. What she didn't understand yet was that knowing the tourist side of the city was of little value when it came to delving deeper – exploring the official and judicial side and, most especially, exploring the seamier underworld of the place. Nonetheless, her plan was to start by talking with authorities and then to try to retrace Malcom's movements on his last night to figure out *what* might have gone wrong by discovering *where* it might have happened. Additionally, if he'd been kidnapped, Brooke also wanted to be on hand to arrange payment. Of course, Jesus stepped up to be her driver. For him, the answer about what happened to Malcom kept evolving: "The first time when I told Malcom is missing, maybe he go away, you know, because, I don't know, maybe they fight and he go away, he don't wanna stay here for a few days."

That theory didn't last long. First of all, Malcom wasn't known as the shy retiring type who would flee an argument and banish himself. Secondly, if he did banish himself, he would have gone to Los Chonchos and Jesus knew he wasn't there. So, as the days rolled by and Malcom didn't show up, Jesus began to think something else might have happened. "I think it's the kidnap," he told me, "They have him somewhere, you know, tried to take his money, that's what I think."

His assumption wasn't far-fetched in a country like Mexico where – though numbers have been falling in the past few years – still more than 600 people were kidnapped there in 2021.[2] That's a considerable improvement from a few years previously when more than a thousand a year was the norm. At one point, kidnapping was almost a cottage industry. Officials pointed fingers at the cartels. There were few, if any, convictions. And almost nobody ever turned up again once they disappeared. Malcom was a *gringo* and clearly had money, so he might have been an obvious target for the local cartels. In the back of his mind, Jesus didn't believe the cartels were involved. He thought there was another suspect: Marcela. He didn't confront her, but he thought that kidnapping Malcom might have been Marcela's way of bleeding more money from him. Brooke was working on a similar theory. She thought Marcela might have something to do with kidnapping her father. She half hoped that eventually someone might contact her and start demanding money. That way she could get Malcom back safely and then deal with whoever was responsible. But by the time she reached Puerto Vallarta on November 4, no ransom demand had been received.

Naturally, as the last person who had seen Malcom, Brooke was interested in talking to Marcela. She had mixed results. Prior to heading down to Mexico, Brooke reached out to Marcela via Facebook Messenger (now simply Messenger). The chain of messages between the two women started on November 2. Initially, the messages were quite normal. The kind of exchanges you would expect between an anxious daughter and a caring partner. But as they progressed, the exchange seemed to get a little more bizarre. Initially, Marcela seemed co-operative. In response to Brooke's first inquiry, she replied, "What do you need to know I will try to help you." But that "count me in" attitude didn't last long. Within hours, Marcela started to sound defensive. Now that might have resulted from an interaction that Marcela had had with Malcom's friend April. In my experience, April can be quite aggressive when she is on the phone and she is trying to find something out. I initially called her to talk about her role in the search for Malcom and within minutes I was on my back heels and she was peppering me with questions. And she certainly didn't feel any obligation to pull punches and question my motive about why I was involved in Brooke's story – the insinuation was that I was out to make a fast buck. Ultimately, she cut off communications with me and refused to participate in the documentary or the book. Early on in the search for Malcom, April had some kind of exchange with Marcela. I was never privy to April's side of the conversation, but Marcela does make a reference to April's call in her messages to Brooke. The literal translation of her messages reads,

> April is thinking is an idiocy. I have nothing to hide, you are welcome right now and you can looking even in the last corner of this house. Please you just ask her doesn't to talk to me like that, my only mistake was not to check who picked up your dad. She thinks our relationship is not okay but we were better than ever. Every afternoon we made love.

April seemed to have made some accusation about Marcela being involved in Malcom's disappearance. Brooke tried to be conciliatory, telling Marcela, "I don't think you hurt him. But we need to find him." Oddly, Marcela replied to that message by talking about how drunk she and Malcom had been the night before and assuring Brooke she was in contact with the police. So it's possible Marcela was just feeling defensive as a result of her interaction with April and that's why her texts to Brooke became more unusual. But it's also possible there was another motive to her defensive attitude – she might have known more than she was saying. Brooke began to try to get solid facts from Marcela, asking questions like, "Which agency did you file the report with? Police station? What restaurant did you go to and how many drinks did he have? Was he drunk?" Marcela became more evasive. She ignored many of the questions and while she did give Brooke the name of the restaurant they had visited the night he disappeared, she also kept talking about how drunk Malcom had gotten during the evening. That struck Brooke as odd, because while Malcom loved to smoke weed, his friends all said, he seldom drank.

Brooke kept probing, "What time did you go to Andales?"

Marcela replied that she didn't remember the time.

"What time was dinner?"

Marcela said, "We got out from the house around 9:00 p.m."

"What time did he get up the next day?" Brooke asked.

Marcela said she didn't remember. All she remembered was that she took him up a coffee. For an event that had only occurred a couple of days earlier, one that should have had a lasting impact on her, Brooke thought Marcela wasn't remembering much.

Then Brooke started asking about Malcom's money. "Have you accessed any of his accounts this week? Can you access the safe?"

Marcela acknowledged she could, but when Brooke asked her directly about taking money out of Malcom's account, Marcela ignored the question. The whole exchange left Brooke feeling a little uneasy. That feeling was exacerbated when she received an emotional phone call from Marcela:

> She called me, sobbing. It was strange because when I make a phone call, I'm not crying. I'm calm and then maybe I'll tear up. But she was crying the minute she was making that call. I said,

> "Where's my dad?" And she claimed he got in a cab with someone he didn't know to go to Los Chonchos and she didn't walk him out so she didn't see who it was, and that he left with all his luggage.

This unsolicited call left Brooke puzzled. For someone who couldn't remember many details about her birthday celebration the night Malcom disappeared, Marcela had seemed to be able to go into some detail about Malcom's departure from his house on the Sunday morning. Brooke probed a little more,

> because I already knew my dad is a creature of habit and he would never go with a cab he doesn't know. He would never go at the time of day she claimed he was going. He would never not respond to Robb. He was very particular. And so I said, "I have a lot of questions," and she said, "I have questions too." And I said, "What are your questions?" And she said, "Where did your father grow up? What are your father's parents' maiden names? And what school did your father go to?"

Brooke was gobsmacked by those questions. In the midst of an emotional exchange about someone who was missing, possibly kidnapped, she felt the questions Marcela was asking were out of context. To Brooke they indicated Marcela was probing for information that would give her a clue about passwords Malcom commonly used. That truly seemed like an odd thing to do at this point in the conversation. Brooke checked her dad's bank account. To her horror, she saw that someone had been draining his chequing account at breakneck speed. On October 29, the day Malcom disappeared, someone had withdrawn nearly $700 – three separate times. The following day, another $700. The day after that, another $700. On November 1, they'd taken $675 out. In four days, nearly $4,000 had been withdrawn. Brooke called Marcela and asked her "if she had been accessing my dad's bank account. She admitted she had and she said that he had told her to take some money so she could go on a trip. I know there's no way my father would ever give anyone that bank card."

Instead of clarifying the situation, Brooke's conversations and texts with Marcela had only served to muddy it. Nothing Marcela said was adding up for Brooke. She hoped she could clear up her questions in person when she got to Puerto Vallarta. When Brooke's plane touched down, she was met by Jesus and Robb. April had already joined her en route. They decided the first place they should stop at was the offices of the Canadian consulate. Brooke was counting on them giving her a lot of help and advice. She thought they might go with her to the police station and act as a liaison to put a little weight behind Brooke's inquiry. She was wrong. "My first experience at the embassy seemed fine," Brooke says. "They were nice enough. I needed a lawyer and they had a list of lawyers. April looked at the list and she liked that there was a woman on there, so we went with the female lawyer. She came immediately and met us."

Robb remembers the first encounter with the consulate: "They weren't very much help, but we went there and said isn't there somebody – I mean Interpol or somebody – something we can do here because he's been missing now for days. And I know [Brooke] filled out a report." Ultimately, other than offering a list of lawyers who spoke English, the consulate did very little for Brooke. That inaction would come to typify the lack of involvement Global Affairs Canada would have throughout Brooke's investigation. And there was even a small problem with the list of lawyers the consulate handed over. According to Brooke, there were no suggestions about which ones might be *good* ones: no indication of who specialized in civil matters, who was a criminal lawyer, or who had experience with immigration issues.

Choosing a lawyer almost became akin to throwing a dart at a board blindfolded. Whether her lawyer was competent would be a matter of luck. They chose Norma Alicia Rodríguez Ibarra. For Brooke, the most memorable thing about Norma was her physical appearance: a leggy 40-something blonde with a propensity for a great deal of makeup and very tight short dresses. Brooke remembered that she always wore incredibly sexy clothes. Aside from that, Brooke didn't believe she was very effective. Norma would be the first of three Mexican lawyers Brooke would go through in the first few months of her search – all in the hope of finding one that was more interested in helping to find Malcom and less interested in merely presenting regular invoices. I took one look at some photos of Norma and asked Brooke what she was thinking, hiring someone that presented themselves in that manner. Appearance isn't everything, but Norma looked more like someone you'd meet on a booze cruise than someone who would command the respect of Mexican authorities. It turned out in this case that the proverbial book could be judged by its cover – Brooke says Norma accomplished little with the authorities.

With Norma in tow, the group headed off to file a report at the local police station, located in a rundown old building on the northern outskirts of town. We went there to get some shots while filming in 2021 and the place looked more like an old factory building than the centre of Puerto Vallarta's law enforcement. But Brooke felt it was critical that they stop at the police station early in the search – she wanted to make sure they were aware of what had happened and if the situation developed, if they needed their help for any rescue, then she wanted them onside. She was also uncertain about whether Marcela had followed through on her promise days earlier to file a missing person's report.

When they got to the station, Brooke was shocked by the attitude of the police. "The police did not have any interest," she recalls. "They thought he was just drunk somewhere in a jungle or that there was no case at all." Robb got the same impression: "They didn't seem very concerned. From the lawyer's translations, it seemed like their attitude was that he'd probably just gone off somewhere without telling anybody. According to the police, people did that all the time in Puerto Vallarta." But Robb knew it was not like Malcom to do that.

Brooke and her companions left the police station feeling somewhat underwhelmed.

Brooke and Robb's feelings about police indifference weren't entirely correct. Though they may have seemed indifferent when taking Brooke's statement, and while the first prosecutor she met may not have acted with a great deal of speed, the investigating detective, José Luis Del Real Arellano, did make some preliminary inquiries in those first few days. He took a team out to Los Chonchos to search Malcom's tree house and ask around, they went by Malcom and Marcela's house, and they asked for copies of Martín's phone records. It was a burst of activity that wouldn't be duplicated very often as the investigation wore on over the years.

Having struck out with the two official offices that might have helped, Brooke and the group decided they would retrace Malcom's steps on the last night he was seen. They had a rough idea of where he'd been from Marcela – the Blue Shrimp for dinner and then Andales for drinks. But the staff at the Blue Shrimp couldn't recall seeing Malcom there. Brooke believed that if he and Marcela took a table on the beach, they might have gone unnoticed. Oddly, when they checked for a charge card receipt, the owners could not find one. Of course, he could have paid cash. But there was something else that bothered them, Robb says:

> The manager, he was always there, really nice guy, and he knew Malcom quite well. So I went and spoke to him and he goes, "Wow, no, Malcom was not here." So I kind of mentioned he's been missing and the guy, he goes, "Be very careful." He didn't want to say too much because he was kind of nervous when he found out that Malcom was missing.

The fact that the manager was so nervous reinforced the group's theory that Malcom may have been kidnapped and, if that was the case, they certainly couldn't dismiss the fact that the local cartels could be behind it – even though Jesus was skeptical. Having struck out at the Blue Shrimp, they went on to the next location. Andales Bar sits on a lovely cobblestone street in the Romantic District. The façade is highlighted by stained glass panels that line the street and a papier-mâché donkey on the adobe tile awning. The bar is much bigger than it looks on first inspection – it covers three storeys and spills out onto the sidewalk. It always seems to have a healthy crowd sitting around with drinks. According to Robb, "We knew he probably would go to Andale's because that was another place [Malcom] liked. We were asking around, well, you know, is it possible to view the camera, the video?"

The manager led them upstairs to his office and allowed them to look through the security video taken the night of October 27 and the early hours of the 28th. That's when they got their first break. Brooke recalls,

> I recognized Marcela's dress. There's a number of different camera angles, but the first one I saw was them coming out of Andale's bar and I recognized the dress because it's a pink dress, and it's not something that Marcela would normally wear and I remember her wearing it in a Facebook image. I remember thinking that's unusual for her, that's not her style.

Eventually, they found video that recorded Malcom and Marcela from the time the couple arrived at the bar at 11:20 p.m. until they finally left at 12:29 a.m., so it's possible to know what happened, and when, at this bar with some accuracy. Luckily, the couple had been seated at a table right underneath one camera. Every detail of what they did during that time was recorded. The video was crystal clear. While the first look at the video provided little more information than a timeline, subsequent viewings would prove to be instrumental in breaking open the case. As the group ended their second day, they had reason to be a little more optimistic. They felt they had finally picked up Malcom's trail.

Within a day or two of Malcom disappearing, Marcela had promised Brooke she would contact the police. Yet, according to police records, Marcela did not file a missing person's report until November 5, some eight days after he was last seen. That statement was given to René Ortega Roldán. He later took the lead as the prosecutor in charge of the investigation. I was given a copy of that statement. Much of it was fairly mundane – Malcom's address, age, passport number, etc. – but Marcela also shared some information about how they met. Her statement was encumbered with the police's additions of addresses and the like. I haven't changed the somewhat stilted result because I want to remain as accurate as possible in my account of these details:

> I got to know him in the year 2011, because some friends introduced him to me. We started going out and I noticed that he was staying in Posada de Roger, which is located in the Playa Olas Altas, and from our co-existence we decided to enter a relationship. It was then that at the beginning of the year 2013, two thousand thirteen, MALCOM bought a house for me in Paso Real Avenue, number 141 in the Colony Las Aralias of Puerto Vallarta. Now, he was no longer coming to hotels, instead he was coming and stayed in his house with me.

Marcela also told police in her statement that she was suspicious of a couple of people she thought might be connected to Malcom's disappearance. She pointed the finger at a group that sold time-shares in Puerto Vallarta:

> MALCOM sent me an email chatting that he bought a time-share in MIRAMAR GRAND CLUB & SPA with address in the street Paseo de los Cocoteros, number 139, in the South Hotels area of Puerto Vallarta, Jalisco. But on his return from Canada, he mentioned to me that the time-share he bought was a scam and that

> he was trying to get his money back from a guy he deposited the money to, because they never let him use the time-share which he has paid.

Marcela suggested that police should investigate the men who allegedly ripped off Malcom for his time-share.

The second person Marcela suggested might be involved with the disappearance was the woman who managed the property where Malcom had his tree house. Marcela only talked about the fact that Malcom paid a monthly upkeep fee to the woman, but Marcela's brother, Marco, went a lot further when he made his statement. He implied the group was a bunch of gangsters:

> I think it is important to mention Mrs. Teresa De Jesus Valencia Hernandes, who is the elected community member in the Suchitlán Refuge, municipality of Cabo Corrientes. She says she is the lessee of the land where the Los Chonchos huts are built. This lady I consider that she charged too much money for the rent of those lands. I don't know exactly how much she charged for the land where the cabins are built, but it strikes me that this lady once went to Malcom and my sister's house. This lady was very well dressed and was accompanied, or rather she was being looked after by a young man who was armed, dressed in civilian clothes.

Essentially, he was saying that Malcom's landlady at Los Chonchos turned up with a bodyguard packing a gun and police should look into them because they could be involved. It is possible Marco and Marcela thought they were being helpful to police by pointing out other suspects, but it's also possible they may have been trying to set up some red herrings to send the police off in a number of dead-end directions. Ultimately, these two pieces of information would prove to have no value in the case.

The time-share wasn't run by the cartels but was a scam engineered by an expat Brit. And Robb tells me Malcom had nothing to do with the payment of fees to the landowners at Los Chonchos. Everyone with a tree house pooled their money, and Robb took care of the payments. The owners had no reason to be upset with Malcom, and the story about them visiting his house to get money had little credibility from what I could gather.

There were some other interesting details that Marcela shared with Ortega.[3] These provided important points of comparison for Brooke when she started assembling the information she gleaned from her investigation. Marcela described their final night and Malcom's alleged departure the following day. For someone who was hard-pressed to provide Brooke with anything other than vague descriptions of the night before Malcom went missing, Marcela suddenly developed a very sharp memory, stating,

> I would like to mention that MALCOM has talked to me, for several days, that he wanted to go to CHONCHOS to clean it up, because the rains the floor get slippery, and being so. On Saturday 27th, of this year I went out with MALCOM for dinner. In that occasion I asked for UBER from the application in my mobile phone, he said that he wanted to leave to Cabo Corrientes early the following day, but he got drunk. Then it was until 2 p.m. two of the afternoon of Sunday, October 28th of this year that MALCOM picked up 3 suitcases, one big, another medium and the last small, besides a big wooden one, a nice packer like make of nylon, a bag full of beers, he say good bye to me and he said to me he will be back November 3rd, of this year. He was wearing beige short pants with flowers, a black T-shirt, black sandals with rubber, he was carrying his phone, his old iPad and the new iPad, as well he was carrying cash, but I do ignore the amount. He was

> carrying his bank cards; I did not see by what means he left the house because I was taking care of my dad in the same house because he is very sick and I am the one assisting him. That is the reason why I did not see how MALCOM left, that day.

That's a huge amount of precise detail for someone who couldn't remember what time he left when she talked to Brooke. So now Marcela could remember details. Why was that important? Because it gave Brooke a baseline from which to work when she began adding up facts. Brooke had gotten to know her father very well during the past few years. When she looked at what Marcela was saying, she found reason to doubt much of the statement. And Brooke wasn't shy about sharing her suspicions with the authorities. In her statement to Ortega on November 5, she told him,

> He usually talks to JESUS on the phone to notify him of this situation, and that in this case my father did not tell JESUS anything. Besides the fact that when my father goes to Los Chonchos, he does not usually do it so late, but he goes in the mornings without exceptions... Honestly, he should have left his house between 01:30 and 01:45. The last boat that leaves Los Chonchos is at 03:00 in the afternoon... it takes an hour to travel, but right before getting on the boat my father has to buy groceries, so it is incongruous that my father left the house at 02:00 two in the afternoon.

Yet Marcela was stating to the police that Malcom had left for the water taxi at 2 p.m. Brooke said Malcom was too much of an obsessive personality to leave things that late. And it wasn't just the timeline that wasn't working for Brooke in Marcela's statement. Apparently, nobody but Marcela saw Malcom leave the house. This was odd, because their house was on a very busy street right across from one of the more popular bakeries and cafés in the city. It's a haunt for expats. While we were filming in Puerto Vallarta, we stood on the street for a couple of hours taking pictures. A steady stream of cars pulled up to pick up baked goods. In fact, the street was a bit of a choke point, with stop-and-go traffic occurring regularly. When we went inside for a coffee, there was a considerable lineup. In between one of Brooke's trips to look for her father – she made a total of three – Jesus put up missing person signs all around the neighbourhood; in fact, he did so all around Puerto Vallarta. Yet not a single person on the street had seen Malcom walk out of the door at 2 p.m. on a Sunday carrying three suitcases, a nylon bag, and a bag full of beer. All that luggage creates a pretty high profile for a casual viewer. So, while it was possible nobody would have seen him standing waiting for his cab, Brooke believed it was unlikely. Marcela also told police,

> I can mention that, before departing, MALCOM handed over to me the debit bank card number 4506 XXXX XXXX 0620 belonging to the bank CIBC associated, I believe, to the account number 01140 XXX XX XX232, because with that one I will pay a washing machine that it was going to be deliver to my residence.

That card was on Malcom's personal bank account. Brooke swears Malcom never gave his personal bank card to Marcela to use. He had one issued for her on a separate joint account. So why would he suddenly hand over his personal card? It just didn't make sense. Additionally, Marcela had just finished telling police earlier in the statement that "He was carrying his bank cards." So those two statements seemed to contradict each other. In Brooke's statement to Ortega, she tells him, "My father is a very suspicious person when it comes to money, and he would not give his cards so easily to MARCELA." What also didn't make sense was that earlier Marcela had told Brooke the money had been taken out of the account in order for her to take a small vacation. Now she was saying the money was to be used to buy a washing machine. Four thousand dollars seems to be a lot to pay for an appliance or, for that matter, a short vacation for one person. Every way Brooke looked at Marcela's statement to police it was riddled with contradictions.

Marcela claimed in her statement that "Malcom did not have a car." That's not strictly true. He had recently purchased a car. He had placed it in Marcela's name, so by the letter of the law, Marcela was right. But Brooke said in her statement, "I am also aware that in February 2018 two thousand eighteen, my father bought MARCELA a Toyota brand vehicle, Avanza type, Champagne colour, automatic, model 2018 two thousand eighteen." According to Brooke, Malcom drove that car. Everyone knew it was Malcom's vehicle. In fact, when he thought Marcela's son, Andrés, might be using it without his permission, he was so upset that he installed a GPS device in the van that would send him an email each time it was started. The email would provide him with the co-ordinates of where the car was at the time. That way he could tell if anyone was driving it without his permission. That action would prove to be critical a little later as Brooke started digging deeper into what had happened. But for now the bottom line was that, within days of arriving in Puerto Vallarta, Brooke found herself believing very little of what Marcela and her family were saying. She described Marcela's version of events as "careless and not with a lot of effort or thought put behind it." Ultimately, she told the police in her formal statement, "I have come to request that an exhaustive investigation be carried out into the events that gave rise to my father's disappearance."

After running out of conventional approaches (for now) to searching for her father, Brooke continued looking for him during her first trip, using what many might describe as more unconventional methods. Prior to flying down, she and April had consulted psychics to try and figure out where Malcom was being held. Now Brooke isn't the first person to try this method. In fact, occasionally, police will use psychics as an act of desperation to try and get information on a crime. In this case Brooke consulted a number of them who claimed to work regularly with the police. Brooke says, "Everyone was saying the same thing – the description of where we were being told he was being held – and they all sound the same." All of them talked about a jungle location, a hut where Malcom was being held, the sound of running water, possibly near a mine of some kind. April and Brooke spent time poring over maps trying to narrow down a place that matched those criteria. But they soon realized that in mountainous rainforest – like the area around Puerto Vallarta – that was the equivalent of looking into a January snowstorm and trying to track a single falling flake. There were dozens of mines, hundreds of rivers and waterfalls, thousands of square kilometres of jungle. The psychic connection proved to be a bust, though Brooke would keep in touch with a few of them, hoping for more information.

Meanwhile, Brooke, April, Robb, and Jesus kept returning to the police station daily and returning to the consulate to see if they could get more assistance. Finally, on October 9, after five days of searching, Brooke had to return to Canada to take care of her two young daughters. She also had dozens of pieces of information she'd been given that needed to be cross-checked to see whether they were worth following up on. Nonetheless, she felt a huge sense of disappointment when she headed for the airport. She had been convinced she would be able to rescue her father during this trip. She believed he had been kidnapped and she would be able to sort out any payments and get him back. "That was a super hard flight back," she recalls, "because I did think my dad was still alive and he was being kept somewhere, and it was really hard to get on that plane. It definitely felt like a failure, and I guess it's the same for anyone who has a missing loved one, it's so time sensitive, it was brutal."

Less than three weeks later, Brooke would be back and while there she would make a discovery that would break open the entire case.

CHAPTER THREE

MALCOM

This story, while primarily Brooke's, also revolves around Malcom Madsen, so when I started working on the documentary and book, I thought it only fitting to do a deeper dive into his personality and history. I think knowing who Malcom was helps to put his choices into context, and understanding his choices is critical to understanding what happened. He was, to say the least, an enigmatic figure. I say that because I've talked with several family members and many of his friends and former partners and I still find it difficult to get a clear picture of Malcom. Brooke was aware of her father's enigmatic nature and she believed he cultivated that persona, intentionally keeping people in the dark about his inner self:

> Malcom has always had an art of keeping the people in his life separated. He kept a lot of his female friends away from me and vice versa. He kept everyone [separate], like a jigsaw, where every piece was kept apart. Had we all managed to bring our pieces in together, to put the picture together, we would have all had a little bit of information. We would have known that something was going on, but he was so good at keeping us all away from each other.

This almost obsessive need for discretion didn't just apply to his life in Puerto Vallarta and to keeping information about Brooke and Marcela separate; it applied to nearly all facets of his life. When I talked with his nephew, Steven Bowles, he was only able to talk about Malcom's real estate skills and some anecdotes about the "cool" room Malcom had at his family's home, but little else. His good friends Gordon and Michele

Chan spoke eloquently about his work life and the parties they used to attend together and fondly remembered trips to Jamaica but knew very little about his personal life beyond that. Former girlfriends and wives knew details about when they were together but were mostly uninformed about other parts of his life. Brooke didn't know about large parts of his life – most notably his relationships with other women and some of his interactions with his other family and friends.

Given that Malcom's life was such a jigsaw puzzle, I worked to bring many of these people together and have each of them tell me the pieces of the Malcom story they knew. This is my attempt to combine all of those pieces and present more of a complete picture. Full disclosure, though, this history isn't complete. It is a much fuller version of his life than has previously been on the public record. Of course, at the heart of Malcom's discretion – some might call it secrecy – lay a very private person. Several people told me he was so private, he didn't even like to have his picture taken. Some research for this book has brought out a few main themes to his life. What they revealed was someone who might diplomatically be described as a "complicated man." Less diplomatically, he could be described as a lost and confused soul.

There is one trait Malcom possessed that virtually everyone agreed with. He was described as "childlike" or "innocent" or "trusting." However he's described, it suggested the same conclusion – Malcom could be seen as a little naive. In some cases that made him a delightful puckish creature. In other matters, particularly those related to women and money, he was dangerously oblivious. Let's start with the money.

Over the years, Malcom's naivete led him to be the victim of a couple of fairly obvious scams and he lost quite a bit of money. In 2004 he got sucked into a fraud involving a Panamanian company that supposedly held the rights to a newly invented GPS device. In a statement taken by the Mexican authorities that were investigating the fraud, Malcom admitted he bought two different batches of shares.

> In November of last year Ron Praxton told Malcom about some GPS systems for global positioning and indicated that it was an opportunity to make money and then he bought 5,000 shares for an amount of ten thousand US dollars which is equivalent to approximately thirteen thousand five hundred Canadian dollars and [Ron told Malcom] that he was in Panama although the central office was based in Florida United States, and the GPS system would be Made in Costa Rica. Once [Malcom] bought the shares, he never heard from Mr. Praxton again.[4]

Given that someone had just taken $13,000 from Malcom and then gone silent, you'd think that would have been the end of any relationship with this Panamanian/US/Costa Rican company. Yet despite this rocky beginning and a number of puzzling and sometimes hostile interactions between Malcom and the company, inexplicably he was persuaded to buy more shares.

> I bought some shares and wanted to know how the company was doing, he got aggressive on the phone and told me that I only had a unit equivalent to 5,000 shares and that I had to buy half a unit more to make good money, when the shares began to trade in the open market I would sell half a unit 5,000 shares and that I would double or triple his profits if this cell phone company went into business with the company and that I could sell the other half a unit in the market in a year, when the shares rose in price. Even so, I resisted and Mr. Johnson was very rude [and] said to buy the other five thousand shares to complete the unit of the shares, and if not, then I had nothing to do with the witness and that I would have to sell the shares on the other hand, so I bought another five thousand shares for the sum of ten thousand dollars American.

Why Malcom would buy more shares from someone being "rude" to him on the phone is perplexing. Of course, having the benefit of hindsight, the explanation Johnson gave Malcom makes absolutely no sense. He seems to be just spewing out bullshit to bafflegab Malcom. And he was successful because Malcom got sucked in a second time. Of course, ultimately the whole venture was proven to be a scam. The court concluded, "The people who said they were in Panama were actually in Costa Rica and they issued something that has no value and that the Company has no value." Several of the fraudsters involved were jailed and the rest disappeared into the woodwork.

Fast forward a few years and Malcom was again on the wrong end of another scam. In 2010 or 2011, Malcom invested in a time-share operation in Puerto Vallarta (Marcela mentioned this deal in her statement to the police). The words "time-share" and "Mexico" are virtually synonymous with "scam." Several years earlier, in my *W5* incarnation, I'd investigated a whole series of time-share scams in Cozumel. We'd even gone down and done some hidden camera work to catch them out in their lies – massive promises until they had money and then just try and book some time. In general, I learned that buying a time-share in Mexico should immediately set off alarm bells. It's not impossible to get a real time-share, but it is highly improbable and any offer should be approached with the utmost caution. This particular time-share was associated with the Grand Miramar Hotel. If you do a quick search online, you'll see a multitude of people complaining they were ripped off on their investments by this group. Most of them say they made the deals with a man called Richard, whose last name I can't mention because I can't contact him and give him a right of reply to the allegations against him. But he was a British expat who worked out of Puerto Vallarta and who is now supposedly working around Cancún. He's not the only one mentioned in the online reviews – a litany of names surfaced relating to fake contracts sold on the property – but his name came up a great deal, as this very typical complaint shows:

> We tried to use the contract for the first time last year 2015 for two weeks. We were put in a two-bedroom two-bath in building that looked like it was furnished in the 1980s and the location was remote. At the update in 2015 Richard xxxxxx told us for additional money he could give us a legitimate contract. We refused his offer. He told us to pack up and leave he was calling the Mexican police to throw us out. The police never came. We were unable to obtain a 2 weeks reservation in 2016 because we had a fraudulent contract... Richard xxxxxx is still selling fraudulent contracts now.

Malcom bought one of those time-shares. We know this because he complained briefly about the deal to Marcela in an email sent on April 28, 2018:

> I never talk about Grand Miramar time-share because it's very upsetting to me. There are a bunch of crooked people who did not keep up to their promises. Since I refuse to pay the maintenance fee since the beginning which is now eight years, they will not let me use it which is fine by me because I never want to be near the place. It goes further where they also like more [from] me... That's why I never talk about it to you or anyone. Maybe it's a little embarrassing to me that I was taken advantage of.

Malcom was always bitter about the money he lost and, according to Brooke, was always trying to browbeat the company into refunding his money – right up until he disappeared.

It's possible to see the house Malcom purchased for Marcela in Puerto Vallarta as evidence of yet another con he fell for. He paid a quarter of a million dollars Canadian for the place. That's a fair chunk of change in Mexico. Yet rather than properly set up a trust through a bank and lawyer to maintain ownership (that's how most people do it), he decided to save the few hundred dollars a year for the fees to maintain the real estate trust and put the property in Marcela's name. To be fair, Marcela put a lot of pressure on Malcom by encouraging him to make this decision. She talked to him in emails about how much he could trust her and put the house safely in her name. Malcom went for the idea, even though his friend Robb tried to persuade him it wasn't the way to go. What this meant was that, according to Mexican law, Malcom bought a house for Marcela. Yet he didn't seem to really understand that fact. So where did this naivete come from? Possibly its roots lay in Malcom's childhood and the fact he was raised in a somewhat rarified environment where money was never really a concern.

Malcom was born in Toronto in September 1950, the second-youngest of Marius and Belle Madsen's five children – the others being Marcia, Rocky, Stephanie, and Dana. They were an affluent family. In fact, some might consider them to be very wealthy. All that money mostly stemmed from the northern Ontario gold rush of the 1920s. Marius, a Dane by birth, was a man of adventure. From a very young age he'd set out to explore the world, seeking adventure wherever he could. And he certainly found it. When he was 19, he worked aboard a Danish schooner named the *Dagny*. In 1920 the schooner was caught in the ice 50 kilometres off the coast of Greenland and sank. The crew, including Marius, made it onto the ice and eventually found their way to the mainland. They were stranded for a year on this barren shore. They managed to salvage enough supplies from the ship to survive, but it was truly just eking out an existence. Eventually, Marius and a ghostwriter wrote a book about the year called *Shipwreck and Struggle*. Following that escapade, Marius moved to Canada, where he eventually decided to hunt for gold in northern Ontario. He was one of a handful of prospectors who searched for gold in the Red Lake area and discovered what would become one of the richest goldmining strikes in the world. The Madsen Red Lake mine was one of the big three in that region. According to one source, during its lifespan it produced 2.62 million ounces of gold.

From there, Marius went on to create a respectable business empire. He was, by all accounts, a commanding figure. According to Malcom's sister Marcia, "He was powerful in the sense that he was considered a Bay Street boy, meaning that he had a lot of clout. He was a mining man, prospector... and then he had several other companies that sort of attached themselves to my dad or he got them as he went along in life." Marius was perhaps the epitome of the Teddy Roosevelt-like man of action – he "talked softly and carried a big stick" according to Marcia, and "he wasn't boisterous, he wasn't loud; he was very soft-spoken but you listened when he talked." But Marius passed away at the relatively young age of 67. Marcia recalls the tribute that was paid to him when he died: "He had a very big funeral procession at a church. There was a lot of people there, so he was well respected." But if Marius was a strong silent figure, Malcom's mother Belle was the strong assertive type. Some might even call her domineering. Marcia says, "If anybody was strong in the family, it was my mum. My mum was the one that was the powerhouse, you know." With two such strong figures as parents, it's not surprising the children had what might be called a disciplined upbringing. According to Marcia, "I knew my parents loved me and the rest of us, but it was important to them that we had that antiquated kind of growing up. My mother sort of believed children should be seen and not heard." According to Marcia, that didn't mean they were neglected or abused in any way: "They did the best for us when it came to schools and proper healthcare and clothes and things, but we were never spoiled." Marcia tells me that while her parents were strict in some ways, they were very easy-going in others – Marcia thinks they gave the children room to grow because they were allowed to explore the world around them in a rather untethered way. Particularly when it came to bringing various animals into their Royal York Street house:

> My parents had the attitude that we could have pretty much whatever we wanted as long as we took care of it. I had a raccoon. I do remember my mom bringing a small [crocodile] up from Miami... and so my brother did have a small crocodile. If we didn't take care of them, my father was very strong in his way of dealing with us.

Marcia says that attitude instilled a deep respect in all the children for nature: "We grew up knowing how to love and take care of animals, not necessarily people but animals." Malcom was particularly fond of less conventional animals – "spiders and snakes and things like that," Marcia recalls. You can see that seed deep within Malcom in his later life. When he sold real estate in Toronto, Gordon and Michele talked about the myriad of animals he kept in the house – a ferret, black widow spiders. Gordon and Michele tell a story about going over to Malcom's house one day and seeing a tank full of baby black widow spiders. The next time they went over, the tank was almost empty. Malcom casually explained that the smaller spiders had escaped through the mesh and were somewhere in the house. The jewellery he became so skilled at crafting was mostly based on animal themes.

In 1959 Malcom and his family moved to Jamaica. His parents had purchased a hotel, the Casa Maria, and the family went there to supervise the renovation. They were there for a year, along with a tutor to make sure the children's education was kept up. Brooke believed it was a formative year for her father – he enjoyed the freedom to explore the surrounding jungle. Brooke felt that year of freedom became a defining one for her father and that he spent years trying to recapture that freedom. Malcom deeply resented the move back to Canada, which, according to Brooke, he felt had robbed him of an important part of his life. Once back in Canada, Malcom graduated from high school in the late '60s, probably 1968 or 1969. He didn't attend university or college. Between finishing high school and starting work in real estate in the mid-1970s, nobody seems to be able to recall what Malcom was doing. Steven Bowles recalls him living at home in his parents' basement, but he has no details beyond that.

Malcom met Brooke's mother, Dale Mullins, in 1975 when he was 25. Marcia introduced them and, like Marcia, Dale was a model in Toronto. At 31, she was one of the few women Malcom had a relationship with who was older than he was. Dale was tall and slender with blonde hair and a striking face. The camera loved her, and I can see why she had a great career. Marcia said Malcom and Dale hit it off right away. Brooke said they shared a number of odd interests together – they both loved making jewellery, they both collected miniatures, and they both loved flying kites. Not the kind of hobbies that are common, so I'm sure they were delighted to find each other. They also shared an interest in just hanging out. As Marcia describes it, "When Dale and Malcom met, they were both having a good time together; they enjoyed each other."

That seems to be another of the central themes of Malcom's relationships: he didn't seem as interested in long-term serious relationships as much as he was into having a good time with an attractive woman on his arm. Dale fit the bill perfectly. But that "good time" relationship came to a rather abrupt ending in 1978. According to Marcia,

> When [Dale] got pregnant, that's when things went a little bit awry because she wanted to get married and settle down, now she was expecting a baby. And Malcom didn't have that kind of thought in mind. He wasn't the kind of person that you could expect to settle down; it wasn't for him and I think that really hurt Dale.

Malcom was interested in living the life he already had – moving freely from one good time to the next. And so he walked away from the relationship, leaving a pregnant wife alone to raise a child. Dale was very bitter about Malcom's decision to leave. Marcia said, "It was a pretty rough time for the two of them and I think that alienation made Dale kind of go away from the family." There are many who would suggest that move was not among Malcom's finest moments. There are some who suggest it was a staggering act of selfishness. Others look at the situation differently, suggesting Malcom was just too young and unprepared to suddenly start settling down and raise a family. Regardless of the motivation, Brooke certainly doesn't remember him being around a lot as she grew up.

In the mid-1970s, Malcom started selling real estate in Toronto. He worked for a company called Terry Martel and mostly sold commercial real estate. According to his friends, Gordon and Michele, he was pretty good at it. And he must have done fairly well because he drove a Mercedes sports car and owned a nice house overlooking the Don Valley in Toronto. Brooke said selling real estate wasn't really his passion; it was more of a way to make money, but he was considered skilled enough that when his family decided to sell some large commercial properties they had in the north end of Toronto, they asked Malcom to shepherd the deal through. The family was pretty tight-lipped about the whole thing, but Malcom's work resulted in each person walking away with a sizable chunk of cash – several million each, according to a couple of sources. But while real estate paid the bills, Malcom's real passion was making jewellery. Brooke says, "His summers were completely spent making his jewellery and going to different shows every weekend all over Ontario. He would do all the different festivals and he loved that. And he loved his jewellery. He was very proud of the work he made, he was very proud." Brooke showed me a selection of his work and, truth be told, I thought he was a pretty talented artist with an eye for the unusual and an attention to detail that made his pieces stand out. One piece in particular that I loved was an old silver spoon he had bent around and then fashioned into a Viking helmet and face shield. Another piece was a bracelet designed to look like the bones of someone's spine. Other than a couple of brief periods when he moved to New Mexico and Vancouver Island in the 1990s, Malcom spent the bulk of his life in Toronto. He retired sometime around 2010 and began to turn his attention towards a life in Puerto Vallarta.

There's little question Malcom was a restless, even troubled, person. There's lots of stories told that suggest he was always searching for some kind of meaning or purpose in his life. Ironically, he may finally have resolved some of those issues when he started spending a lot of time in Puerto Vallarta, or more specifically at Los Chonchos. I've talked already about how he found a real spiritual home once he bought a place at his remote jungle location. Brooke says, "He always said he just needed an island and the love of a good woman. He really enjoyed his time in Mexico."

After he had purchased his tree house, Malcom still flew in and out of Puerto Vallarta and spent time there with Marcela, but he was happiest at Los Chonchos. He could explore and putter the whole day away – helping other tree house owners whenever they had a problem. Robb recalls one such occasion:

> I had a raccoon living under my house. He got an old crate, got some wood that was there. There's not like electric saws or anything, [but he] made this door that would slide, drilled a hole, put a nail in it, ran a piece of wire from the nail to a little thing inside this cage where he put an apple… and the next morning we caught the raccoon and let it out. I mean he made a trap out of nothing.

Robb added, "People would be without hot water because their hot water heater wasn't working. He would know how to bend it and fix it and they'd have hot water. Or if something electrical wasn't working, he would do that. And he would, he would do that for most anybody." The few pictures of him at Los Chonchos often show him smiling. That's unusual because there are not a lot of pictures of Malcom and he wasn't the grinning sort. Los Chonchos seemed to affect his whole persona. Whether he was working on repairing one of the houses with the local manager or overseeing a cookout on the beach, he was smiling away or goofing around, like with a slingshot on his balcony – you can see the pleasure on his face. Malcom also continued to explore his love of wildlife while he was down there. Robb explains,

> I mean, he had a terrarium that he would collect scorpions in and he would feed them bananas, the little flies would come in and he would take them out once in a while. He had little tweezers... But at the end of his trip, he would take them somewhere into the jungle and let them out. He was that kind of person. He wouldn't kill a bug.

Finding Los Chonchos seemed to finally bring some level of peace into Malcom's life: contentment that had been sorely missing. Up to that point, he had been on a 60-year quest for spiritual fulfillment. A quest that took some pretty bizarre twists and turns – starting with his belief he was an alien.

Malcom always seemed to be on a quest to find spiritual fulfillment (whatever that meant to him). After years of searching, Malcom found something he could believe in that gave his life some shape and purpose. He decided he was an alien being. While the details are a little vague, it goes something like this: either he already was an alien being from another dimension, time, and space, now inhabiting a human body, or in another version I've heard he was an alien spirit that was still inhabiting some location in space that would ultimately find its way through to him and he would be complete. I've heard both versions. There are also a few snippets of information about the group Malcom belonged to – the Genesis Alliance. Marcia's take on the whole alien belief cult was

> What they believed in was that he was born on another planet and that in being born on another planet, his soul was floating around in space and these cherubs or demigods – whatever you

> want to call them – were going to, I guess, bring these cherubs or these demigods back into his soul so he could basically live happily ever after.

In the 1990s, the Genesis Alliance gave workshops across the United States and Canada and charged a healthy sum for each one. It was led by a couple known as Phoenix (Rene Burkee-Rogers) and Andromeda (Karen Ronstad) who set up in Santa Fe, New Mexico, in 1992. The local papers there suggested they were running a cult, but the two denied it vigorously. You have to remember that the early 1990s was a time rife with various cults and spiritualists – people claiming they channelled entities that ranged from former Dalai Llamas to Genghis Khan. I remember attending a "channelling" session as a reporter working for the CBC in the late 1980s. We went into this room filled with rugs and pillows and sat on the floor waiting for the channeller. He eventually came in and sat down and after a few minutes took a deep ragged breath and began to talk to us, allegedly in the voice of some great spirit who was now in his body. It all seemed like so much bullshit to me, but a lot of people were convinced. Malcom was one of those people. Patti and Robb vividly remember Malcom waxing on about his extraterrestrial origins, even when they met up with him after he moved to Los Chonchos in 2012. Patti says,

> I remember one night he and Brooke were visiting and we went down after dinner and we were sitting and talking with him and he was going on and on about extraterrestrials and UFOs and I finally stopped him after about an hour and I said, "Malcom, it's obvious to me that you're very passionate about this, but I don't have a clue what you're talking about."

Despite the outlandishness of the belief, Patti feels Malcom's spirituality was a captivating part of him. "He was just this quirky, unique soul, not a malicious bone in his body, but he thought deep about a lot of stuff." Robb added,

> He thought these aliens came down and settled and they're under the ground there and he actually had the one tree in front of Los Chonchos carved with this bone, like the Egyptians have. And he goes, "They're here, they're here, that's what I believe in and that's who, that's the religion I believe in – and they're still here under the ground and they're watching us."

Now this might seem pretty far-fetched as a system of spiritual beliefs, but Malcom was deadly serious about it. So serious that in the early 1990s he left Toronto and moved to New Mexico where he joined the group full-time. Marcia says that decision was a game-changer. She feels it changed the very core of who her brother was: "Malcom was a very fun, very sweet, very sort of loving individual. But I felt that through various things he changed and then he got involved with the cult." Malcom's family was horrified by the idea that he'd joined this group and started trying to get him out of it immediately. They hired a deprogrammer, threatened to cut him off financially from the family trust, and appealed to him on a personal level – anything they could think of to get him to leave. His brother Rocky claims that at one point they'd had Malcom removed from a plane when he was about to return to the Genesis Alliance. His sister Marcia adds,

> We made him come into my mum's place for the weekend and listen to the exit counsellors because they're pretty powerful people, they're people who have already gone into the cult themselves and now they pull you out. They worked on him hard all weekend, believe me, it was the most gruelling thing I've ever seen because I was witness to all of it. And in order to get him to come and sit down, we had to take things away from him, tell

> him that there's no financial support. I mean, we had to do a lot to him to get him to succumb.

Eventually, their pressure worked and Malcom came home. But the residual effects, according to Marcia, lasted for a long time: "I think my brother was going into some sort of trances off and on, even after he was out of the cult." To be fair, not everybody sees Malcom's involvement with the Genesis Alliance in such a negative way. In 1992 Malcom met a woman named Nikki Michalski. Eventually, they got married. She was giving seminars for the Genesis Alliance – workshops, she said, to "awaken people and make them more aware of themselves." She described the whole philosophy as one more focused on empowerment than on aliens coming to Earth. In fact, when I spoke with her, she described the whole alien issue as really more related to believing in some cosmic energy or power as opposed to ET-like creatures hiding on our planet. She described the Genesis Alliance as a group that really spent more time trying to discover what within us was impeding our individual growth. She also said she and Malcom were alarmed by the actions taken by his family. She claimed "his mother hired someone to kidnap him while he was in Toronto." Nikki also described pressure that Malcom's family put on him to work with a deprogrammer as "a little scary." Nikki believes that, ultimately, the continued pressure of the family led to the breakup of their marriage and to Malcom leaving his life in New Mexico and returning to Toronto. Of course, what's interesting is that even though Malcom left the Genesis Alliance, he didn't stop believing in his alien origins. According to Marcia, he always had a hunger to find some kind of spiritual meaning in life:

> Malcom was tormented after he came out of the cult. He was searching for something and he was searching when he went into that cult, but he was searching even after it. I remember him poring over religious books when he was living up at my mum's

> place and trying to find the answer, and I talked to him about it sometimes and after a while it became too hard to kind of help him along to make any sense of what he was saying.

Ironically, Malcom seemed to finally find some kind of spiritual balance at the end of his life. One night at Los Chonchos, just before he disappeared, he was explaining his beliefs to a couple of neighbours. One of the neighbours asked him to repeat his core beliefs and recorded the conversation. Malcom talked about finally accepting who he was and everything that happened to him as the foundation for a peaceful life: "I am divinely guided," he said. "I am always at the right place at the right time... everything is orchestrated for my growth... whatever happens is all part of my growth, whatever happens."

Malcom also believed he'd found the same balance in his relationship with women at the end of his life, particularly with his daughter. In 2008 he had decided, according to his sister Marcia, that he wanted a deeper relationship with his daughter. Brooke says,

> I think it's important, probably, for people to know that it wasn't always the perfect relationship, far from it. I was more or less raised by my mom. Well, I *was* raised by my mom. My dad? There are stages in my life when he wasn't around. He was either living in a different province or just too busy with work.

But Nikki says that while Malcom often thought about Brooke, he just wasn't comfortable showing his feelings towards her. She asserts that, when it came to Brooke, he didn't seem to know how to have a relationship. It "wasn't something he did naturally on his own. I had to encourage him to have a relationship with Brooke. We spent time with Dale and her spouse, Stewart, and got along well." She also pointed out that she believed that any money Malcom got from his family went to Brooke. Brooke isn't so sure. She vaguely remembered her mother getting a few hundred dollars a month. Another one of Malcom's partners, Josie Schywiola, also says Brooke wasn't much in the picture when she was Malcom's partner, and that she would only see her at office gatherings. "I would meet [Brooke] at the office," Josie remembers. "Most of us would meet her at the office. He had a couple gatherings at his mother's house when there were parties and birthdays; she would have been at those. But did Malcom and me take her out? No." All this weighed heavily on Malcom, according to Nikki:

> I think Malcom felt guilty somewhere along the line, for what had happened, but he wasn't capable at the time of making it up to either one of them. And I know that when Dale died, I was at that funeral or the wake and Malcom was determined then to get close to Brooke and make amends with her and make her part of his life, which was important for him because Dale wasn't there to be supportive because Dale was very, very close to Brooke. I mean, Brooke, she was her everything.

Malcom was well on his way to succeeding with his goal of improving his relationship with Brooke by 2011. Brooke liked to talk about how her relationship with her father was starting to transform after her mother died. He began to show up for birthdays and family celebrations. He was around for the birth of her oldest child. When he was in Canada in the summer, he visited Brooke often and she in return would fly down to Mexico when he was there. Brooke had some fond memories of Los Chonchos and Puerto Vallarta. The summer before he went missing, the two travelled to Denmark to explore Malcom's family roots. It was a journey towards reconciliation that Brooke had hoped would continue for a long time: "I needed to continue a path, a journey with him, to kind of mend our damaged relationship… we didn't get that, either of us." Brooke adds, "I feel like we were just starting to get back on path, like really connect, when he went missing, which is really sad. It had begun but it hadn't finished, so he was sort of ripped away; we both didn't get that opportunity, which we both needed, I think."

Oddly, in a certain way, Brooke was about to get to know her father much more deeply than she had ever imagined – just not in the way she might have wanted to get to know him. When he disappeared, Brooke was able to take a deep dive into his personal life and learn a great many details about her father, some of them disturbing. Ultimately, what she saw was a man who was at times charming, at times insightful, but also often naive and evasive: a man whose relationships with women both defined him and directed him. That combination of traits would ultimately prove fatal for Malcom.

CHAPTER FOUR

BROOKE'S INVESTIGATION

Within three weeks of getting back to Canada from her first trip, Brooke was on her way back down to Mexico. She used the few weeks between the two trips to do some research to try to answer some of the pressing questions raised during the first Puerto Vallarta trip. She started by going over to her dad's house in Sutton, Ontario, and picking up his desktop computer. She fired it up and started combing through his files. It was a treasure trove. When she began to look at his email correspondence, she says, she hit the proverbial jackpot:

> I read all the emails between him and Marcela, which made me cry, made me angry, made me sick, made me hate my dad some days, you know, just hate him, the manipulation and the naivety. He was truly in love with this woman and he could not see how badly she was using him for money.

Brooke shared many of those emails with me, and it's not hard to see what she is talking about. You can readily see an evolution that occurred across the length of the relationship. It began with many expressions of love, a lot of mutual sexual chemistry. Malcom told her, "I love you and really starting to miss you and your lips and your body." Marcela responded with "I miss you more than ever and I need you more than ever also." But as time wore on the focus of the emails shifted. Malcom was still gushing with love in many of his messages, but Marcela's responses were often more about listing her many health problems, the issues she had with her family, and, most of all, her financial woes. Brooke described it succinctly by saying, "Every email, money, money, money. I need more money, money, money." That's not quite the case, but it's fair to say Marcela did spend a lot of time asking about money, asking for money, and reminding Malcom about money: "I took money to go one night to a hotel…5,360 pesos plus 4,000 pesos…I will take 20,000 pesos from your card…I would like to have an additional card in your accounts…I'm checking the notes of everything I've spent…it gives me a total of 43,243 pesos," and so on. Now couples do talk about money, but it wasn't hard to see in the correspondence that even Malcom was losing patience with Marcela's focus on financial matters. At one point he finally snaps: "I had left 18,000 in the safe. What are you spending the money on?"

At the same time, Marcela was pressing Malcom to buy a house. In 2014 Marcela reminded Malcom about a conversation they had:

> Good morning love, I do not know if there the cost of a home is extra for you now, I will investigate it. In any way if you want to buy a house you can used my name to do this. You can do it if you can trust in me mi amor. In any way you said what in year 2015 you will be buying a house for me for my family for you, for when you come here don't have that pay hotel. Do you remember when you said that me? I know that John bought his house and all that buy used the name of Amalia to do, so he avoids any problem. So my love here I am for you, we also are a couple and we are loving or you do not love me more?

It was a pretty hard-sell message. Marcela pulled out all the stops – "you promised," "do you trust me," "use my name," "do you love me." The list of pressure tactics was pretty transparent. And Malcom, true to form, towed the line: "Good morning my love. Yes I remember saying I'll buy you a house in 2015. The house would be for you and your family. As for myself I may consider buying a condominium. That I'm not sure yet."

In 2013 he fulfilled his promise. He bought the house and he did exactly what Marcela suggested – he put the ownership in her name. On paper,

Marcela owned the house outright. Robb Stasyshyn was surprised that Malcom couldn't see what he believed was driving Marcela. He says, "No one could make Malcom see – he was in love with this woman and no one could interject and say, 'You know, you better watch it. How well do you know her?' But I could see that's what she was doing, just taking Malcom for all he had." Malcom's actions also didn't surprise his sister Marcia,

> He was generous to a fault. And I think that because [Marcela] was younger than him, in my opinion certainly not prettier, he thought because he was aging, that this was a good thing. I think that he thought that he had scored a young babe, you know, not really listening to that inner gut that tells you not to do that.

In fact, that sentiment was the consensus among most of Malcom's friends and family. Brooke was convinced Marcela was only after Malcom's money. Malcom's sister, Marcia, was suspicious because she felt it was odd Malcom had never brought this person home to meet his family:

> Malcom didn't say, "Oh, my darling, I love you so much, please come to Canada." He left her down there – and he was up here bragging to people that he could fly in and they'd pick him up and they'd take him and they'd cook for him and they took care of him and it was just the life of Riley. So, in Malcom's way of thinking, it was more like she was beneficial because she was now his bitch and I don't mean to say that in a derogatory sense, that my brother would think that. I mean, I think whatever love he thought he had for her, it was real enough to him, but if you love somebody, if you really, really love somebody, you would bring them to Toronto, you would bring them up here, you would bring them, you wouldn't be able to be away from them.

As I read through more of the correspondence between Malcom and Marcela, I saw a noticeable change in the tone. By 2017 there was trouble between the two of them. There's an interchange about an argument they had, which ends with Malcom saying, "Your words hurt me greatly... My question to you is do you love me anymore? Do you trust me? What do you want?" And by early 2018 Malcom seemed to have decided the relationship with Marcela had run its course. And he wasn't very discreet about who he told about it. He shared his thoughts with Robb, who recounted a conversation he had with Malcom at Los Chonchos during which Malcom said,

> "This is what we've decided. We're not hitting it off. It's just very difficult getting along with her, but what I had decided to do is I'm going to rent them a house and sell my house. But I'm going to rent them a house and take care of their utilities and things like that." Which I thought to myself, that that was kind of crazy. But anyway, it was all set. He goes, "You know, we're not together really, so there's no reason for me to keep the house." And it was all resolved, it was like, it was going to take place, that it was all a cut and dry deal that he had made with her.

Malcom also shared his thoughts with Brooke's partner Zab when the two were travelling together in Costa Rica: "We were talking and he told me he was having problems with Marcela and I think he really wanted to end that relationship, I really, really do believe that. I think he was ready to leave."

The disagreements continued between the couple over a number of matters, perhaps the most serious being that Marcela alleged she had contracted herpes from Malcom. In one email, she claimed he hadn't bothered to tell her he had the virus. Malcom never admitted to infecting her, but he did tell her in one email, "I now understand why you don't want to be in a relationship with me anymore. I'm sorry about that. I do accept that."

Eventually, you can glean from the emails that Marcela was worried about the relationship ending, so she began to backtrack a little, suggesting the relationship could go on. She told Malcom that part of the reason they were having problems was that she'd been feeling under the weather. Even so, by late 2018 Malcom was telling Marcela, "Life has a strange way of unfolding. We stand here today and we can go forward together or not." That email was written on September 27, 2018. So how did Marcela really react to that email? Did she take it as one that kept the door to the relationship open, or could she also have seen it as a statement by Malcom expressing indifference as to whether the relationship continued? A month later Malcom disappeared.

What would have alarmed Marcela even more than his indifference towards the relationship was that in the six months prior to the autumn of 2018 Malcom had started talking about selling the house: "If things don't work out between us, then there are two options as far as the house goes. It could be sold to purchase a condo as I originally had planned to do so before I met you. Or you continue living there and I use it as a place to stay when I'm in PV." Marcela was clearly horrified by the suggestion and responded by saying, "What happen if I don't want to sell the house? If you remember you always said me this house is for you and your family. Then why you want sell it and you want I give you the money when I sell it? My question for you is at any moment have you wondered if I am agree?"

Bear in mind that Marcela had no assets to speak of. She didn't have a job, and had a son with a disability and two aging and ailing parents. Losing this house would be a devastating blow to her and her family. There are several emails that go back and forth at this point in time in which they talk about selling the house and buying Marcela a smaller house, but ultimately Malcom backs down and tells Marcela he won't sell the house without her agreement. And, of course, disposing of the house wasn't as simple as Malcom thought it would be. Under Mexican law, Marcela owned the house. Whether she could have held onto the property if Malcom took the matter to court – he clearly had considerably more resources than she did to launch a civil action – was a question that may have weighed heavily on Marcela's mind. Given that, she might have believed her family was close to being put out on the street. This feeling might have become particularly acute when Malcom travelled to Costa Rica in 2018 and bought a piece of property there. Marcela's emails from this time show she wasn't at all comfortable with this move – again, she may have seen it as a prelude to Malcom's exit from the relationship.

Once Brooke had read through all of Malcom's emails, she became convinced that Marcela was the prime suspect. She certainly had motive to make her father disappear – the end of the relationship and Marcela's ensuing poverty. Additionally, Brooke had discovered one more startling piece of information in her father's computer that would eventually make a huge difference to the case. It was a discovery that shook Marcela's cover story to the very core. Marcela had said in her statement to the police that the car didn't move the night Malcom disappeared. That she and Malcom had gone to bed and slept until the following morning. Her son Andrés had backed that statement up, saying, "I returned around 03:30 or 04:00 of Sunday the 28th of October. When I arrived, I saw my mom's car, a Toyota Avanza, parked in the garage." But Malcom was not a trusting sort. As I mentioned previously, when he bought a new car in Puerto Vallarta, Malcom took some precautions. Brooke says, "He secretly put a GPS on his car and he'd only done it like a couple days prior to him going missing." It's a pretty impressive little device about the size of large box of matches. Brooke explains, "It's called Trackimo… every time the engine starts, it'll send a message to your email, telling you exactly where that car is."

When Brooke was combing through Malcom's emails, she discovered these co-ordinates from Trackimo. The emails told a very different story about what happened to Malcom's car the night he disappeared. In fact, it showed that the car had been driving around all night. Additionally, when she plotted the co-ordinates of the Trackimo emails, they told a very interesting story. Brooke knew from the bar video that Malcom and Marcela had left Andales at approximately 12:30 a.m. on the morning of October 28. Marcela claimed they went home and went to bed. But Malcom's car started up at 12:45 a.m. right outside his house. The next time it started was at 1:40 a.m. At that point the car was parked near a rather remote jungle lot north of Puerto Vallarta, in a state called Nayarit, about a 30-minute drive from Malcom's house. The car started again in the same area at 3:30 a.m. and moved a couple of blocks closer to the jungle area. It started for a fourth time at 4:10 a.m., but this time Trackimo recorded it as being at the main marina in Puerto Vallarta. The final time it started that morning was hours later, at 8:58 a.m. At that point, it was right outside Malcom's house again.

To Brooke the implications were clear: someone had driven the car around the city that night. They followed a route that raised some disturbing possibilities. Brooke believed the route suggested someone may have put an incapacitated Malcom into his car, driven him to a remote jungle area, where they either held him against his will or killed him. The car going to the marina was a bit of a mystery. She thought it could have been a stop to dump a body or perhaps just a stop to drop one of the people involved in Malcom's abduction off for work – there are a lot of large hotels and condominiums right around the marina. And who was driving the car? Tough to say. Only Marcela and Malcom would have had the keys to the car, but Andrés could have easily obtained a set and he might have lent the car to someone else. At this point, with only partial information, it was impossible for Brooke to determine the real story behind the GPS co-ordinates. Brooke was certain, however, that Marcela had clearly lied about the car's activities that night, and it was hard to come up with another explanation about why Malcom's car would have been driving around all night. Brooke knew that to really discover the full picture of what happened she would need to track the cell phones belonging to Marcela, Martín, and Andrés. If they matched Malcom's GPS, that would place at least one of them with the car – the proverbial smoking gun. If they didn't, then it was back to square one trying to figure out who drove the car that night.

At this point, in mid-November 2018, Brooke was still working on the theory Malcom had been kidnapped and would eventually be ransomed. With the new evidence she'd uncovered, Brooke decided it was time to go back down to Mexico for another trip. Before she went down, she also decided she'd need to be more careful this time. If Malcom had been kidnapped, then the cartel might very well be involved. After all, they were the culprits in most kidnappings in Mexico. If Marcela was involved in the kidnapping, then who knew what she might do to protect her interests. Brooke decided she needed some help – someone who could protect her and who was a little more street-smart. "We were a little concerned about my safety at that point," she told me, "because we were scared of Marcela and her family. We knew something was up. I had already gotten some hints from an informant that they were acting weird and talking about large stashes of cash my dad had on him at that time – things they shouldn't have known."

She also felt she needed some professional investigative muscle on the case. She started to ask around and eventually found a guy named Chris Collins, an instructor with a company in Toronto called The Defenders – Brooke knew his wife through some charities they were involved with. Collins declined the job but said he knew someone who might help – a man named Jean-Paul Jauffret, a former director of the police in the city of Ajaccio on the island of Corsica. What's more pertinent is that Jauffret specializes in teaching tactical training – how to be a bodyguard for a VIP. When Brooke contacted him, he told her about a promising student he'd trained while he worked as an instructor for the French Foreign Legion, one Yuri Lysenko, a.k.a. Viktor. Yuri had moved with his wife to Guadalajara, so he lived only a few hours' drive from Puerto Vallarta. Brooke talked to Yuri and hired him to be her bodyguard and private investigator.

The first job Brooke assigned to Yuri was to go to Puerto Vallarta and snoop around before she flew down on her second trip. In fact, she'd wanted him to poke around a number of locations in the jungle near Puerto Vallarta, but Yuri soon put a stop to that idea: "She asked me to go to the jungle, to go to some places that was provided [by some psychics] to try to find her father, but it practically was impossible because a lot of places she provided to me, it was under the mafia section, so it was very dangerous to go alone and try to find someone." Yuri also suggested to Brooke that combing through hundreds of square kilometres of mountainous jungle may not be very productive. "It's impossible to try to search every square metre to try to find someone," he told me when I interviewed him. "It's practically impossible. So, I refuse that." Eventually, Brooke agreed. She shifted gears and suggested that Yuri go to Puerto Vallarta to keep an eye on the people she considered to be the prime suspects: Marcela and her family. Yuri said she asked him to "try to look around the house of [Marcela]. To try to find someone, to try to find something, to try to find some information. So this action I accepted." Brooke gave Yuri all the information she had: Marcela's address, Martín's address, and some locations that had come up as a result of information she'd gleaned from the Trackimo GPS. Yuri went down and set up surveillance on Marcela's house. He says, "I tried to go to this house, tried to find some information about something, tried to look what kind of cars stopped around the house, see if we don't see something unusual."

I've always been perplexed as to why Brooke hired Yuri to be a private investigator. Though he had credentials as a bodyguard, he'd never done any kind of investigative work. If you look online at Yuri's credentials, he shows up as someone who's an aspiring actor and martial arts instructor. He's also a somewhat talented painter. His martial arts and military background certainly give him credentials as a good bodyguard, but he had never had any investigative experience. As someone who has done a fair amount of that kind of work as an investigative journalist, I wondered what she thought he could accomplish. It's like hiring a car mechanic to fly an airplane. He had neither the skills nor the instincts to assess what was going on. In fact, he admitted he didn't really get much while he sat on the house for a few days, trying to get photos of who was coming and going, and trying to follow a couple of cars that pulled up to see if they might lead him to Malcom. He was also skeptical about the job in the first place. Brooke wanted him to follow people because "she thought [Malcom] was still alive, and I understand her position as a daughter. We expect that the person is alive." Brooke wanted to see whether Yuri could tail someone to where Malcom was being held. But Yuri didn't agree with Brooke. He thought Malcom was dead. He felt the timeline was all wrong for a kidnapping:

> Nobody asked for money, this is a reason. If someone kidnaps someone, they ask for money very quick, very quick. If not, you need to, you need to maintain the [person], you need to provide the health, you need to provide the food, you need to provide the discretion of the situation. So it's practically impossible [that he was still alive].

Also, anyone who has ever tried to tail another car by themselves knows this is almost impossible. The movies may show this happening with one car discreetly following another at a distance, but in reality you really need several cars to properly follow someone. On a couple of occasions when I've been along while police are following a suspect, they often bring in aerial support. Nonetheless, Yuri kept hunting to try and find a location where a "live" Malcom might be stashed. He decided he was going to keep an open mind about what had happened to Malcom because, as he put it, "everything could be possible, everything. We don't discard any type of situation. Someone's situation becomes so incredible, the people appear after seven or eight, nine years of disappearance, so… all of situation possible." Ultimately, he found nothing of any use and returned home.

And then something almost miraculous happened. Yuri made a contribution that outweighed his lack of ability as an investigator. He found the proverbial smoking gun. Quite by accident, Yuri and his wife found the most important piece of information that would appear for many years in the mystery of Malcom's disappearance. Brooke had managed to get a good-quality copy of the video that showed Malcom and Marcela having a drink on the last night he was seen. She sent a copy to Yuri. Yuri recalls that Brooke had asked him to see if he could glean a specific piece of information. "When Brooke sent me this video, she imagined that we're going to focus on the taxi driver, on the taxi number or the taxi person who come back to bring him to home, but we found something different," Yuri recalls. Yuri and his wife sat at his computer and went through the footage second by second. As they looked at the video, Yuri said, "My wife detected this type of movement..." Marcela was leaning over and putting some kind of powder in Malcom's drink. While it's easy to miss that slight movement when watching the video at full speed, once it's been pointed out, once the video is slowed down, it's as clear as can be and you wonder how you could have missed it in the first place. She was tampering with his drink. Yuri had some big news to share with Brooke when she arrived for her second research trip. And Marcela had some hard questions to answer.

CHAPTER FIVE

THE SECOND TRIP

Protected by her bodyguard and armed with the extra information – the GPS co-ordinates tracking her father's car and the emails showing the relationship falling apart and detailing the concern Marcela had over the house – Brooke felt she was ready to head down to Puerto Vallarta again. She wanted to talk to the police again, explore the locations the GPS had turned up, and, if possible, see if she could turn up any new information and be available for a possible ransom demand. Yuri took charge of the security for the trip. He believed it wasn't very smart to fly directly into Puerto Vallarta – too many people hang around that airport, according to Yuri, to report on who arrives and leaves. So instead, on November 25, 2018, Brooke flew to Mexico City. Yuri picked her up at the airport. They stayed the night and the following day they flew to Yuri's hometown, Guadalajara. After an overnight stop, Brooke was going to drive down to Puerto Vallarta with Yuri and do a little more searching. But before they left, Yuri casually mentioned something about "the drugging" scene in the video. Brooke said, "We were sitting there and he was talking about the drugging part and I said, 'Wait a minute, we saw she was doing something, but we've never seen the drugging part.' And he pulled up his computer and he put it in front of me." To her astonishment, Yuri showed Brooke the series of events that had been captured on the video. Brooke said, "You can see Marcela sitting sideways and my father beside her and we could tell from what we were watching, in the Andale's bar, that she was doing something in her purse, she was fidgeting, and she had pulled her hand out and she was holding something and she was thinking about it."

Brooke remembers the sequence of the footage clearly. For what seems a long time, Marcela sits on the bar stool, seemingly undecided about something. Eventually, she digs into her purse and draws out her hand, keeping whatever she has in her hand well hidden. Malcom then goes to the bathroom, and when he comes back Marcela seems ready to move ahead. Brooke recalls watching in horror as Marcela "cuts in and whispers something into my dad's ear and while she has his attention away from the drinks, she drops a powdery substance in his drink and stirs it a couple of times, and then allows him to have two or three sips before she pushes it away and won't let him have any more."

I've seen the video myself and the whole scene is reminiscent of watching an accident unfold. If that's ever happened to you, there's this sense that what you're seeing isn't real. This video has the same effect. When you're watching it, you can't believe it's really happening. But after a few plays, you realize you've just seen someone spike another person's drink. Then, a few minutes later, the couple gets up and leaves the bar. As Brooke notes,

> To anyone who might not know my father, it might just look like he's an older man who walks a certain way, because he's shuffling his feet as he's walking out of that bar, and that's not how my father walked. He walked purposeful, he took big, large strides, and he walked fast, and I can tell that there's something wrong and she's carrying two glasses, cups in her hands, and my father goes to try and reach for one of them, to help her I think, and she pulls away. So I can tell her energy towards him is not very friendly.

Malcom was never seen again after this video was taken at 12:30 a.m. on October 28. As Brooke said, "The minute I saw that I knew 100 per cent she was the main suspect." Truth be told, Brooke had pegged Marcela as the main suspect much earlier than that. She encouraged Mexican police to look closely at Marcela during her first statement. But any doubt she may have had was now certainly laid to rest. Brooke was elated by what

Yuri had found and was convinced this definitive evidence, once shown to the police, would lead to Marcela being immediately arrested. Not quite. Brooke was about to be introduced to the complexities of "Mexican justice."

Just before Yuri and Brooke headed down to Puerto Vallarta, while they were still in Guadalajara, Yuri took her to meet a new lawyer, Marina Manriquez Jiménez. Robb had heard of this person and suggested Brooke try her out. Brooke had been told that Marina was a "government lawyer" who would work at no cost on behalf of victims of disappeared people. She had a companion named Victor who worked with her and they brought along a translator. Brooke was only introduced to him as "Teacher." If you're starting to get an impression that this all sounds a little vague and perhaps questionable, then you'd be right. Brooke was very much out of her depth (who wouldn't be) in trying to navigate this investigation. She had no experience as an investigator and little experience dealing with Mexican bureaucracy. To this day, Brooke is unsure about who these people were and whether they had any real connection to the government. What Brooke did know was that when it came time to pick up travelling expenses, the "government" lawyer was not working for free. Brooke was expected to reach into her pocket and pay for everyone. And eventually Marina told her that she needed USD 4,000 to do the work. At that point, stuck in Mexico with no support around her, Brooke had little choice. She paid the lawyer. Brooke's new "team" had a couple of other tasks to accomplish before they left Guadalajara. The first was a meeting with the alleged head of the Dirección de Hechos de Desaparición de Personas – the Bureau of Missing Persons. From the information Brooke can piece together, this may have been Blanca Jaqueline Trujillo Cuevas, who worked as one of the key figures in the Bureau for Jalisco State. The other person at the meeting might have been Sheyka Guadalupe Martínez Torres, also a leading figure in that department. Brooke has never been absolutely positive that these were the people, but when she looked at some photos, these were the people she identified, and it made a certain amount of sense given where and when they worked.

Brooke was encouraged by the meeting and felt the "right" people were finally looking at her father's case. But not much was promised at the meeting except the usual "we're going to do whatever we can" kind of statements. The second chore the team undertook while still in Guadalajara was to meet a psychic who claimed to have more information on Malcom. This psychic, introduced only as "The Seer," predicted the future by reading tarot cards and, according to Brooke, deciphering cigarette ashes. To Brooke's surprise, she had constructed a shrine to Malcom in her house and told Brooke that he was very much alive and being held in some remote area. Skeptics might suggest Brooke was wasting her money on these people, but at the very least she derived a great deal of comfort from speaking with them and they created no real difficulties. So no harm, no foul.

After two nights in Guadalajara, Brooke, her bodyguard, lawyer, and translator hit the road for the six-hour drive to Puerto Vallarta. It's a beautiful drive through some of Mexico's most austere mountains – one of the main areas for growing agave for making tequila and mezcal. I made the drive with a crew in 2010 while working on a story. The last hour, as you come up to the Pacific coast, runs through tropical rainforest – a lovely winding road through the coastal mountains, with some stunning views of the Pacific Ocean. Brooke and her team pulled into Puerto Vallarta with enough time to make it to the police station. They were all very keen to show them the new evidence.

The first thing they presented to the police was the video. After all, Brooke didn't think she had to be a cop to understand that this was significant:

> I thought, oh my god, the gods are on our side. I mean it could have been like a movie set, you couldn't have set up that scene

> any better, with the camera catching her doing that. They could have sat at a different table, they could have sat with their backs, it was beautiful, it was perfect and it should have been enough… but it wasn't.

Brooke carefully pointed out to the police what Yuri had shown her just days before. In Brooke's police statement, given on November 27, 2018, she said,

> I also want to mention that after analyzing the video that we obtained from the ANDALE bar-restaurant, which is located on Olas Alta Street in Puerto Vallarta Jalisco Mexico, we could see that at 00. minute 05 second 08 (00:05:08) from the videos captured inside the bar, it can be seen that my father is in the company of MARCELA ACOSTA and at the same time it is seen that on her legs she is holding a black bag in which with her left hand she is looking inside the pocket for something. Seconds after, with her right hand she distracts my father by pouring something into the drink he was drinking at the time. This is seen at the hour 00 minute 05 second 51 (00:05:51), so following the sequence at the hour 00 minute 06 second 06 it is appreciated that she mixes with her right hand what she poured into my father's drink.

There is no disputing what can be seen on the videotape. Marcela tampers with the drink, Malcom drinks it, and minutes later she is seen leading an obviously staggering Malcom out towards a cab. The direct connection between Malcom's disappearance and Marcela cannot be disputed.

The Mexican police, however, didn't agree. Brooke was surprised by their reaction:

> Well, the first thing they did when they watched it – I watched it with two of them and they were definitely excited, but then this one other police officer came in and he looked at it and he

> looked over at me and he glared at me and he said in Spanish, how do we know she didn't doctor it?

Zab believes that in most other countries in the world this piece of evidence would have been decisive: "I think it would have been all finished that day when they saw the video. The Canadian police force, if they would…" He pauses and snaps his fingers before continuing, "Like that, I think it would be all finished. I think she would have been arrested like the next day. She would have been in jail." Brooke says this moment gave her a first glimpse into how much of a challenge this investigation was going to be. Faced with an incontrovertible fact, the police were refusing to acknowledge its importance. Brooke's first thought was that other factors had to be at play here: indifference, incompetence, or corruption. One thing was certain – there were other forces influencing this police investigation that she couldn't ignore. Jesus was quite certain what other factors were at play. "Money," he said. "I think they paid to the fiscal [prosecutor]…they pay money, you know. That's what I think." Yuri agreed. And he added that not only are the various levels of the justice system corrupt, but that corruption has created an environment of fear that makes a real investigation a challenge. It is, he says,

> a fully corrupt system. It's difficult to do something legal here, difficult to find someone. The person disappears and difficult to find the last person who see them. The people are scared to talk, scared to give some information, provide or get information about someone. Even lawyers, even the investigators, are scared to talk about it. So it's very difficult to find something.

Yuri says the first thing most people think of isn't co-operating with an investigation but protecting themselves and their families, "so the personal protection is most important things here, you need to provide protection by yourself, by your family, in this place, in this time, in this point of life." Brooke was also certain bribery had come into play: "I had heard rumours that there's a lot of corruption within the police force there and that bribing is quite a normal part of life for them. And I believe Marcela was paying someone to not be helpful." Brooke remembered the thousands of dollars Marcela had taken out of Malcom's bank account in the days following his disappearance:

> She had the money, like close to 4,000, that she had taken out of the bank and my father had about 9,000 on him and that obviously was gone, so, even before selling the house, there was a good chunk of American cash that was accessible and would have been appealing to anyone.

Though corruption on this level may seem to be a little difficult to comprehend for many Canadians or Americans, bear in mind that, according to a report by Transparency International, more than half of all Mexicans who have contact with the police are forced to pay a bribe.[5] Corruption is so commonplace that when I was working in Cancún years earlier we expected to have to pay the police on a daily basis to leave us alone. Though we had every right to be filming on the streets of the city, I was aware from earlier work trips to Mexico that it was quite common to have local police come over and ask to see a permit. Of course, there was no permit to show. We had accreditation as journalists from the Mexican Embassy in Canada and that was all we needed. But I soon learned that it was much easier, rather than stand there and argue (a losing proposition), to peel off a $20 bill and ask if I could buy the permit from them. Of course, they were happy to "sell" me the permit and allow us to continue filming.

During the trip we made to Puerto Vallarta to film *Malcom is Missing*, we were pulled over for a routine traffic stop. Our fixer, Gabriel, told us to hide our equipment, put on our COVID masks, and say nothing. The cop came to the window and chatted back and forth with Gabriel. Ultimately, Gabriel reached into his wallet and handed over 800 pesos. The cop saluted us and waved us on. Later over a beer, Gabriel said the cop wanted to confiscate the truck and all the gear at first, then had dropped his price down to 1,500 pesos and ultimately to 800 pesos – about USD 40. That might seem like chump change until you realize an average cop in Mexico makes about USD 350 a month – that's about 12 bucks a day. So, to put it in context, our cop just made more than three times his daily pay with one bribe. In fact, according to one report, there's a well-entrenched system in Mexico that has street cops paying part of their daily bribes to their bosses, who in turn kick some upstairs to their bosses. It's how they all survive. Given that system, imagine what Marcela could have done with USD 14,000. But short of either Marcela or the police and prosecutor confessing to taking a bribe, we'll never know whether money truly exchanged hands. The statistics suggest that money probably did change hands. And certainly over the course of the Malcom investigation so many of the basic steps would be delayed and delayed again and, when they were finally done, be done with so little attention to detail that it certainly seems there was intentional foot-dragging and even interference in the investigation.

But it wasn't just the police reaction to the video that led Brooke to believe the police were corrupt. She had one more compelling piece of evidence that the police showed complete indifference towards – the Trackimo GPS information from her father's emails. She shared this new piece of evidence with the police and invited them to look at the account for themselves. What happened next floored Brooke. It confirmed her suspicions that some kind of corruption was driving the police to muddy the case:

> I gave [the Trackimo] password to the police and the next time when I got back to Canada and I tried to access it, the password had been changed. So I had to contact Trackimo and I got back into it through them and everything had been deleted. Somebody

> had deleted the whole system of where that vehicle had been that night. I asked Trackimo and they said there's a manual little image for a garbage can, that the only way that could have disappeared is if somebody had gone in and trashed it all.

Brooke emphasizes that only two people had the password to that account, herself and the police. She hadn't touched the delete button, so it had to have been someone with the police or prosecutor's office. "That was my first hint that the police weren't working with me," she commented. Fortunately, the police did not have access to Malcom's email account and so the Trackimo emails giving the GPS co-ordinates and times of where the car had travelled were still intact. Despite her misgivings about the police, Brooke had little choice but to keep going back during this trip to try to get them to act on the evidence she provided.

Unbeknownst to her, she had some success. The police just weren't sharing what they were doing. For example, the police may have feigned indifference to the video from Andales, but when I obtained a copy of the police report, I noted that on the same day Brooke showed them the video and made a statement, they went to Andales and obtained the original copy of the video.

Aside from giving the police information, Brooke also pressed them to share any information they had discovered – something that was her right as a victim under Mexican law. They told Brooke they had found the taxi driver who drove Marcela and Malcom from Andales to their home. Brooke was elated. In fact, that night she was so convinced they'd just been handed a very important clue that she and the rest of the group went out and had a bit of a party. It was a short-lived celebration. When they returned to the police station the following day, the police told her they'd made a mistake. They had found the wrong guy. Brooke tells me that she walked out of the police station across to a garden and had a complete meltdown. In fact, according to police documents, it's a little fuzzy about when they actually talked to the taxi driver. There's some suggestion in court documents that they interviewed the man on November 30, 2018 – that would have been while Brooke was in Puerto Vallarta on her second trip. But I cross-checked that date with the original statement from the taxi driver that was filed in the police investigation and there is no date on the statement. So it's impossible to tell when exactly they did speak to the guy. At the end of the day, Brooke may not have been learning much about her father's disappearance from the police, but she was learning a lot about what to expect when dealing with the Mexican justice system. She was also continuing her education with Global Affairs Canada. During her first visit, they'd been singularly unhelpful, doing little more than handing her a list of lawyers who spoke English. This time wasn't much better. Once again, they had nothing to offer. Yuri describes the visit: "Even we went to the Canadian office, to the Canadian consulate, embassy, nothing was happening. They don't want to do something; they don't want to move nothing. It was a really, really bad experience to go there. They do nothing."

If police indifference was the first setback and the consulate was the second, there would unfortunately be a third on this trip. You may recall that while Brooke was still in Canada between trips Jesus had gone around putting up posters asking if anyone had seen Malcom. A reward of CAD 3,000 was offered for information. Two people called in. One from a remote village in the mountains claiming she had seen a man who resembled Malcom walking around her village. She called back the next day and admitted it probably wasn't Malcom and she had been more interested in the money. A second woman called and said a man was living in her building in Puerto Vallarta who looked like Malcom. But when she was pressed for details, she also admitted she was more interested in the money. That was it. Hundreds of posters put up around the whole city and only two bogus responses. At best, Brooke saw her second trip as one with mixed results. She'd learned about the crucial smoking gun evidence contained in the bar video, but she had failed to interest the police in that evidence. She'd also come with the GPS evidence in hand and the only result was that it appeared that someone in the police or prosecutor's office had tried to erase all traces of it. She'd papered the place with posters and nobody had responded. By the time she left Puerto Vallarta on December 1, 2018, she was not completely discouraged, but she was starting to understand this was going to be a long haul.

CHAPTER SIX

THE POLICE INVESTIGATION

When you watch a duck swim, it's a bit deceptive. On the surface the duck looks serene, as if it is doing nothing to propel itself through the water. But under the surface its feet are paddling like hell. As ludicrous as the comparison may sound, it's not dissimilar to what Brooke encountered when she dealt with Mexican police. Brooke often thought they were doing little or nothing to advance the investigation. In reality, and often unbeknownst to Brooke, they were scrambling to try and pull some kind of information together. At least that's what I found when I finally got what I was told was a copy of the police investigation in early 2022. I say "what I was told" because while I've searched through the thousands of pages of what I was given and have been able to find every important document referenced by other sources, and while I did have a Mexican journalist read through the whole file and annotate it and he felt it was complete, I don't read Spanish and so I'm not prepared to say with unwavering certainty that I have every piece of paper associated with the case. What I can reiterate is that I was given over 5,000 pages, and none of the pages that represented crucial steps were missing. I can also say this paperwork was part of the legal disclosure given to Brooke's lawyer and that it was represented to him as complete. Based on that, it appears that, while Brooke was shuttling back and forth between Port Hope and Puerto Vallarta and experiencing a frustrating lack of interest by the Mexican police and the prosecutor's office, both actually did have a number of lines of investigation underway. But there were two problems. First, they were not sharing much of that with Brooke – it may be that they were sharing it with her lawyers and they were not passing it on, but I suspect not. And second, much of the police and prosecutorial activity was not very productive. Much of it seemed to be "busy" work. It took up a lot of time, but it didn't accomplish very much from an investigative standpoint. And what they did accomplish was often initiated and completed so long after the crime that the information became virtually useless.

In 2006 I learned something very useful about the Mexican police. I was involved in an investigation for a documentary about the murder of the Ianiero couple – Nancy and Domenic – near Tulum, Mexico. For those who don't remember the case, it involved a Canadian family who had gone to Tulum (south of Cancún) to celebrate a daughter's wedding and were staying at a five-star resort. On the second morning at the resort, Domenic and Nancy were found in their rooms with their throats cut. It was a brutal crime, yet no money or valuables had gone missing. The case gained a lot of media attention in Canada and there was a lot of pressure on the Mexicans to solve the crime. Ultimately, a corrupt state attorney general came to the ludicrous conclusion that two middle-aged women from Thunder Bay – one a doctor and the other an emergency room nurse – were the killers.

It was clear the case had been bungled from the start – something I realized once the Ianiero family lawyer handed me a copy of the investigation. Basic police protocol had not been followed. The crime scene hadn't been sealed off and members of the public walked at will across the evidence. A huge number of basic investigative and forensic procedures had not been followed. The few activities they had attempted, like photographs and fingerprinting, had been done excessively. So, for example, crime scene photos of every single square foot of the room and adjacent hallways, even locations that were nowhere near the scene of the crime, existed in abundance. They covered every surface in the room with fingerprint dust looking for anything that didn't belong to the Ianieros or the maids. Yet police had failed to question the guests at the hotel in the aftermath of discovering the murders, and had even allowed many of them to check out and take flights home. And a security guard who had been seen lurking around the grounds when he wasn't on duty – one who had special forces military experience – was never considered a suspect, even though he disappeared from town shortly after the murders. I could list a number of other examples of excessive fastidiousness on one hand and extreme sloppiness on the other, but suffice it to say, in my experience, this was the typical pattern for Mexican police.

When I finally started to look at the Malcom case file, I discovered a similar pattern: the Mexican police were detailed about some investigative elements and glaringly negligent about others. There were also some serious problems related to the timeline of the investigation – police took weeks to move ahead with obvious investigative steps, weeks that in some cases negated the usefulness of any evidence they might have found. At the end of the day, I realized the police and prosecutor could have accomplished what took them a year in a matter of weeks had they been more efficient – and possibly more willing. That begs some questions about whether that was simply incompetence, a lack of resources, or whether someone was paying for an intentional slow down. Of course, Brooke thinks the delays were related to payoffs: "They completely expect you to give whatever it is you have." And if you don't give, then Mexican investigations don't always proceed in a logical or timely manner.

So let's take a closer look at Malcom's police case. He was officially reported missing on November 5, 2018, by Marcela – *nine days* after he went missing. She made her report at around nine in the morning. There was little in her statement to cause the police any undue concern. But a few hours later, Brooke went into the police station and gave a statement that should have set off alarm bells. Her statement left little doubt she had good reason to believe that something nefarious had happened to her father. That he hadn't, as police initially suggested, gone on some vacation or stormed off in a fit of pique after having an argument with Marcela.

Brooke had multiple reasons to challenge Marcela's story, starting with the timeline Marcela presented for Malcom's trip to Los Chonchos. Brooke had pointed out in her first statement that it was impossible for Malcom to leave the house at 2 p.m., shop for groceries, and still make a 3 p.m. ferry to get out to his tree house. She also pointed out to them that her obsessive-compulsive father would never change his patterns – he always called Jesus when he needed a taxi. Yet, according to Marcela, this time he inexplicably hopped in a strange taxi. Brooke also told the police, "JESUS says that he asked the operator of a boat my father used to travel to Los Chonchos, and he said that my father did not go to Boca de Tomatlán on October 28." So right off the bat, given Brooke's statement, police had a number of reasons to question Marcela's story. It didn't necessarily mean Marcela was lying or involved, but certainly there was adequate cause to start cross-checking Marcela's version of events. There was more.

Brooke also talked to the police about the peculiar financial transactions occurring with her father's account. She noted that Marcela had "in her possession a BANK OF MONTREAL bank and debit cards, with the number 5007 XXXX XXXX X202, and another debit card number 4506 XXXX XXXX X620 belonging to CIBC bank, linked to the account with the number 0114XXXX XXXX2." Brooke contended those were Malcom's personal cards. Malcom had given Marcela a card on their joint account. But he always kept his own cards separate. So why would he suddenly hand over all his personal cards to Marcela? Brooke told the police, "Because my father is a very suspicious person when it comes to money, and he would not give his cards so easily to MARCELA." Brooke also told the police about the multiple withdrawals Marcela had made from her father's account in the days following his disappearance – more than $4,000 in the three days. Brooke suggested to police that was a great deal of money for someone like Marcela, who had virtually no resources of her own: "MARCELA lived in a very humble room with all her family, and when she met my father, he bought her a house and took care of all the expenses, including parents, children, and siblings – and he paid for food, clothing, shoes, telephones, and other services."

Brooke also pointed out in her statement that their relationship was not in good shape and suggested that Marcela and her family may have been worried that the "money well" was drying up. Perhaps none of this provided definitive evidence that would allow the police to issue a warrant for Marcela's arrest, but all of Brooke's suspicions taken together should have raised some concern. Essentially, someone was missing, and his partner had a motive for making him disappear and had already made a statement to the police that had significant holes in it. In most police jurisdictions that would at least kick off a serious investigation. Not in Mexico. At least that's what Brooke believed.

Yet, when I looked at the investigative record, I could see that the police did in fact start some work. It's only on closer examination you can see that they're both doing a great deal and yet really doing little substantive work. They started by taking a boat out to Los Chonchos. A police inspector named José Luis Del Real Arellano took a water taxi down on November 6, 2018, the day after Brooke made her statement. They spent what seems to be a great deal of time walking around the place, taking pictures of the beach, Malcom's tree house, and the jungle surrounding the area. They carefully laid out the location on Google Maps. They tracked how long it took them to get there, and even how they travelled to the beach by water taxi. They provided a very brief handwritten statement mentioning they'd talked with a worker at the location – someone named Marcelino. They asked him about Malcom, and he told them two things:

> I was told by Ruben (the manager) the day Malcom would be here. Sunday October 28, 2018; for this, we already know that Malcom, always arrives at 10:30 in the water cab but Malcom did not arrive at the time he always arrives, it was very strange to me

> as I said Malcom is a very methodical person and always follows his same routines.

That statement essentially backed up what Brooke had said about it being very odd for Malcom to leave at 2 p.m. to go to Los Chonchos. He was such a creature of habit that even the staff at Los Chonchos knew he always followed the same routines. But here's my question about this first investigative step: Why did they bother to go to Los Chonchos? An officer named Héctor Rafael Hernández Salazar interviewed Jesus on November 6. Jesus confirmed he talked to the ferry operator and Malcom had not been seen on October 28, the day Marcela said he travelled to Los Chonchos. Why didn't the police just go down to the ferry terminal, find the water taxi operator, and confirm Jesus's story? That would have made going to Los Chonchos unnecessary. Why bother spending a whole day going when you have several witnesses who say Malcom never travelled there? But they were being methodical. They wanted to "dot all the *i*'s," so a team was dispatched to take photos of practically every square inch of the place. But given that someone was missing, and possibly in need of help, this trip seemed to be little more than busy work.

On the same day, November 6, another cop by the name of Pablo Ramon Zaragoza Ocho swung by to check out the house that Marcela and Malcom lived in at 141 Avenida Pavo Real. On the surface that also seemed like a good idea – inspect one of the locations that may be associated with a possible crime and start searching for evidence. But inexplicably the cop did not seem to go inside the house. He took a few pictures of the exterior and moved on. Maybe they didn't have a search warrant and, at this point in the investigation, may not have had enough evidence to get one. But without a warrant to search the place, why go at all? Why raise the suspect's level of suspicion? Did they bother to knock on the door to see if Marcela would let them in voluntarily? They certainly were not going to find anything of value on the outside of the house, so what did they hope to achieve? In fact, the police would not do a proper search of the residence for evidence for nearly nine months – long after any evidence found could be useful. The more I look at it, the more that first visit seemed like the police were essentially going through the motions of an investigation.

On July 25, 2019, a cop named Julio Cesar Angulo Moreno finally went by with a warrant and entered Malcom and Marcela's house. He snapped dozens of pictures of clothing, medication that was in the bathroom cabinet, the rooms in the house, some stuff in the garage, but nothing that in retrospect seemed of any real evidentiary value. The warrant stated he was looking for an iPad, a number of cheque books with the Canadian Imperial Bank of Commerce, and a great deal of clothing – shirts, jackets, and jeans. What they could have hoped to gain by seizing clothing nine months after the fact is beyond me, but it fits in with another typical methodology for this case – gather evidence but gather it long after it has any real potential value.

Several academic sources suggest that, when it comes to blood, "a delay of more than 48 hours may make the samples useless." Those same sources state that "other biological fluids have some of the same issues in collection as blood." And, finally, they acknowledge that "hair and fibres do not suffer from decay unless allowed to mildew or mould from exposure to wet." Given that, it's not surprising that when the Jalisco State forensic lab released its report about the evidence gathered at the house, it stated, "Regarding the request for the application of the luminescence reagent, *it was not applied since* in the tour and inspection that is carried out inside the house, *no biological traces were found* [emphasis mine]." I had to shake my head about that one for a while – a forensic lab saying that since it couldn't see any obvious traces of biological substances, it didn't bother to test for them.

While it was way too late to be testing material for blood or other body fluids, they could still have been combing through the evidence for hair and fibres that might have given them some information. But instead they went by the letter of the request and tested for fluids only. Since there was no visible evidence of fluids, they didn't test at all. There may have been a third search of the house. There are a series of colour photographs in the police documents that show the inside of the house, but it is hard to confirm that they are from a third search. No written statements are included with the photos, and they don't show up in the more extensive police report I obtained. The photos simply exist on stationery that seems to belong to the Jalisco State forensic lab. The trouble is that the date of the search is listed as September 2, 2017. If the date is accurate, it means the search took place over a year before Malcom disappeared. There's always an outside chance that the house had been searched for another reason. Marcela's brother, Martín, had recently spent time in prison, and they could have searched his sister's house in relation to that. Maybe, but unlikely. I believe that date to be a typo since I've run into a number of date anomalies on Mexican police documents. It's that phenomenon of being fastidious in some ways and unbelievably sloppy in others. I think the date is really September 2, 2019. That would make this information part of the potential third search of the house. But, of course, I can't prove that theory. So I've treated these photos as unusable as evidence.

During this same burst of activity, police also went down to the bar on November 7, 2018, and requested a copy of the videotape. At this point Brooke had talked about the video but didn't know about the images of Marcela tampering with the drink. Brooke had mentioned the video as a means of establishing a timeline for the night Malcom disappeared. While the police moved quickly on getting a copy of the video, they waited two months to analyze what they'd been given. Ultimately, only after Brooke's second statement on November 27, 2018, in which she pointed out that the drink had been spiked, did someone at the police department isolate the key frames that showed Marcela taking a vial out of her purse, pouring some powder into her hand and, within a few minutes, putting that powder in Malcom's drink. There's little question that, once they'd done that, they knew Marcela was involved in Malcom's disappearance.

Not taking any chances, in March 2019 the police sent the video to the state forensic lab. The lab examined it frame by frame – possibly looking to see if there was any evidence that the image had been manipulated – and made copies of the frame-by-frame cuts, which it sent back to the police stating,

> The required inspection of the contents of the guide brand USB storage device, model GAC074, with a capacity of 16 GB, blue colour, is carried out, the requested sequence of images is generated, which is printed as part of the opinion and recorded on a compact disc, which is attached hereto.

The lab didn't draw any conclusions, but it did certify that the frame-by-frame images it had examined were true images. That means the police were now certain Brooke or her lawyers had not tampered with the original video. So, by March 2019, based solely on the video, the police should have been certain Marcela was a prime suspect. Yet it would take the prosecutor's office a year to issue an arrest warrant.

As the days ticked by, the police took a number of other steps in the investigation. They took a second statement from Marcela on November 12. Her first visit to the police had been merely a missing person's report about Malcom. This time they called her in for a more formal interview. She reiterated the same things she said in the November 5 statement: she and Malcom went out for dinner, had a drink afterwards at Andales, and then took a taxi home. Malcom was kind of drunk, so her son Carlito helped her get Malcom into bed, then they both fell asleep for the rest of the night. They woke up late Sunday morning, and in the early afternoon Malcom took a taxi to catch the ferry to Los Chonchos. That was the last she'd ever seen of him. Marcela's son Andrés and her brother Martín also got called in for formal interviews. There are a few notable points in what they said. Andrés confirms his mother's narrative – that he saw Malcom on the morning of the 28th: "Approximately at 11:00 a.m. I woke up and I saw Malcom seating at a side of the bed… my mom was actually coming up to their room. She was carrying some coffee for Malcom."

In fact, Andrés was the only person who confirmed Marcela's story. Later, when police talked to other family members, including Marcela's mother, nobody remembered seeing Malcom. All her mother would say was that his luggage was in the hall when she left for church and was no longer there when she returned. She did not see Malcom that morning. Additionally, police talked to some of the neighbours and nobody recalled seeing him. But Andrés's statement was more interesting because of what he said by way of an alibi. He claimed he had a rock-solid one that put him in another state the night Malcom disappeared. He said his uncle, Martín Acosta Ramos, had invited him to a rooster fight. Andrés claimed to have spent Sunday afternoon helping his uncle build his new house in a suburb in the state of Nayarit, just north of Puerto Vallarta. After they'd finished working, they went to the cockfights and then to a bar where they hung out until 4 a.m. If that was true, then Andrés was nowhere near Puerto Vallarta when Malcom went missing. Martín said exactly the same thing: "That day we finished at around 19:30 approximately, and from there we went to the 'Palenque of Roosters' within Mezcales, on Mestizos Street, just a few blocks away from my house in Mezcales due to there being a rooster fight. And since I myself raise roosters, me and my nephew love to see rooster fights." He then continues: "Andrés and I were together, with some of my friends having beers. One of them is Nacho, they call him 'Pasadita,' also with Alejandro Peña to whom I know since 20 years ago, and he is missing a foot, and also with the owner of the Palenque: Rogelio Ruiz. And there we were drinking until 04:00 a.m. of October 28th 2018."

Now what interested me about Andrés and Martín's alibi for the night of the disappearance was that it could have been easily checked by the police. Martín specifically mentioned three people they were drinking with in the bar: "Nacho," Alejandro Peña, and Rogelio Ruiz. Martín and Andrés's whole alibi hung on the fact that three other men sat with them drinking until 4 a.m. And yet as far as I can determine, the police didn't bother to find these men and interview them. I've been through the documents of the police investigation several times and I can find no statements. These men could have absolutely proven or disproven what Martín and Andrés were claiming about their movements that night. The police had names and an address. So why wouldn't they simply take half an hour to drive out to Rogelio's bar and talk to them? Remember, they did have time to take a whole day to go to Los Chonchos. It's a bit of a head-shaker. I even reached out to one of the prosecutors I was in contact with – Juan José Mejía Gonzalez – and asked him about this. He didn't reply to my question. The only time these men showed up again was when Martín mentioned as part of his statement of defence that Rogelio could corroborate his whereabouts the night Malcom disappeared. But I note that there wasn't a sworn affidavit from Rogelio in any of the court documents. That made Martín's alibi very shaky and legally irrelevant.

During the early weeks of the investigation, police also took a second statement from Brooke. If she'd been suspicious about Marcela in her first statement, during her second she was downright accusatory. She handed over the information about the video and the GPS on her father's car, but she also handed over a great deal more. She gave police more details on the missing finances, she shared some of her father's emails with the police showing Marcela had a motive for making her father disappear, and she shared a text exchange she'd had with Marcela's other brother, Marco Antonio Acosta Ramos. He had been quite chatty with Brooke in the immediate aftermath of Malcom's disappearance. He'd made some surprising claims:

Marco: I suspected of Andrés Marcela's son.
Brooke: Why?

Marco: I saw couple of things.

Brooke: What did you see?

Marco: Andrés have couple friends. Those friends are bad people and yesterday Andrés call me... He say... Maybe Malcom is kidnapped because the day he left to Los Chonchos (Sunday) He has a lot of money to pay in Los Chonchos.

Brooke: Yes he did. So when do we hear something? Would they kill him? Where is all his stuff? Do you think he drove my dad that morning?

Marco: But when someone is kidnapped, they call for money.

Brooke: Do you think she knows? Marcela?

Marco: Yeah.

It's pretty clear Marco was hinting that Andrés may have been involved in kidnapping Malcom and that Marcela was probably aware of what was going on. Brooke thought it was pretty damning evidence. When she shared all that material with the police during her second statement, it seemed to light a bit of a fire under their investigation. In the next few weeks, the police found the taxi driver who picked up Marcela and Malcom at Andales and interviewed him (more on that shortly). They finally searched Malcom's car on December 5, and on the same day police brought Marcela in for a third statement.

During this third interview, Marcela still clung to the narrative she'd already established, but she made a couple of mistakes in what she said and inadvertently telegraphed a clue that would prove to be a major contradiction a few months later. The first mistake was that she became more specific about the taxi that took them home, stating,

> To one side of the planter, a taxi was parked, and the driver was standing outside the taxi, I remember it was a Toyota Avanza, with a grill in the canopy. Steering towards the driver of this taxi to ask for the service, I opened the door of the taxi so that he

> could get into. MALCOM and then I got into the car together with MALCOM in the back seat. I asked the taxi driver if he would take me to the Aralias neighbourhood.

Marcela didn't know the police had already found the driver. His name was José Guadalupe Ochoa García. And he was quite clear to the police that he did not, as Marcela kept insisting, drive her and Malcom home. Rather, he took them to the rear of a night club on the waterfront called Mandala. García told the police they both got out of the taxi and that Malcom did not have to be helped. His statement contradicted everything Marcela had told the police over the course of three formal statements – lying in a formal statement to the police is a criminal offence in itself in Mexico, punishable by a sentence of up to 20 years in prison. Marcela had lied about the fact that Malcom was so drunk he couldn't walk. She'd also lied about where they went – they didn't go home. The taxi driver also told police that Marcela was in contact with Andrés and Martín and that he believed they were waiting across the street when he dropped them off. Once again, a massive contradiction to what Martín and Andrés had said to this point. Remember, they had sworn they were at cockfights and then at the bar 30 kilometres north of where the cabbie dropped off Marcela and Malcom.

A second interesting point emerges from Marcela's December 5 statement. Brooke had been told by one of her informers that Marcela was tipped off by the police that they were about to search Malcom's car. Marcela seemed to pave the way in her third statement for the forensic team to find something and have a plausible explanation for it by stating, "I consider it pertinent to mention that there may be signs of some vomiting and urine in the vehicle, this is due to the fact that a niece of mine vomited inside the vehicle approximately a month ago and my father, who is ill, urinated inside [the] vehicle." Marcela seemed to be worried that if the police checked the car for any kind of biological markers, they might find something. Marcela need not have bothered with creating an alibi, because five days later, when the police finally searched the vehicle, they found nothing. Their report states, "the Vehicle of the Toyota brand Avanza type, Gold colour, plates JPJ3908, in which the fingerprints and beginnings, fibres, hairs (interior) were made, as well as luminol technique, yielding negative results throughout the interior of the vehicle."

No surprise there. The car had been in Marcela's possession for over a month. She had ample time to clean the car of any forensic evidence – bleach and soap are readily available in Puerto Vallarta. And secondly, as with the house, checking for body fluids long after a potential crime was somewhat of a waste of time. If the police had seized the car within days of Marcela becoming a suspect, they may have been able to do a proper forensic examination. But as it was the action smacked of mere showmanship.

By late August 2019, the Mexican police, according to their own reports, had sufficient evidence to arrest the three suspects. Malcom was still missing. There was still a possibility he was being held somewhere, but the chances of this being the case were remote. More likely he was dead and the suspects had killed him that night and disposed of his body. The police knew Marcela, Martín, and Andrés had lied during their statements and that they had taken Malcom's car to a jungle location for several hours during the middle of the night. They also knew Marcela had emptied Malcom's accounts within a few days and was now trying to sell the house. They had video of the start of the crime – Marcela drugging Malcom's drink. That all added up to means, motive, and opportunity, the classic parameters for prosecution. That should have added up to more than enough evidence to lay charges and issue arrest warrants for the three suspects.

But the police and the prosecutor did nothing of the sort. Mexican journalist, Jorge Olmos Contreras, wrote in the online publication, *Vallarta Uno*, on July 12, 2020, "On the contrary, it seems that René Ortega Roldán and the Investigative Police gave Marcela Acosta Ramos enough time to make money, with the sale of a house that the Canadian Malcom bought her, to later escape justice." He went on to say,

> Worst of all, is that the family of the disappeared Canadian is the one that has been providing data, evidence and others to the Prosecutor's Office so that the case progresses; that is to say, they did part of the work of the Public Ministry and now of the Investigative Police, despite the fact that it is a typical police task, and that it requires nothing more than common sense to execute it.

The inexplicable behaviour of Ortega and the police left Olmos asking, "When will the Public Ministry, René Ortega Roldán, be able to carry out a clean, hygienic process and will the investigating police comply with their assignment and bring those implicated in this crime to justice?" Olmos wasn't the only one who had observed that Ortega and the rest of the Bureau of Missing Persons were moving at a glacial pace. A report released in October 2022 was scathing about the lack of activity, inefficiency, and outright corruption that existed within this office. Among making other points, it stated, "When actions are not carried out or are omitted, either due to ignorance or fraud, they are also carrying out actions that could be classified as…crimes of corruption…it is necessary to generate true accountability mechanisms to reverse this situation."[6] The report was frank about the fact that the Bureau of Missing Persons in Jalisco was corrupt and showed little, if any, concern about the cases that were being brought forward, and had a rate of solving crimes that was painfully inadequate. From the date Malcom disappeared to the date an arrest warrant was issued, it ultimately took 16 months for Ortega's office to issue a warrant. It took a further four months to make the first arrest. Marcela was finally picked up on July 13, 2020. Martín wouldn't be arrested until September 2020, and it would take a further year to finally arrest Andrés in September 2021. And none of these steps would arguably have happened without significant pressure being brought to bear by Brooke on the police and prosecutors, forcing them to finally act.

CHAPTER SEVEN

MARCELA

Aside from Malcom and Brooke, the other central character in this story is Marcela Acosta Ramos. I wanted to paint a clearer picture of who she is and what might have motivated her. But despite a great deal of research, there wasn't really very much to be found when I went looking. Brooke and the rest of Malcom's family knew surprisingly little about her – other than their belief they all held that she was some kind of a "gold digger." What little can be found comes partly from what turned up during the police investigation into Marcela. A little bit more can be found in her correspondence with Malcom. But on the whole there's not a lot. For example, I can't find any references to her making a living in any way – other than a vague mention of her working as a clerk in some store and possibly as a security guard after Malcom went missing. So how she supported herself and her children during the years leading up to her meeting Malcom remains a mystery. Of course, she regularly had male partners and it's possible she depended on their money, but she said nothing to Malcom about receiving any kind of alimony or child support. Here's what we do know.

The police social evaluation report dated October 13, 2020, states that she was born in the village of Hostotipaquillo in Jalisco State in 1974, about 100 kilometres northwest of Guadalajara. It's in the middle of a large stretch of mountainous jungle. It's not on any main road, and to get there you have to get off Highway 15 and take what appears to be a dirt road north into the hills. Perhaps the most notable nearby population centre is the town of Tequila. Online sources say Hostotipaquillo has just over 10,000 people and the town web page brags about being founded when the area was conquered by the Spanish in 1530. The townsfolk also seem very proud of a historic church called the Temple of the Virgen del Favor built in 1615. The area has some mining activities and a little logging, but it appears that agriculture has always been the main activity that supported the town. To sum up with a couple of apt clichés, this is the proverbial one-horse town in the middle of nowhere. There's no mention of what her father did for a living, but the odds favour him working as a farmer. All the police report said about her childhood was that she was the eighth child of nine and that "her basic needs and affective were partially covered." Given the translation, I take that to mean she had food, clothing, and a roof over her head, but little more.

There's a strong possibility Marcela didn't have a great deal of formal education. Online sources about the town indicate that only 23 per cent of the population finish primary school. One thing I learned about these early years was from Marcela when she told Malcom she didn't like her mother. We also know she was married at a very young age. The police report says she got married in 1991 at the age of 17. She had two children: Andrés, born in 1992, and Carlito in 1993. Marcela was still a teenager when she became the mother of two children. That may not have been unusual in the rural area she came from. Her mother had nine children, which suggests she began bearing children at a similarly young age. The report added that the relationship between Marcela and her first husband "disintegrated due to the divorce of the couple, after 12 years," but it does not give very much information on why the relationship fell apart. However, that timeline would make it around 2003.

At some point, Marcela and her family moved to Puerto Vallarta. There isn't a mention of when, just a conversation that Marcela had with Malcom about the family owning some property in the "pink zone" – the red-light district. She talked at some length about the problems they had selling the property because squatters had moved in and taken it over. Under Mexican law, according to Marcela, that gave them some rights to the property. She also talked with Malcom in the email chain about another man she had a long-term relationship with whom she refers to as "the teacher." In an email to Malcom on January 10, 2013, she mentioned him a couple of times and not in very flattering terms: "My last relationship I had was before I met you was with the teacher about told you ... He never trusted me, doubted all the time, that I was faithful, he also in some way cheating me ... When he died I felt guilty about his death." Oddly, one of the things she did tell Malcom was that her previous spouse died under mysterious circumstances. The story varies, depending on the source, but it was either as a result of an overdose of insulin or a cerebral hemorrhage. In one email, Marcela talks about an ugly fight she had with the man and ends by saying she

> finally told him that men like him could be found on every corner. I think what he was bothered much with what I said. And from that day he began to feel unwell. Three days after, he had a cerebral infarct and he died. He was diabetic and took no care. Each week, he drank to get drunk. But even so it took two years for me to finally understand that I was not responsible for his death.

That's a very interesting snippet of information: the partner she had prior to Malcom died under mysterious circumstances. Also note that she felt she had to explain to Malcom about not being responsible for his death. When you couple that piece of information with the fact that Malcom vanished under mysterious circumstances, that makes for an odd pair of facts. Two of Marcela's partners in a span of about ten years died under questionable circumstances. And, as it turned out, there was a third – more on that shortly.

We find out a great deal more about Marcela after she met Malcom in 2011 or 2012. Brooke didn't have a specific date, but her correspondence with Malcom began in 2012 and ran through until he vanished in 2018.

When she first met Malcom, we're told by Brooke she's living in very modest circumstances. Of course, within a couple of years, Malcom had bought them a large house and they all moved in. She didn't work while she was in the relationship with Malcom. At least there's no mention of any work and she seemed to be totally dependent on him for any money. Malcom paid for all of her medical bills, paid for her son Andrés to take courses as a paramedic, and paid all of the expenses associated with the house. She did seem to have a great number of medical complaints. She was always complaining to Malcom about some health issue – mostly to do with her reproductive system. He always seemed to be paying out money for treatments – mostly in cash. She frequently explained to him that they couldn't have sex because she'd just completed some treatment. And that was pretty much what was on the record until 2018. As I said, slim pickings.

After Malcom disappeared, Marcela continued to live in Puerto Vallarta until she sold the house (sometime in 2020) and moved out of town in early 2021. From information Brooke obtained from one of her informants, we know she moved to a suburb of Mexico City. She also started a new relationship, moving in with a lawyer named Julio Alejandro Márquez Camacho. Here's where the story becomes intriguing again. Within months of hooking up with Marcela, Márquez also died under mysterious circumstances. The Mexican press had a field day with this. As Jorge Olmos reported in *Vallarto Uno* on July 16, 2020,

> Another boyfriend of Marcela Acosta dies under strange circumstances; he was shot on July 4 … An entire new investigation hangs over Marcela Acosta Ramos, the woman who was arrested just Tuesday in the State of Mexico for her alleged responsibility in the disappearance of the Canadian Malcom Madsen, since another of her boyfriends, the lawyer Julio Alejandro Márquez Camacho, died under strange circumstances on July 4 (13 days

> ago) in Tlalnepantla de Baz and relatives of the deceased today suspect Mrs. Acosta Ramos.

Apparently, Márquez was out in the street in front of his house when he was approached by a gunman and shot in the stomach. He died later as a result of a massive infection to the wound. Olmos continued, "The lawyer died near the house where he lived on Convento del Carmen street in the Los Reyes Iztacalq neighbourhood, that is, he was shot there, but no one was identified as allegedly responsible for the crime." Olmos goes on to say, "Now, in the case that concerns us, that of Marcela Acosta Ramos, if her participation in the death of the lawyer is proven, we could be facing a pattern of behaviour of a woman who looks for adult men with money or belongings to win them over and then get rid of them." In other words, Olmos was suggesting that Marcela was some kind of black widow who hooked up with men, took their money, killed them off, and moved on to the next victim. That's unproven, of course, but it is an unbelievable coincidence that Marcela could have had three partners in roughly ten years, all of whom died under mysterious circumstances. I'm not sure how to calculate the odds, but they would probably be astronomical. Of course, the Mexican media felt no constraints in running with this theory – whenever Marcela was mentioned in headlines after that, she's referred to as the "black widow."

Interestingly, the psychological profile done by the police in 2020 provided some support for Marcela having possible sociopathic tendencies. The psychiatrists suggested she "establishes interpersonal relationships superficially and selectively," and concluded, "as for the illicit conduct, she does not recognize any responsibility regarding herself." So, no real meaningful relationships and a lack of ability to accept responsibility for her actions – not a good combination, both of which are a part of most medical definitions of sociopathy. The report went on to conclude that Marcela is "in full use of her mental faculties, that she is capable of distinguishing the good from the evil, which allows her to perceive the moral, social and legal significance of her actions." But sociopaths often know what they're doing is wrong; they just don't care.

That's pretty much everything I could find out about Marcela in terms of facts, but I think there's a great deal more to be gleaned from unpacking her life and circumstances. I think it's clear she grew up poor, was married off very young, and spent most of her life scrabbling to make any kind of a living to support her children. I think that would make any person who was forced to survive in that manner tough – you'd have to be in order to survive. But I think Marcela had a few things going for her: she was obviously smart, in a street-wise kind of way, and she was pretty. Pictures of her as she aged showed a person in fairly good shape but with a very hard and unforgiving face. But early pictures – when Malcom first met her – showed a very pretty woman in great physical shape. Marcela probably had to capitalize on those attributes. Particularly in light of having to support a disabled child – her son, Carlos Antonio Romero Acosta (Carlito), has some kind of disability. Marcela mentioned seizures in some of her emails and, from his appearance, he is clearly afflicted with some kind of handicap. All in all, Marcela really was in a position where she had to scramble to survive. It's not an uncommon position for a great number of young women in Mexico, other parts of Latin America, and throughout the Third World. A position that many Canadian and American men take advantage of – I've seen this first-hand.

A few years ago, I was invited to go scuba diving in Cuba. At the time, aside from working as a producer for CTV's *W5*, I was writing for a number of diving magazines, and the trip organizer was interested in drumming up some publicity. I was delighted to accept the invitation. I regularly went to places in the Caribbean, dived, and wrote reviews. There was one rather cryptic part of the invitation I was curious about. I had been told this trip was "one for the wolfpack." Initially, I thought it meant it was just a bunch of boys getting together to go diving. As soon as we arrived at the resort, I realized the phrase had an entirely different meaning. There was a group of young and very pretty Cuban women waiting for the bus as we pulled in to the resort. As the "wolfpack" got off the bus, three of the men were immediately embraced by young women. There was a substantial age difference. Most of the men were in their late 50s or early 60s. The women all looked to be twenty-something. During the next week I watched these "relationships" in action with some interest. This was a rather remote part of Cuba. The nearest village had little industry. The sugarcane factory had closed and that left subsistence farming for the most part as the only way to make a living. As with Marcela's family, the economic conditions meant that many families would be scrambling to survive. They would have to use what assets they possessed. Sometimes those assets were daughters. By the end of the second day, all of the other men on the trip had linked up with women. In fact, by the third day, I was asked by the trip organizer if I was interested in meeting someone. I declined the invitation. As a result, I was looked on as something of a pariah for the rest of the trip. The "wolfpack" started avoiding me in the evenings. There was little to suggest that these relationships were anything other than sexual. In fact, I noted that during the evening when the "wolfpack" sat around with drinks, the Cuban women would sit at one table talking and the Canadian men would sit around swapping diving stories at another table. There was no attempt to disguise the nature of these relationships. It was purely a matter of hedonistic delight for the men and financial compensation for the women. Everyone seemed comfortable with that state of affairs.

Thinking there might be a good article in it, I did try to talk with one of the young women who spoke English. She was unwilling to tell me any of the details of her circumstances or to talk about her relationship with her elderly Canadian man. As a side note, there was one Canadian woman on the trip who had a very young Cuban man waiting for her when she arrived. I've heard of other examples like this, but often it's associated with the younger man wanting to marry someone and get the hell out of Cuba.

While I was somewhat surprised at how blatant these relationships were, I was not shocked by the fact they were occurring. I had heard about Cuba being a destination for sex tourists, and years earlier I'd also seen it in action in Thailand when I was travelling around. The bottom line is that any time there are men who have money and women who need some kind of financial assistance, the ground is fertile for these kinds of relationships. Malcom's former partner, Josie Schywiola, had some thoughts about the matter based on her own observations, "because there's all kinds of men that I know who have got girlfriends in Cuba and they've got girlfriends in Honduras and they've got girlfriends in these poorer countries." She went on to say, "At the end of the day, when you're in a country where people are trying to survive and eat and feed their children, keep them sheltered, keep a roof over their head, these women will say anything, they'll do anything if these men are prepared to give them money that will help them survive." She also added that, in her opinion, the whole thing is somewhat pathetic:

> I see other men I know going down that same road... they were all kind of womanizers their whole life, but as they got older, they couldn't pull that shit off any more in Canada, you know, but they could pull it off in these Third World countries, they were desired and I think there was this veil here that needs lifting. Buddy, you're desired because you're like a king to them, your money – and a lot of them don't have any money.

Josie stopped short of describing Malcom in that manner: "I'm not saying Malcom was that kind of statistic, but a buck here and a buck down there is like night and day, it can be everything between eating and not eating."

In Mexico, this phenomenon has almost become an industry. If you go online and search terms like "dating" and "Mexico," you'll stumble onto a slew of websites that offer older American and Canadian men a chance to date young attractive Mexican women. There is no attempt to keep these sites or these liaisons discreet. In fact, some of these sites host parties for the men once they get down to Mexico – an opportunity to "shop" for the right young woman. If you do a little searching online, you can find some video footage of these parties. It's a little creepy watching 60- and 70-year-old men trying to party with these young women. Nothing seems quite so pathetic as a 75-year-old trying to look cool dancing to the sounds of a DJ with a smoking hot young woman.

To get a personal sense of this dynamic, I spoke with a friend of Brooke's who we'll call Martina. She's in a relationship with a Canadian man but still spends a great deal of time in Puerto Vallarta because that's where her family and friends still live. I asked her about this business of older men hooking up with younger woman. Right off the bat she said it's "not uncommon to have older men and younger women in relationships in Puerto Vallarta. Right now, I have one friend who is being taken care of by an older American. He rents her a condo and she takes 'care' of him when he's there. In fact, she has a young boyfriend on the side."

Martina said these relationships are usually well understood by both parties. The man provides financial security and in return gets a young attractive girlfriend with benefits. Martina said, "The girls all understand what the deal is – you get something, but not love or family." The whole dynamic repulses Josie: "So these men who think they're kings when they go to these countries, it's like are you fucking kidding me?! Wake up, really look at what's happening, you know, pay attention. There's a price attached to anything."

This is not to say that the relationships don't sometimes evolve into something more profound. In Martina's case, she married her Canadian man. They've been together for 16 years and have two children. She has a network of friends in Canada who have also developed long-term relationships. But that's not always what happens. Martina says it comes down to the person's values. If they're not trying to scam someone, then there's a chance the relationship can evolve.

This conversation with Martina led me to wonder about the kind of relationship Marcela had with Malcom. Was it money for sex or something more serious? Certainly, Marcela seemed aware of the ground rules. She provided Malcom with sex and a place to stay when he was in town, and she expected him to pick up the bills. The problem might have been that Malcom was not fully aware of those rules. When you look at his emails, you realize he believed this was a "real" relationship. He believed the two of them were in love. So it's only natural to him that when he's no longer in love with Marcela then the relationship was over. But when Malcom decided the relationship had run its course and he wanted out, he was breaking the contract in Marcela's mind. And where did that leave her? She was no longer a young sex kitten. She was now an unskilled, middle-aged woman with a handicapped son to provide for and two aging and ill parents. There's a real possibility Malcom's move towards ending the relationship broke the rules of the relationship game and created a deep desperation in Marcela. The kind of desperation that could lead her to extreme acts.

CHAPTER EIGHT

THE THIRD TRIP

As the first year of Malcom's disappearance passed, Brooke, unaware of what was being done, began to worry that the police were doing almost nothing. She believed that while the police hadn't been completely idle, they hadn't really been aggressively following up on many of the leads that were available – leads she had provided. They hadn't searched the locations where Malcom's GPS indicated his car had been the night he disappeared. This was a particular bone of contention for Brooke. Malcom's car had been parked for several hours beside a stretch of overgrown bush in a neighbourhood of the town of Mezcales in the state of Nayarit, about 20 minutes north of Puerto Vallarta. It's not all that big a section of "jungle" – about 500 square metres – but there was lots of privacy available in the midst of this overgrown bush. Brooke was certain it was pivotal to the investigation. She believed it could have been the location where her father was killed the night he was kidnapped. It might even be the area where his body was buried. But despite repeated requests to police to take cadaver dogs into the area, they hadn't made any moves. They claimed the situation was complicated. The investigation was being handled by Puerto Vallarta police. They worked in Jalisco State. Mezcales is in the state of Nayarit.

While it's true this jurisdictional issue can make things complicated, it's not impossible for police to work in another state. There had been other examples during the investigation where the two police agencies had worked together – questioning witnesses, for example. So it was feasible for them to search the area. There just didn't seem to be the desire to do so. But this wasn't the only part of the investigation Brooke was getting increasingly concerned about. As far as Brooke knew, they also hadn't obtained copies of the phone records belonging to Marcela, Martín, and Andrés. Brooke was sure those records could be plotted to track where the three suspects were all night. The records could prove whether they really were at home or at the bar. Additionally, as far as Brooke knew, the police hadn't yet searched the house Malcom and Marcela shared. Brooke decided that the police and the investigating prosecutor, René Ortega, needed a little motivation to move the investigation ahead. She felt this push was better done in person. That meant another trip down to Puerto Vallarta. There was a second reason she wanted to go back. Brooke felt it would be a great time to meet her new lawyer to get a better feel about his competence.

Brooke had never been happy with her Mexican lawyers. She'd begun with Norma Rodríguez, a Puerto Vallarta-based lawyer recommended by the Canadian consulate. That hadn't worked out. Brooke felt Norma spent more time making up invoices than getting solid information from the police. Then Brooke had hired Marina Manriquez Jiménez, the lawyer from Guadalajara. But after a promising start in which Brooke was introduced to some important people in the justice department, Brooke believed her effectiveness waned. Like Norma, Marina seemed to present a great many large bills for her work, but Brooke felt not much was getting done. So, in early 2019, Brooke started to look around for another lawyer. This time she made what appeared to be an even less conventional choice. She was introduced to a lawyer from Costa Rica named Ricardo Ananias Loaiza Morales. She found him through her father's friend, April Aboud. When Malcom was down in Costa Rica looking for an investment property, April recommended Ricardo as someone who could handle the property purchase. Malcom was happy with the work done by Ricardo. He ended up steering Malcom away from a real estate deal that might have taken Malcom for a considerable sum of money. Ricardo explained,

> The people that wanted to sell, raised the value after he agreed on the money, they raised the value 20,000 or something of that sort, and then I told him don't buy them. People that deceive you the first time, they will deceive you a second time... Then we look for another lot. And then he says, you were right, I like the way you think.

Ricardo says the two went on to be firm friends after that. Given that Malcom had already done business with Ricardo, and that he was also April's lawyer, in January 2019 Brooke reached out to him to ask him whether he thought he might help with her case in Mexico. Ricardo remembers that phone call:

> April Aboud call me and then put Brooke on the line, and then she started asking me questions – "Is this Mexican lawyer doing a good job? What should we do, in your experience?" I'm a 27-years criminal lawyer experience. So that's how we connect. And I connected really well with Brooke.

Brooke said she had a very good feeling about Ricardo. He had experience in criminal law and he'd worked international cases before, so she hired him. He wasn't cheap. Over the next year, he would bill Brooke for in excess of USD 100,000 for the work he was doing – that included travel costs, office costs, and his salary. The agreement was Brooke would pay most of the money up front and this money would cover his fees right up to the point of trial, then they would renegotiate. While it was a lot of money for Brooke, she felt it was money well spent. She finally had a lawyer she completely trusted.

Ricardo Loaiza was born in 1972 and raised in San José, Costa Rica. He graduated from the University of Costa Rica with a law degree in 1994 and began practising the same year. The year he graduated he founded his own legal practice. Though he took on a lot of real estate law, he says he was also a practising criminal lawyer and he dabbled in a bit of international law. He was quite proud of the fact that he'd represented some celebrity clients from the United States. He wouldn't say who they were, but he did drop hints about Hollywood. According to Ricardo, these celebs lost some money to a bank in Panama. Ricardo got it back.

Now when I was doing my due diligence on Ricardo, I did find a couple of potential red flags in his history: he was called in front of a tribunal for some misdealing with a property he came into possession of. Something about illegal use of money held in trust for a property or business transaction. He also seemed to have some kind of involvement with a vague company based in Panama. But either one of these flags could be explained away. One as a reasonable mistake; the other as a conventional part of doing business in Central America – it might just make sense to be incorporated in Panama instead of Costa Rica.

So Ricardo was brought in to advance Malcom's case – sort of. One of the first things he established with Brooke was that he believed Malcom was dead:

> I think they kill him. They kill him and they kill him because it's easier to get rid of him. Dead people doesn't talk and he will never fight back for the house in a civil litigation, he will never bring other big lawyers to fight for the house or claim or put a lien on the house. So, for them it was the short way to get rid of him. Just kill him for the trouble he was causing to their family… five, six people living in that house because of Malcom and he was giving them every month, money. Besides the house and the two cars, he was giving them money, so he was – by selling the house – taking away their way of living, so they just kill him.

Ricardo decided that Malcom's threat to sell the house, stop providing money, and leave Marcela and the rest of her family on the street was enough of a threat to galvanize them to act. He suggested that, though the house was registered in Marcela's name, the family had no money to fight a protracted lawsuit should Malcom contest who owned the house. The easier course was to just get rid of Malcom. He believed they drugged Malcom that night, took him to a remote location, and either killed him that night or on a subsequent night. Agreeing with Ricardo's analysis was a very hard step for Brooke. But she finally accepted it in November 2019 and had Malcom declared legally dead.

Meanwhile, Ricardo became more and more her trusted advisor. Brooke says, "Every day my morning starts with... I need to track down Ricardo and talk to him about this." She soon found that Ricardo was much more than just another lawyer. She felt he was a decent human being with a fearless attitude when dealing with corrupt Mexican officials:

> He's incredibly compassionate, he's very smart... I don't think many people can find lawyers that want to do this job. I know a lot of other Canadians are having a terrible time finding a lawyer that's brave enough to even deal with this kind of stuff, especially if they're a Mexican lawyer. He's a brave dude.

And aside from being a "brave dude," Ricardo quickly proved to Brooke he was also pretty street-smart when it came to how things worked in the Mexican justice system. Brooke said, "I was still fairly naive until Ricardo walked onto the scene. Ricardo took one look at the situation and he said there's no arrests going to be made, Brooke, we've got to play this a whole different way."

Ricardo suggested to Brooke that what she had believed was possibly incompetence in the Mexican justice system was, in fact, much more than that: "I couldn't understand why things weren't happening and he explained to me that they were purposefully not happening." When I spoke with Ricardo, he also suggested that he suspected the foot-dragging by the police and prosecutor was intentional. Ricardo also convinced Brooke that she was going to have to take a more aggressive stance if she wanted her father's investigation to move ahead. As she put it, "He made me realize nobody was ever going to help us, unless we made them help us." Ricardo, she said, also had a great number of suggestions about tactics they could use to get around the system in Mexico.

In a system this corrupt, Ricardo seemed aware that certain financial incentives might have to be provided to make the process run smoothly. Brooke said, he "found another avenue. And we didn't actually have to take the avenue we thought we would at this point." That cryptic reference related to the fact that Ricardo was suggesting that money may have to change hands to make the system work more effectively. As Brooke had suspected, it wasn't just happenstance that evidence wasn't being gathered and followed up on. It wasn't being done because someone was making sure it wasn't being done. Money was already changing hands in Ricardo's opinion. Of course, Brooke and Ricardo couldn't be sure at this point who that person or persons were, but they certainly had their ideas about who was paying and who was being paid. It didn't take much sleuthing for Brooke to figure out who that might have been.

The first question Brooke asked was who would benefit from the case not proceeding? The answer was clear – Marcela, Martín, and Andrés were facing a life in prison if the evidence was gathered and the case made it to court. Marcela had Malcom's money – the $13,000 she gleaned in the immediate aftermath of his death. In addition, by late 2019 she'd also sold the house Malcom had bought. That raised an additional $250,000. Marcela did buy another house with part of that money, but one that was more modest. Conceivably, there would have been money to spare. So it's a simple matter to guess who would want the case to go away and who had money to pay the police and prosecutors to make that happen.

On the other side of the equation, the question had to be asked, who had the authority to slow down or even stop the investigation? Brooke believed that path led to only one person – the man in charge of the case: René Ortega. Now Ortega wasn't the only possibility – it could also have been any of the main police investigators or another prosecutor from the Puerto Vallarta office, but Brooke and Ricardo focused on Ortega as the most likely person.

Interestingly, once Brooke concluded what they believed was really going on, she and Ricardo were able adjust their tactics and push the investigation ahead in a more efficient manner. They started with bypassing Ortega's office. Ricardo went to Guadalajara and met with the head of prosecution for "the disappeared" for the whole of Jalisco State. That meeting brought pressure to bear on Ortega's office, which then finally began the process of issuing an arrest warrant. Thinking more tactically didn't mean the whole process suddenly became easy – every step forward was still a challenge, but with Ricardo on her side, Brooke felt they had a chance to succeed. "We've had some up and downs," she remarks. "There's been some very stressful moments between the two of us, but, oh, god, I don't know what I would do if I didn't have him. I wouldn't be here."

Ricardo felt they had to keep hammering away and pushing the police to follow up on obvious leads. So, throughout 2019, Ricardo made trips to Puerto Vallarta to talk to Ortega in person: he demanded to see documents and insisted on being present for certain key investigative steps. On September 8, 2019, Brooke decided to join Ricardo on one of these trips, so she made her third trip down to Puerto Vallarta. This time the two of them would see what they could do to really put some heat on the police and the prosecutor.

Overall, Ricardo had a game plan. He would keep pressure on the police and prosecutor to ensure they issued warrants and had Marcela, Martín, and Andrés arrested. After that he would try to ensure they stayed in jail pending their trial and, ultimately, he would oversee the trial process on Brooke's behalf. He told Brooke that if the trial didn't work out in their favour, he would then take the case to the Inter-American Court of Human Rights, an international court based in San José, Costa Rica.

Now while some of Ricardo's plan seemed logical, this whole

"international court" concept was another red flag for me. He suggested to Brooke they might be able to launch a case with this international body if the Mexicans continued to drag their feet. But after a little research I discovered that's not how the international court works. It's a court that can be appealed to as a last resort, but only after all legal avenues have been exhausted in the country where your case originates. Ricardo couldn't launch a case in this court at the same time as the Mexicans were still dithering around. Besides, the international court is really a human rights court that only has jurisdiction in cases where a clear violation of someone's rights can be proven. In Malcom's case, the connection to a human rights abuse case is somewhat tenuous. It would be a stretch to say his rights had been violated because he had disappeared and the Mexican government had not conducted an adequate investigation to find him. So, given that tenuous connection, there was some question about whether the international court would even look at the case.

There was still one more red flag for me: Ricardo had convinced Brooke they would have to go to Washington, DC, to launch the case and that would require more money. But the court is in San José, Costa Rica, and to launch your case you just fill out the needed forms online. All that had to be done was to submit them online to the office in San José. I was always puzzled about why a lawyer with Ricardo's experience wouldn't have known that.

On her third trip, once again Brooke travelled to Puerto Vallarta with Zab. When I asked her about the week and what she felt she and Ricardo accomplished, she told me, "We spent most of the time at the police station." But Brooke felt that dealing with the cops this time was a little different. With Ricardo leading the way, Brooke was able to finally penetrate the inner sanctum of the justice building. Before, she says she had been forced to cool her heels in the lobby. Now she was able to attend the meetings they had with Ortega. Brooke believed he wasn't very happy she was back in Puerto Vallarta:

> I really realized then how much Ortega disliked me because he made a point of like trying to never look at me and as he was shaking everyone's hand, shaking my hand was the last thing he did and you can tell he just hated it. He never looked at me or spoke to me, like he just hated me.

Brooke also talked about an incident she witnessed while she was inside the justice building that had a profound impact on her understanding of Mexican justice: "These two women came in there just holding this black and white photo of their missing young man and I remember they looked at Ortega like he was such a god – they thought he was going to help them." Brooke says that, from what she saw, Ortega was not the least bit interested in helping these women, no more than he was interested in helping her. She felt he was indifferent to their problems (though, ironically, missing people investigations is what Ortega specializes in as a prosecutor) and that any hope the women had was false hope. There was some basis in fact for Brooke's feelings – at least if the study I mentioned earlier was anything to go by. But while being with Ricardo did allow for some access into the inner sanctum of Ortega's office, there were still obstacles being placed in front of Brooke and her team. Often these were petty obstacles. For example, each time they asked for a document, they were told the photocopy machine was broken. The only way they were able to get copies was to spend time laboriously taking pictures of documents on their cell phones. And they were only given a limited amount of time to take those pictures. It meant that rather than have full copies of key police documents, they would often have to quickly scan through them and try to determine what was critical and then photograph only those parts. In fact, though (once again) Ricardo did not seem aware of it, they could have filed a request in the local court that gave them standing in the case as the victim's family. The police and prosecutor would have been obliged to give them everything once they had that standing. Instead,

Ricardo would often spend hours taking photos of thousands of pages of documents. The photos were often illegible. When Ricardo shared those "documents" with me, many were almost incomprehensible – the edges blurred, sometimes the whole page out of focus.

One investigative step Brooke and Ricardo accomplished during this trip was to finally get the police to go out and search the jungle location indicated by the GPS on Malcom's car. Brooke said, "It bothered me they hadn't searched this area prior." Nonetheless, even though this was something she had wanted to achieve for some time, she was a little nervous about the prospect of going to a remote location with the police. She says Ricardo made her feel safe. The police went with them and searched the jungle location, but without dogs. They also took the time to check all the locations where Andrés had been living and where Martín was building his house. Bear in mind this is a year after Malcom had disappeared. They found nothing.

The police also showed Brooke and Ricardo some of the evidence they had seized from the search of Malcom's house, which they finally searched in late July 2019. They sent Brooke a link where she would be able to view photos of evidence – the theory being that Brooke might recognize an article of clothing. They also returned a number of items to Brooke that had belonged to her father that they had seized during the search.

Ricardo and Brooke also wanted to make sure the police were factoring in all the evidence that had previously been given to them. Ricardo felt the police always seemed to be looking for an excuse to not believe the evidence put before them. Take the example of the bar video. Marcela cradles something in her hand and then at a certain point blocks Malcom's line of sight and leans in and puts something in his drink. She stirs it a couple of times and then lets him drink it. It's a definitive piece of evidence. But you may recall that when the police got the video their initial reaction was to suggest to Brooke that she'd doctored the images. When Ricardo brought it up, he says, "The police reaction was this is just a piece of evidence, we need more." Ricardo wanted to make sure they hadn't just let the video evidence and any other evidence fall by the wayside:

> We wrote for them 14 steps to follow, including everybody that was associated in the video and pointed out there that had a critical interaction with Marcela and Malcom, should be investigated. We point out to them, number one, that there was a side table with four people and during the time that Malcom went to bathroom, where he got hit in the head somehow and got blood, during the time of Malcom missing in the video, one of the old guys, which we assume may be the leader of that wolfpack, went to Marcela and told her something, touch her on the shoulder. That is unusual conduct. When there is a crime in process and there are collaborators, you have to take the specific minutes and seconds of what happened in those critical moments. We point out to the police that there was an alleged taxi driver at the very end, before they were leaving the place, which follow them, and we want to point out to them that what the behaviour and the actions that this other collaborator did, not only Malcom and Marcela leaving the place, follow the guys that were in that, in that table, even the waitress.

According to Ricardo, police reaction to his 14-point plan was indifference. Of course, unbeknownst to Ricardo and Brooke, the police had already done a forensic check on the video. They knew it was legit. They just didn't share that information with Ricardo and Brooke – more of the passive-aggressive behaviour they displayed in general.

Another compelling piece of evidence Brooke and Ricardo wanted to follow up on was the GPS information from Malcom's car. But when Ricardo brought up the GPS, he says, "The police investigators told me that is not credible evidence because we have no way to associate the car to his GPS service. So, I told them it's easy, you write to the company which holds the rights and provides the control for the GPS contract, for the GPS service." The police ignored that suggestion. As Ricardo explained, Brooke took the initiative to do just that.

> Brooke did and then we provided, through a Mexican lawyer, the route that the car took. So, they say, well, you are not able to prove who drove [the car]. And I said, yes, you are right but you have cameras in the marina, you have cameras in the other locations where they made stops and you should look for them.

Ricardo's request to view the footage from the Puerto Vallarta marina was a great idea. We went to the marina to film. It's a very upscale facility, with dozens of large yachts moored in highly secured births. It also has more security cameras scattered around than at any comparable facility I've ever seen. I walked the length of the dock and could not find a single location where I was not between at least two cameras. If police had moved in a timely fashion, they might have found compelling evidence in that video. They knew precisely when Malcom's car had stopped and on what date. How hard would it have been to view the video for that time period from the marina? But they didn't follow up on Ricardo's suggestion. Police also already knew the GPS from the car Trackimo device was critically important. They knew that because they *had* already corroborated the GPS data – the police had obtained copies of the phone records belonging to Malcom, Marcela, Andrés, and Martín, tracked it, and it had told them the full story.

Now you'd think that if someone was going to commit a crime and needed to communicate with others during the event, they'd have watched enough police shows to know what happens when you make a call with a cell phone. Your cell phone connects to the closest tower. If you make enough calls, then you leave a map of your locations throughout the night. That's why criminals often use "burner" phones that can't be traced. Marcela, Martín, and Andrés were not that smart.

The police obtained the records of all of their phones and sent the data off to the forensic lab for analysis. The reports they got back were definitive. Every time any of them made calls, the latitude and longitude of their phone was recorded. The forensic lab was able to track the location of the phones within a metre. The three suspects made dozens of calls throughout the night that Malcom disappeared. For someone supposedly in bed asleep, Marcela was making a call every few minutes – so was her son Andrés and her brother Martín. It took seven months for the lab to complete the analysis of all the data. It sent it back in stages, with Marcela's information being sent in early February 2019 and Martín's by the end of August that same year. When it arrived, the evidence was once again irrefutable. Police saw that the three of them were travelling all around the city that night. At one point they all ended up in the same location: the location shown by Malcom's Trackimo account – in the remote jungle area north of Puerto Vallarta in the state of Nayarit. The police report stated,

> Relevant to the case, taking into account that the cell phone device registered in the name of Marcela Acosta Ramos 3221336740, performs on October 28, 2018, a displacement from the Lázaro Cárdenas colony, in the city of Puerto Vallarta (00:45: 48), Jalisco to the town of San Vicente, municipality of Bahía de Banderas Nayarit (01:44:32 until 02:06:10) returning later, crossing through Nuevo Vallarta and Jarretaderas, in Bahía de Banderas Nayarit (02:21:10) to the vicinity of Colonia FOVISSTE 96 in Puerto Vallarta Jalisco.

Cut through all that wordiness and what the police are saying is that Marcela's phone travels from Puerto Vallarta at 12:45 in the morning of the 28th to the jungle area in Nayarit at 1:44 a.m. and returns home at 2:21 a.m. The route is almost identical to the route shown by the GPS in Malcom's car. The report continued by stating that Marcela was in constant contact with Andrés and Martín – contrary to what she said in her statements about being asleep all night – and concluded:

> It is noticed that this communication activity took place in the towns of Mezcales and Nuevo Vallarta, municipality of Bahía de Banderas, Nayarit, which also *evidences a contradiction* for what Marcela Acosta Ramos declared in repeated occasions, who refers that when she and MALCOM MADSEN left the ANDALE bar in Puerto Vallarta... they took a cab that took him directly to his home in the Aralias colony of Puerto Vallarta Jalisco, place where she refers that they were, they spent the night there without having left home [emphasis mine].

Again, cutting through police jargon, it's quite clear in the report that they finally *got it* – Marcela had lied to them about where she was that night. She wasn't at home at all but driving around the city and in constant contact with her brother and son. Martín's and Andrés's phones showed similar patterns. They were out all night, and rather than sitting in a bar in Nayarit, they were driving all around the city. The two locations they all had in common, based on the phone evidence, were downtown not far from Mandala bar in Puerto Vallarta and the remote jungle area. They were all at the jungle area at around 1 a.m. But once again, as with the video evidence, the police chose not to share that information with Ricardo or Brooke, so they were still under the impression the police were not taking the GPS evidence seriously. Ricardo told me on multiple occasions how often he had asked the police whether they had obtained copies of the cell phone records and asked them constantly to share a complete set of that data with him. He says that never happened, other than a few random pages of phone records he was allowed to photograph.

More red flags here for me about Ricardo. In fact, he was given a complete copy of the phone records in one of the documents sent to him by the prosecutor. It seems he didn't bother to go through it completely and was therefore unaware it contained the phone records. Now there were 5,000 pages to go through, but Brooke was paying him very good money for his work.

Another key investigative step Ricardo and Brooke were anxious about was having Malcom's car searched for blood, fingerprints, body fluids, and hair fibres. They also wanted the police to retrieve the Trackimo GPS device so it could be presented to the court as evidence. Brooke and Ricardo knew that one search of the car had been done a few months after Malcom disappeared. But they had not received copies of the search results after they had been processed by the forensic lab. Ricardo eventually received an abbreviated version of the report. Police said they had checked the car for fluids. Ricardo looked at it and right away asked for them to do a second search.

> They did one for the biological substances, which they claim they found just urine, and I asked them to do a second one for fingerprints because the first one they said there were no fingerprints and I told them that's not possible. Every car has fingerprints, this conclusion is wrong.

Ricardo also asked them to recover the GPS device. This was a no-brainer as the police had suggested they needed to see this device to believe it was real and the Trackimo emails were genuine. So a time was set to do a second search of the car. But from the get-go it wasn't a promising venture. Ricardo and Brooke had no idea what Marcela might have done to clean up the car. As the day of the search dawned, the search became even less promising. The police had not booked a forensic technician to do the work. That left Ricardo, helped by Jesus, scrambling to find a local mechanic who could improvise and somehow find a device that is about the size of a book of matches hidden somewhere on the car. It also meant there was nobody there to re-do the fingerprint testing. The local mechanic was game and brought along a detection device that looked for power signatures from batteries. He went over the car for hours, with Ricardo standing by watching. They found nothing. No real surprise. Maybe the device was still on the car and the battery was dead or, equally possible, as the car had been in Marcela's possession for several months, the device could have been found and removed. Brooke and Ricardo said they knew Marcela was being fed information by someone – in fact, Ricardo claimed on occasion she'd been given key documents from the investigation before he was given them. Brooke suspected Marcela was told about the Trackimo information and had the GPS device removed. It was also possible that whoever Marcela was paying off inside the investigation went into the impound lot and took off the device. The whole experience merely reinforced what Brooke and Ricardo had suspected all along – the investigation was being undermined and it wasn't just plagued by incompetence. As Ricardo said,

> It is frustrating and it gives you a lot of space of thinking that maybe there are other things going on that you are not aware of and that is the worst part because you may deal with incompetence but if there is something in the back of the screen, you don't know what is happening, then you have to be more careful.

Once Ricardo had received the partial copies of the phone records, he and Brooke went over them in some detail. They found another piece of information that seemed critical – Marcela, Martín, and Andrés called several numbers that night that the police hadn't bothered to follow up on. In fact, there were three phone numbers that were called repeatedly throughout the night. Right away, Ricardo asked the police to get the records on these phones and find out who they belonged to. The police ignored the request.

That seemed to be a little odd to me, so while I was talking with reporter Jorge Olmos, I asked him why the police might have dragged their heels on this request. He replied, "They don't want to find out who owns those phones." Jorge's suggestion was that the phones might be connected to cartel figures and the police didn't want to start making that sort of connection. Brooke believed there were some gangsters involved in the kidnapping and murder of her father. She's never been certain about whether Marcela, Martín, or Andrés would have the ability to kill Malcom. She believed it was quite possible they enlisted the help of some people that would be able to do such a thing. That's not a very tough task in Mexico. *Sicarios* (assassins) in Mexico are plentiful and cheap. Now it's possible there was no cartel connection. Certainly, when Jorge started to look into the story, he checked around to see what kind of a shit storm he might be entering into. He told me he couldn't find any connections between Marcela's family and the cartels. So maybe the unknown phone numbers merely belonged to a couple of street thugs Marcela or Andrés or Martín enlisted for the night's activities. Regardless, they were important pieces of evidence the police ignored. In early 2023, the trial prosecutor Juan Mejía was asked by Brooke, yet again, about these numbers. He promised he would ask the cell phone company for the records immediately. It never happened.

That pattern of one step forward and two steps back was how the third trip unfolded. Each time Ricardo and Brooke asked about evidence, the police found reasons to suggest it wasn't credible – often doing so while their own investigation had already shown them it was. To Ricardo's credit, he was undaunted by this resistance. He kept presenting them with steps they could take to satisfy their own investigative standards. He kept asking for documents and bugging them to take legal steps against Marcela, Andrés, and Martín. On September 12, after only four days in Puerto Vallarta, Brooke decided to wrap up her third trip. It was clear to her that they were not going to get much co-operation from the police. It was also clear the police were being very secretive with what they had found. The main thing Brooke had gleaned from the trip was that she now strongly suspected that the police and the prosecutor were actually working against the investigation. Brooke knew by now it was going to take something more than requests to the police to figure out the case. She was beginning to suspect she might have to go public to turn up the heat on the police and the Canadian government.

CHAPTER NINE

THE MEDIA

It took Brooke a year before she finally decided to use media attention to pressure the Mexican and Canadian authorities. She says she felt more might be accomplished if the whole incident didn't become a media circus. But sometime after her third trip to Puerto Vallarta, as she approached the one-year anniversary of her father's disappearance with little progress occurring, she decided to go public. But Brooke had little experience with the media and she certainly didn't have the resources to hire a publicist. She started reaching out to journalists in both Canada and Mexico, trying to get some interest. She also began to use social media in a much more strategic manner. Initially, she didn't have much success with mainstream media. But as a couple of key publications started paying attention, her campaign picked up steam. Ultimately, this tactic would prove to be one of the most effective she had at her disposal. In my opinion, the impact of these "allies" cannot be underestimated.

Brooke's campaign began with social media. She started Facebook and Instagram accounts both called *Justice for Malcom*. Brooke kept up a constant series of posts. What made the social media push particularly effective was that Brooke expanded it beyond just being a platform in which she kept subscribers updated about events related to Malcom's case. She also began to include the stories of other Canadians and Americans who had loved ones that disappeared in Mexico. That drew in a much wider audience – people who could relate to what Brooke was going through because they and their families were also going through it. The more families that were included, the more their friends and family began to subscribe to *Justice for Malcom*. Brooke began to post a series of video diary entries on the pages that proved very compelling. Each time she experienced a major event, she would record an entry on her phone and then post it. This gave people an intimate view of what Brooke was thinking and feeling. I suspect this personal touch drew in a great many people. Today, the Facebook page has nearly 2,100 subscribers. That may not be in the same viral territory as celebrities and social media divas, but it's still a respectable number for what amounted to an amateur social media campaign. Of course, another critical aspect of the social media pages was that they would eventually capture the attention of the mainstream media. CTV News wrote an online feature about her struggles; she was invited to an interview with the CBC radio show *As It Happens*; a number of local radio stations invited her on as a guest. But the real boost came when the *Toronto Star* weighed in.

In the fall of 2019, reporter Kenyon Wallace reached out to Brooke. He said he came upon her story as a result of an editor who saw something online, "and Brooke was quoted in it, talking about her dad and somebody forwarded me that and said 'What's going on here? We need to look into this…' So then I just reached out to Brooke." Kenyon was shown the infamous bar video by Brooke and he knew he'd found gold: "I don't think she had shared the video with anybody at that point. I was able to convince her to give me the video."

As I discovered during the 40 years I spent working in the news business, it's not always the fact that you get to a story first that counts. It's more often what you do with the story once you find it. Though Kenyon wasn't the first to talk about the story, he was the first to realize the significance of the video and build his story around that compelling image. It's not often you get handed video in which you can actually see the beginning of a crime. But Kenyon, a thorough investigator, didn't just run with the pictures. He took the time to do the rest of the legwork. He went through every document he could get his hands on. He reached out to everyone he could think of for some kind of information – including Marcela. "Every time I wrote a story," he told me,

> I reached out to her out of courtesy, you know, out of journalistic due diligence. Initially, we had a number for her, as well as an email and her Facebook account, which was still active... So I sent numerous messages trying to seek comment from her, as well as other people involved.

Kenyon also made repeated attempts to contact someone in the Mexican justice system who would comment.

> I always would email or call the investigators, the DA's office, any way I could try and get a hold of anybody I was going to talk about in the story, I wanted to make sure that they had an opportunity to respond. And I did manage to reach a lawyer for Martín and Andrés, Manuel Vega, who speaks Spanish... But they never really gave us anything. I reached Ortega, once, and he made me put my questions through their media relations department at the DA's office and they never even responded.

Regardless of the lack of comment from Marcela, and from within the Mexican justice system, Kenyon felt he had more than enough for a fully substantiated story.

Kenyon's first article was published on November 29, 2019. And, as expected, it caused a stir here in Canada. In it, Kenyon certainly wasn't shy about pointing fingers:

> It's been more than a year, but Mexican police and Global Affairs Canada officials haven't rushed to find the retired real estate agent and jeweller. Madsen's daughter and only child Brooke Mullins has pleaded with them to help find her dad. Frustrated with their indifferent and sluggish responses, Mullins started investigating the case herself.

Kenyon pointed his readers towards some of the facts that illustrated both how poorly the Canadian government had responded and how the Mexican justice system's response had been less than adequate: "There's not really a rigorous urgency, in terms of quickly investigating serious issues because as we all know, the longer you wait in a missing persons case, the less likely it is you're going to find the person."

I talked with Kenyon when I was preparing the book and documentary. He was extremely generous in sharing his research and his thoughts. He said that after his first article his main conclusion was,

> It just seems to me like beware, buyer beware, traveller beware... What I'm amazed by is like, Brooke is a unique case because she has resources. If you didn't have the money to fly to Mexico or hire lawyers or get your own private investigators, the only reason why the progress in this case has been made, is because Brook has resources to force it to happen.

That's the same conclusion I've come to about travelling to Mexico: buyer beware. When people ask me if it's safe, I tell them, "most likely." But I also add that if you do run into a problem with the law, you will be in a world of hurt.

Kenyon would go on to write a second article in July 2020 and a third in October 2021. Each time he published a story, there was a demonstrable cause and effect – an almost immediate knee-jerk reaction by the Mexican justice system. Following Kenyon's second article, Martín was arrested. Did his article cause that? Hard to say for sure, but the same cause and effect can be seen when Mexican journalist Jorge Olmos published pieces in *Vallarta Uno*. And when I spoke with Luz Nagle, a law professor and member of a number of United Nations committees looking at corruption and justice, she said the only time she ever sees a court case in Mexico proceed in any kind of transparent manner is when there is outside scrutiny either by the media or by a foreign government.

By the time Kenyon published his third article, the Mexicans certainly knew they were the subject of a great deal of external scrutiny – an over-watch that Kenyon maintained for years. In fact, he told me the case had become more than just another investigation. It left him deeply impressed with the kind of tenacity Brooke had shown during her journey.

> I think what impresses me most is her loyalty to her father, even though she didn't grow up with him… Even though he wasn't around for a large part of her childhood, she seems to have come to terms with that and they kind of seemed to have, in recent years, before he disappeared, they seem to have reconciled to some extent and she seems to embrace that wholeheartedly. So you have to admire that. It must have not been easy. And then to spend four years and countless hours trying to get justice for her father, [who] was largely absent in her life when she was a child, that's… that takes a lot of dedication that I'm not sure other people would have been able to or would have had the inclination to do.

Kenyon also felt that, to a large extent, this story fit his very definition of why he became a journalist in the first place – it wasn't just a good narrative.

> Ultimately, in my view, why I do journalism… is because I believe that journalism has the power to do good, if done properly. And I like to approach my work with the goal of not only informing, entertaining, educating the public, but also with the hope that it might improve something in society, whether it's a government institution or making somebody's life better or helping somebody who's disadvantaged or shining a light on an important issue that maybe has fallen by the wayside. So any time I write something that has some positive impact, whether

> it's forcing police to do more investigating or pointing people towards something that's wrong or even, in some cases, a new law being enacted... it's very gratifying and that's ultimately why I do what I do.

While Kenyon made the biggest splash with the story in Canada, and his articles clearly had an impact on the case in Mexico, no single journalist had as great an impact on the course of events as Jorge Olmos, reporter and managing editor of *Vallarta Uno*, the online publication based in Puerto Vallarta. It's not a huge player in the Mexican market, but as the old saying goes, it punches way above its weight. Virtually every week, Jorge publishes an article about dishonest politicians, sleazy business deals, and corrupt police and prosecutors. Given the violence directed towards journalists in Mexico, I'm actually surprised Jorge is still alive. In fact, when we talked (we interviewed him in Mexico City), I asked him about whether he'd ever been threatened. "Several times," he replied. "The most delicate was one day when they wanted to practically kidnap me. The others are threats by telephone, but sometimes strong threats like, if you continue writing such and such things or about delicate issues related to drug trafficking, something will happen to you. Journalism in Mexico is risky."

Jorge said he survived by keeping a low profile: "In Mexico, the lower the profile, the better it is not to expose yourself especially when you write about sensitive issues such as drug trafficking, the disappeared, fraud." Describing his situation as "delicate" was a bit of an understatement. In Mexico, 2022 was the deadliest year on record for journalists being murdered – one UNESCO report pegged the number at 19 killed.[7] The average number has been well over ten per year. When Jorge talked about keeping a low profile (we hid his identity in the documentary), I was well aware he would face serious consequences if we made a mistake.

Brooke was put in touch with Jorge through her first lawyer, Norma. Jorge said,

> One day she contacted me and told me that there was a very interesting subject, a missing Canadian, and I was interested in the subject because she showed me the photographs of the video that they took in the bar "El Andale." And you can clearly see where Marcela puts a little powder in the glass of this Canadian man… and I got interested in the subject and that's when I started to learn more about it.

The result was almost a symbiotic relationship in which Jorge got great stories and Brooke got exposure for her cause – exposure that kept the pressure on the police and prosecutor in Puerto Vallarta. Brooke described Jorge as someone who "doesn't like injustices and he wants the truth to be always told. He cares about his country very much. He's a very passionate man." And she admitted that many of the people who came forward to help her did so after reading Jorge's articles. "He has been very, very valuable. He brought me lots of information… he's brought me a lot of my informants because of his articles. Mexicans read them and they care and they want to be involved. He's great."

Jorge says he didn't start working on the story because he wanted to be a crusader; he started working on it because it was a compelling story. The picture was enough to hook him into starting some deeper research. What he found drew him even further into the story was that "we learned at the beginning that Mrs. Marcela Acosta, she was the first to report the disappearance of Mr. Madsen, from there we began to take all the investigation, according to the documentation that was presented to the prosecution, and we saw that there were some inconsistencies in the statements of Marcela Acosta and what had really happened on Sunday 28."

Once he'd found "some inconsistencies," Jorge began to find other interesting facts:

> I read the whole file of the investigation of the Special Agency for Missing Persons and there is very strong evidence that involves

> Marcela Acosta and her brother and her son Andrés in the case. In a conspiracy to disappear this Canadian citizen, there is terrible evidence such as taking him to a place in downtown Puerto Vallarta when they said they took him to his home. There are the telephone conversations that the same prosecutor's office and the investigating police officers discovered. So I do not believe that [the evidence] is something that is being held [together] with pins in this case. On the contrary there is enough evidence to point out that this lady is very guilty.

During the next eight months Jorge would write three articles about the story. The first was an overview. From the beginning, Jorge saw the money as being pivotal to the case. In his first article, he talked about the USD 9,000 Malcom was carrying and asked what had happened to it. Jorge's work hit some kind of a chord with the police and prosecutor working on the case. Ortega's office finally issued an arrest warrant for Marcela within a few weeks of Jorge's article. Jorge says this is just sometimes the way things work: "Look, sometimes here in Mexico, you know [this is] how justice is sometimes... they don't take interest in an issue unless it starts to appear in the media, that's when they start to work a little more, otherwise sometimes they leave the cases in the archives."

In his second article, published on July 12, 2020, Jorge came out swinging against the prosecutor in the case, René Ortega. He accused him of dragging his feet on the case and allowing Marcela ample time to raise money and get the hell out of town. He pointed out in the article that while the arrest warrant had been issued on March 5, 2020, it was now July 12 and nothing had been done about it. He pointed out that

> the behaviour of the Public Ministry has been quite suspicious, since more than four months have passed since the arrest warrant was issued and in all the time that the case has been going on, [the prosecutor] has only promised the relatives of the Canadian

> that the police, the investigator "will soon arrest them." But the weeks go by and everything remains the same. Malcom Madsen does not appear nor has the main suspect in Malcom's disappearance been caught, that is, the Mexican Marcela Acosta Ramos, who was his girlfriend.

He also wrote that, thanks to the inaction by Ortega's office, Marcela had fled the jurisdiction, "therefore, today we find that the suspect is on the run and we reiterate, she has a significant sum of money with which she can provide means of concealment and recruit possible collaborators to prevent and complicate her arrest." Following that article, the very next day, on July 13, 2020, police arrested Marcela in a suburb near Mexico City. Those events seem a little too close in time to be a coincidence.

Encouraged by the success of his articles, Jorge's next piece came out within a few weeks of the second one. It was a barnburner with a headline that screamed, "Another boyfriend of Marcela Acosta dies under strange circumstances." Jorge was the journalist who discovered that after Marcela left Puerto Vallarta, she had become involved with a lawyer named Julio and he had been gunned down in the street within a few months of the relationship beginning. Jorge connected that death with Malcom and an earlier partner of Marcela's. He was the one who coined the phrase "black widow" with reference to Marcela. Other media outlets picked up the juicy story and it got a lot of play in Mexico.

Once again, within weeks of Jorge's third article, the police made a move. This time they arrested Marcela's brother Martín, one of the co-accused. Three articles, three significant responses. Yet Jorge was very matter of fact about the impact his work had on the case. He said the people who really deserve the credit are the families who conduct the investigative work, "the relatives come and they start to investigate on their own where their father was the last time, where he went, who he was with him, what his partner was like, his partner's family. They start to investigate a little more and sometimes they contribute more than the public prosecutor's office."

Nowhere was Jorge's point more apropos than in Malcom's case. When I looked through the case the prosecutor finally filed with the court, most of the evidence was information provided by Brooke. Jorge agreed that, without Brooke's work, the case would never have moved ahead: "The information that was handled in news portals, even in Canada, and the pressure from the embassy has been decisive for this case to move forward. Three people have been arrested, but unfortunately we still do not know where Malcom Madsen is."

Jorge's work had another benefit on Malcom's case. Once it became a sensation in the media, the case attained such a high profile it rose above the level of petty corruption – at least according to Jorge. This meant there was now a chance the case would be dealt with fairly. Jorge believed there might have been some payoffs happening at the beginning of the investigation that slowed things down, but he said he didn't believe that could be the case anymore:

> Sometimes Mexican justice has a bad reputation, but there are also honest judges and auditors who in this case I do not believe that they would lend themselves to a *cochupo,* as they say in Mexico, a bad deal. I believe that the trial will go forward. I insist because of the evidence and it will end badly for the lady who has a criminal behaviour.

And he thinks something else good came from all the media attention. He's been through the case files and thinks the case is not going to end well for Marcela:

> I think she will reach the end of the trial and she will be sentenced there, she will be in prison for a long time, because I don't see any other way for her to go free, even though Malcom's body

has not been found there is strong evidence, and the day of the trial will come, the final trial and she will be sentenced, that's what I think.

Malcom's case isn't the only one Jorge has championed. He's written a number of articles about "the disappeared" in Mexico. He acknowledged it is a massive problem, one the authorities seem overwhelmed by. Jorge isn't quite sure how they can begin to control this problem. The cartels are involved in many of these cases and that adds a huge danger factor for any authority that has any intention of looking into a case. The system is rife with corruption and there just doesn't seem to be any political will to confront the issue. Jorge has sent me a number of recent studies that all agree there is an almost insurmountable problem surrounding the "disappeared." Those studies, however, don't seem to change anything. Jorge adds that when Brooke began her crusade to find her father, "I don't think she would have realized this issue, how complex it is and how big it is. I would put it as if she stepped in a swamp, but the swamp is very big." It's a swamp we ventured into when we began investigating Brooke's story.

The most common question I get from people after they've seen the documentary, *Malcom is Missing*, is "How did you find the story?" As I mentioned earlier, we owe the documentary to pure chance. Truth be told, we owe a tip of the hat to Kenyon Wallace at the *Toronto Star*. We didn't see his original article, but in the summer of 2020, while staying in Vancouver, my partner Jari and I came across an abridged version in the *Vancouver Sun*. It was only a couple of paragraphs long and it talked about a Canadian woman who had been fighting Mexican authorities to do something about her missing father. That rang a bell for me. During the 17 years I worked for the investigative show *W5*, I'd done a number of stories about Canadians who'd run afoul of Mexican justice. I knew how potentially slow and bureaucratic or just plain corrupt the whole system could be. This story sounded as outrageous as some of the other ones I'd worked on, so I went online and began to do a little research.

One of the first things I discovered was the Facebook page called *Justice for Malcom*. I scrolled down the page and was astonished at some of the evidence Brooke Mullins had amassed during the past year and a half – including actual videotape footage of what looked like a crime being committed. I scrolled through the names of people who belonged to the group and to my delight I found someone I knew. David Weisz was a colleague of mine. I had spent a number of years teaching research methods to graduate students in the School of Journalism at Ryerson (now Toronto Metropolitan University). I had struggled a bit with the section on data journalism. I was certainly using the techniques of that method of research, but the manner in which I crunched data was cumbersome and my geo-plotting was positively painful. David, on the other hand, was a wizard with the software and techniques of data journalism, so I'd brought him in to help me teach that section. I was so impressed with him that I asked him if he would privately tutor me in some of the more advanced techniques. For several weeks, David dropped by my house and showed me how to properly use a number of pieces of relevant software. These lessons stood me in good stead and I've used them on virtually all my documentaries to sort out and find significant information in large databases.

I called David and asked him if he would introduce me to Brooke. Within a day or two I was on the phone talking with her. I soon realized the story was much more involved, much more emotional, than any of the print stories had described to this point. After several long conversations about her investigation, I asked Brooke if she would be interested in letting Jari and me attempt to put together a documentary project. She agreed and we went to work. Without getting into all the tedious details of how a producer operates in Canada, suffice it to say that within six months we had found a broadcaster, raised the financing, and we were in production. A year after that, the feature-length documentary aired on CBC's Docs Channel on November 20, 2022. On May 5, 2023, it dropped on the CBC streaming platform, Gem, and it was finally broadcast on the main CBC channel in January 2024. It was both a gruelling and rewarding project, but that's not why I felt a mention of the documentary was needed in this book. I'm talking about this because the research we did along the way put into place a third damning piece of evidence.

It didn't take too long after we'd begun our work to be introduced to Ricardo. He seemed to be a fount of knowledge, so I kept going back to him to ask questions. One of the points he kept talking about was how he had been hounding the police to get complete copies of the cell phone records belonging to Marcela, Martín, and Andrés. Ricardo told me that when the police appeared reluctant to believe what the Trackimo evidence showed, "I told [the police], that's so easy to corroborate or invalidate... trace the phone records of each of them." He went on to say that if the police would only hand that information over to him, he could then trace the movements of the three suspects and be able to see whether they were in the same area as Malcom's car. It sounded like a reasonable argument. Particularly when Ricardo passed on to me what he said he'd been given so far – a handful of badly photographed pages that were so incomplete as to be virtually useless. I tried to geo-plot the partial records, but not much of a picture was painted. So much for that line of research.

But in the winter of 2022 Kenyon shared some files with me – files Ricardo had sent to him nearly a year earlier on December 19, 2019. As I combed through the files, to my surprise I found pages and pages of phone records. I cross-checked the phone numbers against the police statements given by Marcela, Martín, and Andrés. These statements listed the phone numbers of the accused. Sure enough, the phone numbers in the pages Kenyon had passed on to me matched the phone numbers in the police statements. These were the so-called nonexistent phone records. And following each set of records there was a synopsis completed by the police that tracked the location of the phones throughout the night and plotted that information on Google Maps. The locations were an exact match for the movement of Malcom's car. There was little question the three accused had followed the same route Malcom's car had travelled and at the same time. What's more, the police had made that connection between the two pieces of information. The last few pages of their report contained an executive summary. The police concluded that all three accused were in the jungle area at the same time in the early hours of the morning of the 28th. They also concluded that Marcela, Martín, and Andrés had lied in their statements to the police. Typically, the police had not bothered to share any of this information with Brooke. At least not directly.

According to Ricardo, he had been pressing the police for more than a year to get the phone records and analyze them and compare them to the GPS information from Malcom's car. He claimed the police had led him on – they had not bothered to tell him they had already obtained the records and made the critical connections. If Ricardo was right, then holding back this information was a colossal act of obfuscation. Someone in the justice system had intentionally misled Ricardo about a critical piece of evidence. But that theory – presented by Ricardo – was not complete. In some ways, Ricardo's lack of knowledge about the phone records could be seen as a self-inflicted wound. He had been given a massive amount of documentation in the early winter of 2019. Those 5,000 pages contained all the phone record information. Had Ricardo fastidiously read through the documents, he would have found them. There would have been no need to spend the next year asking for those records. Now perhaps Ricardo was overwhelmed with the volume of information he was receiving. He was working alone. But most lawyers would go through any documents they received on behalf of their client. And there weren't just a few pages of this phone data tucked away. They jumped out immediately when I scrolled through the PDF documents. There were dozens and dozens of pages of phone numbers and maps plotting the numbers.

Shortly after we found the cell phone records, I got on the phone to Brooke and told her about them. Right away, she knew it was an important piece of evidence. She described it as "huge considering [that in] her first statement, Marcela claimed they went straight home, that she went home and went to bed – so why is her phone travelling somewhere with, on the same path as my father's vehicle? That's just another example of how she lied. Everything she's said has been a lie." And the police knew about Marcela's lies all along. They'd submitted these reports to the prosecutor between February and August 2019. There was little doubt after this information was available that Marcela was the prime suspect. Yet little happened in the investigation and prosecution of the case for a year.

Apparently, this is Mexican justice.

CHAPTER TEN

GLOBAL AFFAIRS

While the media were busy turning up the heat on Mexican authorities, the people who should have been doing this – Global Affairs Canada – appeared to Brooke to be doing very little. Stated more accurately, they *chose* to do very little. In my experience (and Brooke's), it is possibly one of the most indifferent and privileged Canadian government organizations that exists. Here's what my experience – gathered over 40 years of working as a journalist – tells me: if you think that when you get into trouble overseas the consular services of Global Affairs will have your back, then think again. They will *not* have your back. They will most likely do little to help you. I've seen it in case after case throughout my years of working overseas on stories about Canadians in a jam. And never was my hypothesis more clearly demonstrated than in Malcom's case. A closer look at their involvement (or lack thereof) would, I believe, give readers some helpful context to why Brooke's struggle with the Mexican justice system was so much harder than it needed to be.

Canada has an embassy in Mexico City. It also has consulates in several major cities and in key resort towns, like Cancún and Puerto Vallarta. Mexico is a major tourist destination and hundreds of thousands of Canadians visit Puerto Vallarta every year. As a result, Canada is very important to Mexico when it comes to its bottom line. Canadian tourist dollars accounted for $1.33 billion in 2019 according to the *Mexico Daily News*. We rank second – after the United States – in numbers of tourists that visit the country every year. I saw one figure that put tourism as being responsible for 8 per cent of Mexico's GDP.[8]

Additionally, Canada has a massive economic relationship with Mexico.

We're part of the United States–Mexico–Canada Agreement (USMCA), and according to the Canadian government, our relationship is worth $41.7 billion each year in trade. And, finally, Canada also has a large temporary foreign worker program that provides thousands of Mexican citizens with work and keeps millions of dollars flowing back to families in poorer areas of Mexico. So why all these numbers? Because I think it's important to illustrate one fact: given our economic importance to Mexico, Canada could have a great deal of influence in that country. If we chose to flex our economic muscle, we could "suggest" a great number of actions when it comes to how our citizens are treated. While Global Affairs cannot directly interfere with internal matters, like police investigations, it does have the ability to ask for updates on the process, arrange meetings to talk about the case, and even offer some scientific and technical support if it might help. That kind of scrutiny can't be overstated. The Mexican government and justice system – as seen by how sensitive they were to any public criticism in the media – respond very quickly to queries by the right people. And Global Affairs is well aware of this – at least when it comes time to use its influence, it has shown it's more than capable when the right incentive is applied.

Take the case of Brenda Martin. I mentioned her earlier in the book, but I think a closer examination is called for. In the fall of 2007, when I was working for the CTV current affairs show *W5*, I had heard some vague stories about a Canadian woman named Brenda Martin who was being held without charge in a Mexican prison. Through her family I was able to reach Brenda by phone and, after speaking to her for about an hour, I hung up the phone, gobsmacked by the story she had told me. She was living as an expat in Puerto Vallarta. To make ends meet, she took a job as a cook for a wealthy Canadian businessman – Alyn Waage – who lived in a swanky mansion up in the hills behind the city. But within a few months of taking the job, the federal police suddenly swooped in on the expensive house and arrested everyone in it. It turned out Waage had been running a rather extensive confidence game, defrauding people in a number of different countries, including Mexico.[9] The Mexicans charged Waage and at the same time charged Martin with knowingly accepting money that had been obtained through fraud. Martin steadfastly maintained the only money she received were her wages as a cook. She admitted she had invested in Waage's company because he told her it was a growing concern. The amount she invested was a pittance. We're not dealing with millions – we're dealing with a few thousand dollars. Nonetheless, Martin was thrown in a Mexican jail where she rotted for several years without ever being convicted of a crime. According to Martin, Global Affairs did little to help her during that time. She told me its support amounted to a couple of visits to the prison, but it gave little assistance in addressing her abysmal living conditions in jail and her legal problems. Yet Martin claimed she had been beaten and sexually assaulted by other inmates, taken into court proceedings without a translator (she spoke only English), and virtually cut off from contact with her friends and family. She claimed she had repeatedly asked the local consulate in Guadalajara for assistance.

That was the situation when I found the story at *W5* and started working on my own investigation. I contacted Global Affairs and asked whether it could provide any information. Of course, it declined. I say "of course" because in the 40 years I worked as a journalist, I can't recall one instance in which Global Affairs agreed to speak about its actions. It maintained that position throughout the process, citing privacy concerns, even though Martin had given us full permission to talk to Global Affairs. Undeterred, I contacted the prison authorities in Mexico, and after weeks of negotiations, to my surprise, I was granted permission to enter the prison and film an interview with Martin.

Along with a crew, I flew down to Guadalajara and travelled out to a grim-looking prison on the outskirts of the city. It looked like the set for a Second World War POW camp escape movie. The prison was situated in the middle of a large field, surrounded by 15-foot concrete walls and topped with barbed wire. At regular intervals there were well-manned guard towers overlooking the interior and to keep an eye on the exterior as well. We were told it was one of the highest security prisons in Mexico. All this for a cook, I thought. Getting through security with our equipment was tense. While the guards were polite, they had to search everything and put us through multiple scanners. We were finally ushered into a mostly bare activity room – a table in one corner and a few chairs scattered around.

Within minutes Martin turned up. I could see through the windows of the room that looked into the main courtyard for the women's section of the prison. It was filled with some hard-looking people. Martin, by comparison, was a slight woman who looked thin and fragile. She made her way across the courtyard escorted by two guards. When she entered the activity room, she came up to me and put her arms around me and started quietly weeping. She thanked me for paying attention to her plight. When she'd calmed down, we sat down and the reporter I was working with started the interview. The stories she told were horrifying – physical assault, isolation, food that was inedible. By this point, she'd been locked up for more than two years and still hadn't been convicted of a crime. For Canadians, the idea was unimaginable. Later I learned this was not an uncommon state of affairs in Mexico. I was told by our fixer, Gabriel, that people often spent a dozen years or more locked up without ever being convicted. As part of our story, I decided Global Affairs' excuses about not speaking to the media for privacy reasons had to be challenged. So, after asking again for an interview at the local Guadalajara office and being refused, we turned up at the office unannounced one afternoon. They were not happy. In fact, they would not come out to the lobby and engage with us. They left us as a problem for the locally hired receptionist. Not a lot accomplished, but as an image representing its indifference, I thought it demonstrated a lot: Global Affairs felt it owed nobody an explanation about its actions – even when its actions seemed egregiously wrong. We filmed the rest of the story and, within weeks of returning to Canada, broadcast it on our show.

Once broadcast, other national media in Canada picked up on the story and it caught fire. Suddenly, Brenda Martin's name was in all the headlines. She was being interviewed almost daily by various media outlets. And that exposure had a huge impact on the Canadian government and on Global Affairs. Suddenly, we learned Global Affairs was negotiating a transfer for Brenda Martin to a Canadian jail. In a matter of weeks, Global Affairs switched from a position of "we can't interfere" to being very much involved. The plan was that Canada would request that Martin finish her sentence in a Canadian jail, and once she arrived back on Canadian soil, she would be released on "parole." That way, while Martin was not exonerated, she was at least free. Mexico agreed, but first, in order to make her eligible to be moved, they convicted her of fraud and sentenced her to five years in jail. Martin got her transfer and was flown back to Canada. Shortly after arriving – after a token time in a Canadian low-security jail for appearances – she was released. What does this sorry tale illustrate? Other than another example of the dysfunction of the Mexican justice system, the bottom line was that when Global Affairs wanted to exert influence, it could have a great deal of sway in what happened when a Canadian was entangled with the Mexican justice system. The problem is, it doesn't often choose to use that influence. Global Affairs always seems more concerned about Canada's trade relationships and not rocking the financial boat. And that approach costs a lot of Canadians a great deal in unnecessary pain and suffering.

Take another example: In 2011, also while at CTV, I heard about Pavel Kulisek, another Canadian rotting in a Mexican jail under very unusual circumstances. He and his family had decided to take some time off from a busy life in Vancouver – he ran a small building contracting business. Pavel and his wife, Jirina, and their two girls bought an RV and headed down to Baja, towing a couple of motorcycles in a trailer. Pavel was a passionate dirt bike enthusiast. You could see that in the home video they shot along the way. Much of it was Pavel and his kids firing up their cross-country motorcycles in one remote area or another. Once they got to Baja, they liked the lifestyle so much they decided to make the change permanent. They bought a little house and moved in. They thought they could make money to support themselves by selling real estate.

Of course, once there Pavel became deeply involved in the local dirt bike circuit. At one cross-country meet, he was told the race was a team event. He would have to have a partner to compete or he couldn't enter. He was uncertain about what to do until another solo rider approached him. He introduced himself as Carlos Herrera and offered to team up. Pavel agreed. They rode in the meet and got along so well that they eventually teamed up for a couple of other races. In fact, they even got together socially a few times. Carlos had a wife and four kids and they had a couple of family barbeques together.

Then one day Pavel got a call from Carlos. Carlos told Pavel he was sitting with Eduardo at a local hot dog stand just blocks from Pavel's house. Pavel told me he owed Eduardo some money for construction supplies and that he wanted to pay the debt off. He jumped on his ATV to whip down and take care of the debt. Jirina says that when Pavel didn't return from that quick errand she began to get concerned. After several hours she was in a panic. She started looking for her husband but could find no trace of him around the town they lived in. The local police couldn't help. She contacted the Canadian consulate. It knew nothing at first, but within a few hours it called her back. It seemed that when Pavel turned up at the hot dog stand, he, Carlos, and Eduardo were suddenly surrounded by police and arrested. The next thing Pavel knew he'd been flown to Mexico City and was being paraded in front of the media. There's a funny yet horrifying clip that may still be available online on a Mexican television's site of the whole "gang" lined up at a hangar at a military base. Each "suspect" is allowed to make a statement. When Pavel is asked about why he was there, all he could think of to say was "I'm on holiday." It turned out Carlos was really Gustavo Rivera Martínez, one of the alleged leaders of the Tijuana cartel. Eduardo was actually Marcos Assemat Hernández, a supposedly corrupt cop with convictions for drug trafficking and, according to the police, also a member of the Tijuana cartel.

As Pavel had been seen in their company, they charged him as a co-conspirator and threw him in jail. He rotted there for more than three years – again without ever being convicted. His wife Jirina contacted me – having seen some of my other work – and asked for help. Again, we asked Global Affairs what was going on and it replied that it could say nothing. This time the Mexicans would not let us interview Pavel, but with Marina's help (and a huge inventory of home video) we were able to tell Pavel's story. Once again, our story created a media chain reaction and became such a source of embarrassment for the Canadian government that eventually it arranged to have Pavel transferred back to Canada, but not before he'd tried to kill himself during the last few weeks he was in jail. He was released once he arrived home. Yet he still suffered for years from the effects of that experience. So it seems that only when the right pressure is applied – a possible public outing – does the Canadian government choose to help its citizens who get into trouble overseas. That's certainly what Brooke believes: "I believe that if this was, you know, the prime minister's father, that we wouldn't be sitting here having this chat. I totally believe that for the right people, things are done immediately."

Brooke says she put a huge amount of effort into trying to get Global Affairs to help her with both her investigation and her interactions with Mexican authorities. The result? Not much, according to Brooke: "We do feel like it's all about the relationship between Mexico and Canada and the trade, that they don't want to interfere. I don't think Canada makes it clear how dangerous Mexico really is." At one point during the 2020 federal election, she even tried to confront Justin Trudeau. His handlers politely diverted her away from Trudeau's "meet and greet" on the streets of Port Hope. That didn't mean she gave up trying to get Global Affairs to do its job. But her experiences were fairly uniform when it came to getting help – mostly indifference. She had started contacting Global Affairs within days of Malcom disappearing, trying desperately to get its attention. Of course, she went to the Canadian consulate in Puerto Vallarta and asked for help. She dutifully went back and checked in with the Puerto Vallarta consulate each time she returned and, according to Brooke, its involvement remained marginal. In fact, when we travelled to Puerto Vallarta with Brooke, she went to the office yet again. It was closed. This was possibly due to COVID restrictions, but the emergency help line did nothing but take Brooke to a phone tree where she was asked to leave a message. Brooke says, "I've never had a good experience in this office or with the people that work here." She continues,

> They do not care. I don't know if it's because they are just overworked or there's just been so many missing people or missing tourists in Puerto Vallarta that we're just a number now, we're just a file, the loved ones of the person that's missing and they just don't care. They're just exhausted maybe or we're just a number and not people anymore because they've been doing it for so long.

In fact, Brooke believed the consulate actually undermined her investigation at one point: "From the beginning, they recommended a lawyer that was very overpriced and took advantage of me and other people as well." She continues, "They also gave this lawyer information, when I stopped working with her, that I feel like they should have not given her because for my own safety. They should have had my back and maybe told me that she was looking for me when I was back in the country." (After Brooke fired her, Brooke's first lawyer, Norma, continued to bill her for some months – Brooke refused to pay the bills.)

ABOVE: A freeze frame from the video from Andales Bar shows Marcela spiking Malcom's drink. It was the defining piece of evidence in the case against her.

LEFT: Marcela and her son Andrés, the third suspect in the investigation.

OVERLEAF: Brooke with Malcom in Denmark prior to his disappearance.

AMNESTY
INTERNATIONAL
KROEN

ABOVE: Malcom's refuge in Los Chonchos, Mexico – modest to look at but surprisingly luxurious.

LEFT: It took months to convince the police to search the remote jungle area where Brooke believed her father's body might be hidden.

RIGHT: Hundreds of copies of this missing person poster were circulated in Puerto Vallarta after Malcom disappeared.

PERSONA DESAPARECIDA

Nacionalidad: CANADIENSE
Edad: 68 ANOS **Sexo: MASCULINO**
Piel: BLANCO
Estructura: ALTA Y DELGADA
Altura: 189m **Peso 60Kg.**
Vestimenta: camisa gris con manga cortas y pantalón negros.

Fue visto por última vez que la vimos fue en el Ándale Bar, subiendo a un taxi amarillo el noche de sábado 27 de octubre de 2018 a las 00:30 Puerto Vallarta. Estaba acompañado de una mujer de pelo negro largo, con una cola de caballo y un VESTIDA ROSA.

Agencia Consular de Canadá en Puerto Vallarta
Plaza Península, Local Sub F. Blv. Francisco medina Asencio 2485
Zona Hotelera Norte 48300 Puerto Vallarta Jalisco - México
De lunes a viernes, de 9 a 13 horas.
NÚMERO DE CASO 18-PVRTA-4680861
TELÉFONO (322) 293-2894
pvrta@international.gc.ca

Se ofrece una recompensa de <u>$ 3,000 USD</u> por información verídica que conduzca a localización de la persona.

ABOVE: Suspicion finally focused on Marcela and her brother Martín Ramos.

LEFT: Malcom and Marcela out for a night on the town.

ABOVE: Marcela serving time in the jail in Puerto Vallarta.

LEFT: An early picture of Marcela just after she met Malcom.

Brooke also showed me dozens and dozens of emails she had exchanged with Global Affairs, prompting it to take action. Other than one case officer named Imad Kaddouh, who seemed to actually care about the case and tried for a time to get regular updates from the Mexicans, the majority of the correspondence was a litany of unfulfilled promises, downright misinformation, or transparently thin emails spouting formulaic words of encouragement: "We continue to monitor this case closely and will be sure to keep you informed when we receive or obtain updates. Kindly do the same on your end in case your lawyer and/or private investigator is informed of development before our consular officials." Or,

> It should be clearly noted that the local authorities have the full responsibility – as they are the only ones with appropriate jurisdiction locally – to investigate the circumstances surrounding your father's disappearance, and not consular officials with Global Affairs or officers of the Government of Canada.

At one point in early 2019, one case officer even wrongly informed Brooke she had no right to any of the court filings that existed on the case:

> If information is released to you before the investigation is complete, it could compromise the local investigation and fodder [*sic*] a defence for the perpetrator. While we are sympathetic to your frustrations and interest in seeking a resolution to the case, you do not have a right to the interview records or forensic results from an active police investigation. (To note, this information would not be shared to the family of a victim in an active criminal investigation in Canada).

In fact, if the case officer had taken time to look into Mexican law, they would have discovered that families of victims in Mexico do have a right to access case files. In fact, they can file for full standing in the case and the authorities are obliged to hand over everything they have. Not only was this Global Affairs case officer wrong, but their misdirection was leading Brooke away from information she had every right to obtain. Even when they did pass on information to Brooke, they often seemed either confused or uninformed about what events had actually transpired. In one email dated July 2020, Brooke was told,

> As discussed on the phone, our consular officials did not receive any official letter or email from the Mexican authorities regarding Marcela Acosta Ramos' arrest. However, we have received the email that *you* forwarded to us from the lead investigator Lic. René Ortega stating that Marcela was arrested.

Our own government officials, who allegedly were in constant contact with Mexican justice officials, couldn't say for sure if Marcela had been arrested. Brooke had found out weeks before and had to tell them what was happening. This wasn't an anomaly, according to Brooke: "I usually tell them what's going on. I update them and they feel that's kind of embarrassing for sure." Brooke went on to suggest that all Global Affairs was doing, at best, was acting as a source to confirm information she already knew – and even then, its officials were often indifferent about how effectively they were communicating: "They just confirm everything. If I have a question, it's like telephone tag, you know. [The Consulate] talks to the Canadian Embassy, the embassy talks to the DA's office, and then the information comes back. We just get confirmations."

As time progressed, Global Affairs' performance did not improve. In fact, in some ways Brooke says it worsened. In September 2021, I received an email from Brooke saying, "Alex from Emergency Watch & Response just called me to inform me that my father was arrested on Friday." A case officer at Global Affairs told her that her dead father was under arrest. He clearly hadn't bothered to closely examine the case files – Brooke's father was missing and declared dead going on three years by this point. As Andrés had been arrested that month, possibly the case officer was referring to that, but they could have at least taken the time to check the rudimentary facts of the case before passing on wrong (and painful) information. More recently, when Brooke asked for an update on the case, the officer who made the request on Brooke's behalf was sent a single scanned document by Mexican authorities. She passed that page on to Brooke as an "update." But when Brooke and I examined the page closely, we quickly realized it wasn't an update at all. In fact, it was one page of a court document dealing with setting a date for a hearing. Out of context, it meant nothing. Brooke complained about the complete lack of attention to detail shown by this officer – had the case officer even looked at the document, she wondered? Why would anyone accept this as a so-called update? Brooke complained and in response she received an email in August 2022.

> I am sorry to hear that you are concerned with the information transmitted to you by our Department. I can confirm that on July 21, 2022, consular officials in Mexico sent an official communication to the Prosecutor's Office (Fiscalia General del Estado de Jalisco) requesting an update on the investigation. As conveyed to you by AXXXXXXXX, the Prosecutor's Office responded on July 26 and provided the document in Spanish which we have duly transmitted to your attention. No further or additional information or documents were provided by the Prosecutor's Office with regards to your father's case.

Still no acknowledgement that anyone at Global Affairs had bothered to read the document; no clarification on whether it had asked the Mexicans for a more complete update; no suggestion about a query on why the Mexicans had sent this document in the first place. Brooke thought the whole situation smacked of indifference at best and incompetence at worst.

But that incident wasn't the worst encounter Brooke has experienced with Global Affairs. The one that offended Brooke the most happened during a Zoom meeting in August 2021 to discuss a deal Marcela was proposing to a prosecutor named Sonja Alvarez. Alvarez had called a meeting to lay out the terms to Brooke. I sat in on the meeting as Brooke's guest. There were a couple of people in the meeting who did not have their cameras turned on. One of them turned out to be a representative from the Canadian consulate. Though the meeting lasted for nearly two hours, the person behind the thumbnail never showed her face. And when everyone went around and introduced themselves, she was the only person who refused to give her name and would only say she was there on behalf of the consulate and at this time it had no comment. Possibly the anonymity was a precaution she was taking as a result of living in Mexico and having a job as a government official, but Brooke found the whole situation emblematic of Global Affairs' general indifference – a faceless image that contributed nothing of any value. Brooke keeps track of all of these interactions with Global Affairs and hopes one day someone will listen and act. "I just have to keep logging these," she tells me.

> I need to have that paper trail showing what I've been requesting, so that later on, I have that trail to say, "Listen, I kept banging on your doors, I was telling you that something totally... terrible and illegal and criminal was happening over there, not just with my dad's case but with authorities, and you know, nobody's done anything."

There was one exception to this pattern of government indifference. Not surprisingly, it made a huge difference. It wasn't as a result of any action by Global Affairs; rather it was as a result of a letter sent by Northumberland–Peterborough MPP, David Piccini. He wrote a letter in December 2018 and asked some very hard questions of Pamela Goldsmith-Jones, the parliamentary secretary to the minister of foreign affairs. He stated quite plainly, "Most of the progress the family has made investigating this case has been out of their own volition." He ended the letter by stating, "We are hoping for immediate assistance." He also wrote to the Mexican ambassador in Ottawa, trying to solicit some assistance in preventing Marcela from selling the house.

That letter triggered a significant response from the Mexican government. We know that, because of it, Brooke managed to get a copy of a letter dated January 16, 2019: It was a letter between the Mexican ambassador to Canada, Arturo Hernández Basave, and the attorney general for Jalisco State, Gerardo Octavio Solís Gómez. Hernández states plainly that, "to date, the results of the investigation on this matter have been ineffective." He also suggests that the prosecutor "carry out all procedures necessary to locate the whereabouts of Malcom Robert Angus Madsen as promptly as possible, thereby avoiding a potential negative impact on the Canada–Mexico relationship." What happened next wasn't really known to Brooke, but in looking at the timeline of significant events we created around the Mexican investigation, shortly after this letter was sent, a flurry of activity took place, including the police finally searching the car and completing their reports on the phone activity of all of the main suspects.

Meanwhile, Brooke was trying to keep up the pressure by writing a few notes of her own. On January 13, 2019, she wrote to Global Affairs – to Pierre Alarie, Canada's ambassador to Mexico – and said,

> It feels very much like our own government is also not doing much to resolve the many issues raised by my father's sudden disappearance. Perhaps that has been a failure of communication on both of our parts, but I do hope this letter will afford us both an opportunity to establish an effective line of communication from your office to me.

The official response from Global Affairs was tepid. The minister responded with a polite note of sympathy, and another department head responded with a stock letter spouting platitudes like "certainly sympathize with your desire for justice and closure" and "only Mexican authorities have the mandate to investigate missing persons," and inviting her to go to their website. *Toronto Star* reporter Kenyon Wallace recounted in one of his articles that Global Affairs had written to Brooke and said,

> Thank you for taking the time to share your concerns with us. I realize that this situation is causing you much distress. Please know that Ambassador Alarie, Canadian consular officials in Puerto Vallarta and Mexico City and the consular team at Global Affairs Canada's headquarters in Ottawa have all been working together on your father's case since learning of his disappearance.

More empty glad-handing. Even in late 2019, when Kenyon started calling to ask questions for the *Toronto Star*, all he got was the same vague statements: "Global Affairs Canada told the *Star* that its consular officials in Mexico are in contact with local authorities but offered no other details, citing privacy laws." When I contacted Global Affairs, asking for a response in 2021, I was simply told the same thing. That, despite the fact Brooke had written to Global Affairs and told it I had her full permission for it to share any information with me.

The whole experience left Brooke coming to much the same conclusion that I had years ago, that "most people believe that this would never happen to them, and hopefully it never will, but if it does, you are completely on your own." She adds, "The Canadian government will not support you in any way, nor will Mexican authorities." And yet there's certainly no lack of people employed by Canada in the various consulates and the embassy in Mexico City – some 266 spread across ten different offices. Yet, with all those people in all those offices, at the end of the day nobody could seem to find the time to do much more than hand Brooke a list of English-speaking lawyers.

Despite severe misgivings, I decided to reach out one more time to Global Affairs. So in 2022 I again sent an email to Global Affairs asking for an interview. I also asked Brooke to send a note to her handler giving them permission once again to talk to me about her case. We got the usual stock answer from them about not being able to discuss specific cases because of people's rights to privacy. Brooke took another approach. She filed an Access to Information (ATI) request in February 2021 for a copy of her file. According to the Access to Information Act, she has every right to do so. For more than three years, all she received from Global Affairs were emails telling her they were sorry they had not sent her the ATI, but they were doing their best to get things in order. Raymond Brault, ATI consultant for Global Affairs, wrote to her in October 2022, saying he had the information and just had to sort through it to see what he was able to release.

Brooke heard nothing for months. She wrote again in January 2023 and got yet another response in which Brault said much the same thing: "I have commenced my review of the documents that are relevant to this request (GAC's file reference P-2020-01086) and due to my heavy workload and shifting priorities, I have not yet completed my review. Nonetheless, I would like to assure you that this request still remains one of my priority files to complete as soon as possible." He suggested that if she was unhappy, "you have the right to file a complaint to the Privacy Commissioner of Canada. In the event you decide to avail yourself of this right, your notice of complaint should be addressed to Mr. Philippe Dufresne, Privacy Commissioner of Canada." That email was the Global Affairs equivalent of "If you don't like it, lump it." They're not saying we've really messed up here and are way behind in giving you this information. They're saying we're working on it at our own speed, and if you don't like it, tough. Appealing to the information commissioner could take another two years to look into the case given their backlog. Remember that the federal government is supposed to deliver information for an ATI request within 30 days.

Brooke finally got the information in September 2024, four months shy of four years after she asked for it.

The final approach I used to pry some response from Global Affairs was to ask for an interview to discuss in general terms what it thought its responsibilities were to Canadians who got into trouble in foreign countries – a kind of what we can and cannot do interview. In late 2022, I corresponded back and forth with Global Affairs for a few weeks with promises of an interview but finally received this email from a spokesperson named Grantly Franklin:

> Global Affairs Canada is committed to providing effective and efficient consular service to Canadians around the world. Each consular case is unique and the assistance we can provide will vary depending on circumstances. The Government of Canada's ability and success in resolving consular cases are conditioned, in many instances, by the laws and regulations of other countries as well as the quality and level of cooperation offered by persons and organizations outside the Government of Canada. Due to the provisions of the *Privacy Act* and to protect the privacy of the individuals concerned, we cannot disclose information on specific consular cases. For additional information, please refer to the Canadian Consular Services Charter, which provides an overview on the consular services available to Canadian citizens as well as the limitations of those services.

A stock answer that tells Canadians little about what Global Affairs will or will not do to protect them. Will it step in and help with corrupt police? It depends. Is it able to get you help if you're being assaulted in prison? Can't say. If you've been robbed and beaten, will it come and help you? Maybe yes, maybe no. Frustrating, but in my experience absolutely typical of Global Affairs Canada.

CHAPTER ELEVEN

THE ARRESTS

The police investigation entered a dormant period between the fall of 2019 and the spring of 2020. Brooke's third trip to Puerto Vallarta in September 2019 had caused an initial flurry of activity, but after that investigative work seemed to die down. Of course, it's not possible to say what might have been going on behind closed doors – there may have been intense activity – but no major goals were achieved. At least not if I use court documents as a yardstick. As I've said already, what did finally spur some activity were media articles in Mexico that began to be published in 2020. Only weeks after Jorge's first article in March 2020, the prosecutor's office finally issued arrest warrants for all three suspects – it took 17 months. It would seem that having the three primary suspects under threat of arrest would be great news, but there were problems – no surprise – with being able to serve the warrants. In the time it had taken to issue them, the three suspects had scattered. Marcela had moved to somewhere near Mexico City and Martín and Andrés had fled north to the state of Nayarit. Authorities in Jalisco State showed little interest in rounding them up. In fact, according to Brooke and Ricardo, the arrests would never have happened if they had not gotten directly involved with the process. Here's how that happened.

While there are some documents to back up parts of this part of the story, mostly I had to rely on interviews with Brooke and Ricardo for the main points. That's because the arrests and how they came about ventured into the seamy side of Mexican justice. Because of that there's really not much I can do to verify details. Once you start talking about "incentives" being given to authorities and cops that are "shaking down" people in order to have them do their jobs, then clearly there isn't likely to be any kind of paper trail. What's more, I couldn't find any of the authorities involved who wanted to talk to me. So, though I can't verify the details on how these events happened, I can say that the story Brooke and Ricardo tell is not implausible. Basically, Brooke and Ricardo had to give money to the police to have them serve the arrest warrant on Marcela.

This is not an uncommon experience in Mexico. Getting someone in the justice system to do their job and having to pay for that privilege happens routinely. While I won't bore you with the details about the research we did on the Mexican justice system and corruption, I do think it's worth touching on a few salient points to put what Brooke and Ricardo did into some kind of context. The information we found doesn't paint a pretty picture. One report on corruption in Latin American and the Caribbean from 2019 stated that half of all people in Mexico who had contact with the police paid a bribe.[10]

In fact, corruption is big business in Mexico. In 2015 the Mexican Institute for Competitiveness estimated that the country lost $53 billion annually to corruption. And every report I examined indicated the problem does not seem to be getting better; it's getting worse. According to an article by the think tank and media organization InSight Crime, "An average of 1,688 corruption cases were registered for every 1,000 active-duty police officers in Mexico in 2017, according to a survey conducted by the National Institute of Statistics and Geography. That translates to 1.6 acts of corruption for every police officer at the national level."[11]

Let that sink in for a moment – each and every cop in the country is responsible for close to two acts of corruption per year. Given that there will be a few cops who are not on the take, this statistic probably means that most cops are responsible for more than two acts of corruption per year. What this phenomenon translates into is surreal: at one point the InSight Crime article goes on to say authorities arrested one town's entire police department in the state of Chihuahua. I'll say that again – the entire police department arrested for corruption. Another example cited points out that, in the municipality of Tehuacán in Puebla State, 205 officers were rounded up and charged with corruption. So, while I have no way of independently corroborating what Brooke and Ricardo tell me about having to deal with corrupt cops, it would seem to be an anomaly if, during the course of their many years of dealing with Mexican police, they did not encounter corruption and either have to pay money to someone along the way or drop the investigation. They chose to pay.

Here's the known facts surrounding the arrests of Marcela, Andrés, and Martín: An arrest warrant was issued in March 2020 for all three. Marcela wasn't arrested until July 13, 2020, near Mexico City. Martín was arrested on September 24, 2020. He was picked up somewhere in the state of Nayarit. It may have been at the house he was building near the jungle where Malcom's car spent so much time the night he went missing. Andrés wasn't arrested until September 24, 2021, and he was also living in Nayarit. For both of these arrests, the prisoner transfer documents from the Nayarit police to the Puerto Vallarta police force are the main documents I have that told me what happened. Those are the bare facts. But it's the story behind those simple facts that is really compelling: a more complex and at times seedy narrative.

According to Brooke and Ricardo, since the police showed a great deal of indifference about moving ahead to arrest the three suspects, the two of them were forced to do a huge amount of work to make up for that deficiency. In other words, they were forced to start playing the justice game by Mexican rules. Brooke's understanding of this reality began when she hired Ricardo: "I wouldn't have known [if] I had to do it without him. I didn't even know what I was up against until he clarified. I didn't know that there was no way the police were going to arrest Marcela." And Brooke believed the inaction by police went way beyond incompetence or indifference: "They issued the arrest warrants, probably, I'm going to take a good guess, and warned [Marcela, Martín, and Andrés] and then just sat on it for months and months and months and months." In fact, though Brooke had a legal right to know about major events in the case, she wasn't informed in a timely fashion about the fact that warrants had been issued: "I guess it was just to make us go away. He never told us or he never told Global Affairs; he never told the Canadian Embassy. None of us in Canada were informed that there was an arrest warrant and yet Marcela was given a copy of the arrest warrant – she had her own arrest warrant." The fact that Marcela had a copy of the warrant, and was able to leave Puerto Vallarta before it was served, screamed payoff to Brooke. "Somebody warned Marcela and Martín and Andrés that these arrest warrants were out for them and they left town."

Of course, there could be another explanation for how Marcela knew about the arrest warrant. She might have had a good lawyer who was watching what documents were filed in court and passing on that information. Regardless, Brooke wasn't about to just stand back and watch all her hard investigative work slip away because of police indifference. And here's where Brooke's relentless networking paid off: "It's one thing for me to be like a squeaky wheel or a little dog just yapping at them, but when you bring in the media, everything starts to change. That's how I got Marcela, I brought in the media."

Jorge Olmos wrote his first article about Brooke's father on January 27, 2020. About three weeks later, on February 14, 2020, someone named Alfonzo Hurvide contacted Brooke through Facebook Messenger. He claimed to be related to Julio Alejandro Márquez Camacho – Marcela's latest boyfriend. Alfonzo and the rest of Julio's family had heard about Marcela's nefarious past and that made them concerned about the relationship. Alfonzo was willing to tell Brooke exactly where Marcela was living if Brooke was interested in having Marcela arrested. But at this point Brooke didn't know about the warrants, so she politely declined the offer. But in June, Alfonzo was back. A warrant did exist, he told Brooke, and for the right price he could arrange to have a couple of local police officers pick up Marcela. Shortly after Brooke received that offer, Julio was gunned down in the street near his house. He was taken to hospital and treated, but an infection set in and he died a few weeks later on July 5. Julio's family, including Alfonzo, immediately connected Marcela to the shooting because they said she was one of the few people who knew when Julio took his daily walks and where he went on those walks. For an assassin to intercept him, they would need to know the time and place when he was out and about.

The messages to Brooke became more persistent. Alfonzo sent documents to prove he was not lying about knowing how to find Marcela – copies of her personal documents, picked up on the sly when he was visiting. The arrest could be made, according to Alfonzo, for USD 100,000. Ricardo stepped in and started to negotiate. He got the price down to $10,000 to pick up Marcela, and $5,000 each for Martín and Andrés. The cops also wanted additional "expenses" paid for – meals, travel costs, and a drone for surveillance. Ricardo made the deal and on July 13, 2020, two police officers picked up Marcela.

By this point, Alfonzo revealed his real name. In order to get paid, he sent Ricardo and Brooke his name and banking information. He was Sebastian Sanchez Marquez. He was related to Julio – possibly a step-brother or the son of Julio's sister Julieta Miriam Márquez Camacho. I tend to think this version of events is the one closest to reality. Brooke has provided me with copies of the messages that passed between her and "Alfonzo" and has shown me the computer records they sent as proof of their ability to deliver.

Having said that, I should note that Ricardo told me a slightly different story. But as I've gotten deeper into this story and reviewed the primary evidence, I've tended to give less and less credence to what Ricardo said. He really didn't seem to be familiar with the court documents. Nevertheless, I'll relay what he told me. First, he says, the people who contacted them were from within the prosecutor's office in another state: "These people were part or had association with another DA office, in a different state in Mexico." Later Ricardo claimed the people who contacted him were a vague group of "four or five people, two of them are police officers." He is also very clear that, from the start, it was all about money: "The only purpose they call me, to sell me information. They never wanted to do a co-operation or assist the other Puerto Vallarta DA's office; they wanted money." Regardless of the differences in the two stories, Ricardo agreed with Brooke that two things were on the table: information on where Marcela was located, and an offer that, for the right amount, local police could be hired to finally serve the warrant. Ricardo also believed that if they had ignored this odd arrangement, Marcela might never have been arrested. Brooke says that once Ricardo told her money was on the table, she felt she had no choice but to go along with the process: "I had to pay them a lot of money to get them to do their jobs. I had to buy them equipment. I just paid for their lunches, whatever they needed." Brooke continued,

> I had heard that this is what happens down there. I had been asked for bribes at the very beginning and I refused. I said I wasn't going to be a part of that, absolutely not. It's funny... it's a slippery slope, right, to just suddenly find yourself doing something you never thought you would agree to, maybe out of desperation or because you're so close. You've found the person, you have their location and suddenly no one will go and arrest them unless they're offered big sums of money to do so? It became, *What is her arrest worth to me?*

Once they had the intelligence of where Marcela was located and they were in contact with the police willing to do the job for a price, the stage was set for the arrest. Money was paid, an address was provided, and the police went over and arrested Marcela.

Once Marcela was behind bars, Brooke began to work on getting the other two suspects arrested. Once again, she turned to her tried and true method of exerting pressure by generating media attention. More articles turned up in *Vallarta Uno* and the *Toronto Star*, both raising questions about the inaction by the local prosecutor. In July 2020, Jorge Olmos and Kenyon Wallace both wrote articles – Jorge's was about Marcela's "black widow history," and Kenyon's was about Marcela's recent arrest. Less than a month after those articles were published, on September 24, 2020, police finally picked up Martín. There are not many details about his arrest, but a court document stated that two officers – Francisco Javier Genaro Dominiguez and Heini Hediguer Jimenez Amaton – travelled from Puerto Vallarta to Nayarit and "in accordance with existing agreements will take custody of this man charged in relations to the case number associated with Malcom." The arrest had been ordered by Jaime Navarro Hernández, the director general of prosecutions for Jalisco State. It all seemed to have been done by the book – no money changed hands – more than likely it was done as a result of feeling the pressure of the media attention and unwanted political scrutiny. Though Brooke and Ricardo did not pay police to arrest Martín, Brooke says that when Ricardo paid the first two cops to pick up Marcela, part of the deal was they were also supposed to pick up Martín. However, she says they didn't seem in a hurry to complete that work, and while it was possible these cops called in some favours from other Puerto Vallarta cops to do the work for them, it's more likely Navarro was behind the arrest. Regardless, Brooke said, "I'm very relieved Martín's been arrested. We've always believed that Martín is the brains behind the operation, so for him to be arrested was very important." At this point in the case, no more arrests would be made for nearly a year. But there was some other fascinating activity that started to bubble to the surface in August 2021. A new prosecutor entered the scene and made an interesting offer to Brooke.

The appearance of a new prosecutor is not unusual in Mexican cases. Ortega had not been removed from the case – he was still the investigating prosecutor. But in the Mexican justice system, often several prosecutors will be involved in a case – one to investigate, one to prepare the case for court, and one to try the case. Sonja Alvarez, a prosecutor based in Guadalajara, seemed to have been brought in to prepare the case for trial. Shortly after she became involved, she reached out to Brooke and asked for a meeting – as I mentioned to earlier, Marcela wanted to make a plea deal. Now it might be somewhat perplexing for many Canadians and Americans to try and get their heads around a justice system that would even consider a plea deal in what appears to be a murder charge. That was certainly Brooke's initial reaction: "I think mostly shock. I didn't think I would be able to have a say or I'd be involved in a plea deal. It didn't make sense to me that they would be asking me. I thought that was something the authorities would be dealing with." But this was not a murder case. The accused were charged with making someone disappear. And under Mexican law plea deals can happen in order to find the bodies and bring some peace to the families. But the authorities cannot move ahead without the consent of the family of the victim.

After some consideration, Brooke took another view of the situation: "I have to be honest, I definitely felt a little elated for the fact that she's actually admitting that she was involved, the fact that Marcela admitted that she knew what happened to my father that night. So that was kind of like mixed feelings, confusion, but some elation for sure." Here's how the deal was laid out. Sonja Alvarez contacted Brooke through Ricardo. She asked for a meeting on Zoom to explain a new proposal. On August 8, 2021, about half a dozen people gathered in a Zoom meeting to hear what was on the table – this was the same meeting I referred to earlier in which the Canadian consulate employee said nothing of any value. It took a long time to get the meeting underway, but eventually Alvarez was joined by Jaime Navarro, the head prosecutor. After much humming and hawing, Alvarez finally got down to it. As Brooke explains, "The deal was that Marcela would tell me where my father's body is in exchange for a lesser sentence. I believe she wants to serve eight years instead of 25-plus and she wants the same deal for her son." In fact, according to court documents, the prosecutor was asking for 50 years as an appropriate sentence. So eight years was a very favourable deal for Marcela.

As I sat there listening to Alvarez, it struck me that Marcela had just confessed to murder. If she was admitting she knew where the body was, then at the very least she was confessing to some role in the kidnapping and killing of Malcom. But there's an interesting point about Mexican law that comes into play in this kind of situation. In no way does Marcela's offer act as a confession. Even though she was admitting she knew where the body was buried, it could not be held up in court as tantamount to confessing to the crime. Apparently, this is connected to an effort to find more bodies. Nobody would ever come forward if what they said would ensure they were found guilty. So killers get a break. Brooke listened to the offer but was skeptical from the start:

> I don't feel that eight years is an adequate amount of time for what she took from my father. I certainly think he had eight years left; he had a lot more time... She's not interested in telling me what happened to my father, she just was giving the bare minimum to get what she wanted. And she certainly wasn't offering to return all the money and possessions she stole... and there was no regret or remorse, still, for what she'd done.

As the meeting wore on and other people began to speak, another agenda surfaced. Alvarez started to focus in on what *else* the prosecutors wanted – they wanted the case to go away. They seemed to be sick of having to deal with Brooke, the Canadian government, and the media. So Alvarez started talking in vague circles about the need to wrap the case up by Christmas. Brooke observed, "I was more or less, in my opinion, threatened by the Guadalajara DA that if I did not take this plea bargain – assuming it was a true case and she did disclose where his location is – I may not get the outcome I want. She may not serve time – more time – in prison in the end."

In the weeks after the meeting, Brooke and Ricardo discussed the deal and decided to make a counter-offer. They suggested that Marcela should serve a minimum of 18 to 20 years, that she would show them where Malcom's body was buried, and that she would return the money she got from selling the house. That counter-offer elicited virtually no response from the prosecutor's office. Eventually, Ricardo sent them a letter stating that if they did not respond by January 15, 2022, then the deal was off. As far as Brooke knew, nobody answered his letter.

After the plea deal died, there was really only one more significant event in the case during the rest of 2021. On September 24, Andrés was finally arrested. And this time it was clearly a police operation that scooped him up north of Puerto Vallarta in the state of Nayarit. Brooke believed that yet again a media outlet instigated this action – in this case, our documentary. We had begun principal photography a week earlier. As part of the preparation, we were in contact with the prosecutor's office in Puerto Vallarta and Guadalajara. Brooke says, "You know what, 100 per cent the documentary gets to claim Andrés's arrest, that's you guys... This documentary is the reason Andrés was arrested because they knew I was going to say that it was not because of them that the first two arrests were made. They needed to step up and do something." Whether in fact that was the case was hard to say, but the timing was rather coincidental. After Andrés's arrest, Brooke felt she'd taken a major step ahead in her father's case. All three principal suspects were now behind bars. According to Brooke, there was a lull in the case: "Now that Andrés has been arrested it feels like it's slowing down. I don't know if it is though – there's always a surprise around every corner."

In fact, there were going to be several surprises around corners in the next six months. For a start, more than three years after the case began, the prosecutors finally filed their cases in court. And what they had against the accused was stunning.

CHAPTER TWELVE

BODY PARTS

People are often the best source of information. When I taught at Ryerson (Toronto Metropolitan University), I would tell my graduate research class that people could provide them with information faster and in many cases more directly than painstakingly combing through documents. That's not to say I wanted them to ignore documents – they're needed to corroborate stories and to make sure the details were correct, because people can also be the least reliable sources. However, having someone tell you the inside story will get you to the end result much more efficiently than staring at page after page of documents.

Brooke learned this very quickly. She liked to talk about her "informers." She described them as "good informers" and "bad informers." That designation was not a complicated moral or ethical one. In fact, the vast majority of them were really not "informers" in the true sense of the word. An informer is someone "who informs to the police or another authority." What this network really consisted of was a large group of people, mostly in Mexico, who were feeding Brooke information on the quiet. In the journalism business, I'd call them contacts or sources. Regardless of the semantics of the situation, for Brooke, good informers were the dozens of ordinary Mexican people who offered to help her and provide information. Surprisingly, some of them were even feeding her details from inside the justice department. Many were keeping an eye on Marcela and her family in an informal way. Some were just passing on bits of information they'd heard through the proverbial grapevine. Brooke made friends with a number of them and still keeps in regular contact.

"Bad informers," according to Brooke, were people who sometimes had information (and sometimes didn't) but whose real motivation was simple – they wanted money. Not always. Sometimes it was an odd desire to cozy up to the notoriety of her story. They came out of the woodwork once Brooke's mission became public. People liked to claim they had provided Brooke with critical information, when in fact they had done nothing of the sort. One woman I met in Puerto Vallarta claimed to have connected Brooke with reporter Jorge Olmos. When I asked Jorge about this person, he looked perplexed. He asked who she was and I described what she looked like and where she was from. Jorge shook his head and said he had never heard of her and that he was connected to Brooke's story by Norma, Brooke's first lawyer. But for some reason this "informer" wanted to feel a connection with the investigation, feel she was instrumental in solving the mystery. A life in need of more excitement? Possibly.

On the plus side, Brooke certainly did have some "good informers" who provided her with first-class information. She won't tell me the names of some of them, but Brooke often knew about internal matters in the investigation and about the private lives of the main suspects long before anyone else had officially given her the information. She seemed to have eyes all over Puerto Vallarta – Marcela and her family couldn't make a move without Brooke hearing about it. One group of what Brooke calls "bad informers" stands out above all the rest. They were the people who claimed to be related to Marcela's most recent boyfriend – the ones who blew the whistle on Marcela and enabled Brooke and Ricardo to have her arrested. They always seemed to have something for sale. Even after Marcela was arrested, Sebastian Sanchez, aka Alfonzo, kept contacting Brooke and Ricardo. Eventually, Alfonzo claimed he had something that was a key piece of evidence. Brooke says, "I wasn't surprised when I was told there were body parts. After reading the emails and knowing how Marcela really felt about my dad, I could totally see her being capable of keeping souvenirs. Nothing surprises me anymore." Alfonzo spun a story about how, after Marcela had been arrested, he and his family had gained access to Julio's home – where Marcela was living – and searched it. They found Marcela's computer – the one Malcom had purchased for her. They also found identification papers, medical documents and, according to Brooke, they found something else: "I woke up one morning to a text message from an informant, to tell me that he just remembered that Marcela kept some of my father's teeth, as well as other things that were body parts that were collected from my father."

Specifically, Alfonzo and his cohorts explained they had found two of Malcom's teeth and two jars with what they claimed were parts of Malcom's body. The story changed from time to time, but it was most often his eye and one of his testicles. Brooke explained, "She was keeping them under her bed in a little bag full of crystals... There were two teeth. They were in there with that little sack that I think was kind of like a totem to bring about wealth and such and maybe protect herself from my father, from him as a spirit coming back to get her." To prove they were not making up this story, Brooke says Alfonzo

> sent [Ricardo] a lot of photos and then he sent me images of the photos and some of the more shocking photos... my mind didn't even grasp at first what I was looking at. I just kept looking through documents and then I suddenly thought, man, wait a minute, what was in those jars? And Ricardo told me that they were possibly body parts.

Now, of course, for many people this would sound like a scam from the get-go. But two facts made Brooke and Ricardo stop and consider what was being offered. In the first place, these people, though clearly only interested in money (and possibly revenge for Julio's death) had provided good intel on where Marcela was living. They'd also brokered the arrest. And Ricardo said, "What made me, inclined me, to believe that maybe it's true is the fact that they have Marcela's computer and they show it to me in real time and I found intimate and private information that would only belong to Marcela. So if they had the computer, why the [body parts] were not to be credible?"

Ricardo has little doubt that Marcela and her two accomplices had the motive to go to such extremes as collecting souvenirs. They were furious that Malcom was about to tear down their world: "It is very, very likely that she wanted not just to disappear him or kill him, just to [kill him] in a certain way that it will be a symbol to the family of Malcom." In other words, Marcela didn't want to just get rid of Malcom; she wanted to send a message to Brooke to back off from any attempts to try and take her house away. Taking some body parts might be a way to send that message.

What doesn't make sense about Ricardo's theory is that a threat from Marcela only works if the person being threatened knows about it. Brooke knew nothing of the body parts until Alfonzo and his cohorts started asking for money. So Brooke remained skeptical for some time about the body parts. There were months of negotiations. Brooke and Ricardo wanted a sample of the tissue so they could test it for DNA and compare it to Brooke's DNA to see if it was a match. While the informers didn't refuse that request, they delayed and avoided the issue and dragged the whole process out, all the while constantly pushing towards getting the money. What finally tipped the scales for Brooke was her conclusion about what these body parts could mean as decisive evidence. If Marcela was in possession of parts of her father's body, then there would be no doubt she was guilty of more than just drugging him. She would be guilty of conspiring to kill him: "I don't know if I definitely believe them, but can you take the chance of... not finding out if it's true? It's kind of a very valuable thing... you're playing a horrible game of chess with these people and was I willing to not find out if they're my dad's teeth?" There was also an emotional level to the negotiations. As Brooke puts it, "You're in this weird limbo of like are you happy if they're your dad's teeth or you're not happy. It really draws in every kind of emotion you've ever not really developed in yourself. It's weird."

Weird or not, Brooke decided she couldn't take a chance on not getting access to such potentially compelling evidence. She dispatched Ricardo to Mexico City to negotiate the purchase but not without a degree of trepidation. As Brooke confessed to me, "I don't like being outsmarted and these people have been manipulators from day one and everything is trying to get to their advantage, and I'm going to feel sick if they screwed me over on this one."

In April 2021, Ricardo flew to Mexico City to see if he could make the deal. Brooke was still anxious. "Well, I'm still struggling with it because we don't know if it's his teeth or not, so it's damned if you do, damned if you don't. If it is his teeth, it's like wonderful in a way but horrific. And if it isn't his teeth, it's wonderful in a way but it's horrific because of the means I had to go through to get them." The asking price was USD 5,000. The meeting was set up in front of a large international hotel in downtown Mexico City. But from the start the ground began to shift. Early in the day, Brooke got a call from Ricardo. The group had changed the price. Now they wanted USD 20,000 for the body parts, the computer, and the other personal items. They also wanted to put off the exchange for a couple of days. When Ricardo tried to negotiate, he told Brooke they cut off contact. Brooke sat in Port Hope anxiously waiting to hear from Ricardo. Hour after hour passed and nothing happened. Brooke tried to call Ricardo back. He wasn't answering. It seemed as if the whole scheme had completely unravelled. Finally, in mid-afternoon, Ricardo called Brooke. He told her he had re-established contact with the group and they were talking – they might do the deal today, but they were firm on the price. Also, they still would not consider giving a tissue sample to them for testing first. The bottom line was that Brooke would have to buy blind, without any real proof she was getting her father's body parts.

Ultimately, Brooke gave Ricardo the green light to pay. Brooke was phlegmatic about the increase. "That far into the game," she says, "I didn't care, I just wanted to get results. I wasn't getting them doing it my way."

The meet was on. They told Ricardo to sit outside a downtown hotel and they would make contact. I was in on the call with Brooke and Ricardo, and once I had the location, I called a local camera crew I had been in contact with earlier in the week and had them set up across the street to secretly film the meeting. Ricardo was nervous from the start: "We met in a different hotel the previous visit I make to Mexico... when we were negotiating – they say to me, look over the window... we are here, and there was a police patrol car over there, they are with me – take a look." The threat was clear to Ricardo. They were stating they had police protection and could use that protection or muscle anytime they chose. Ricardo was worried: "It is very likely when we do the trade-off, they maybe set me up because they are police, they may have another car and then they may prosecute me for, not for the payment but for the assistance I was given." In the video shot by our crew, you can see Ricardo pacing up and down in front of the hotel drinking a coffee. Ultimately, he does settle down on a bench, but it's clear he's anxious.

Eventually, the people did show up – three of them. One of them looked very much like the pictures Brooke gave me of Julieta – Julio's sister. She was with two guys: one man, whom we never saw but acted as a kind of guard off-camera, and another man who kept close to Julieta – was it Sebastian, aka Alfonzo? Ricardo took them out in front of the hotel where we had a clear glimpse of the group and had them sign some paperwork. That struck me as a little ludicrous. I mean, getting sleazeballs like this to sign a contract? What would it mean to them? Probably nothing. But Ricardo felt he had to impose some semblance of order on the transaction. Julieta got the money and headed off to the bank, according to Ricardo. But they didn't all leave, he said, "because some money was paid in cash, they [left] me [with] a sentinel, what they call a hawk in Mexico, *un halcon*, to stay in the hotel while I was in the restaurant, and I was warned that I could not leave or I will be watched until they will go to the bank and make sure the dollars I gave them in cash were real."

Julieta also didn't want to take any chances after they'd confirmed the cash was real. Ricardo says he went up to the restaurant in the hotel and had some lunch, "and this guy was staying in the lobby watching me, watching me." Even after lunch, when Ricardo went for a walk to meet our crew, "I was followed after…I went out in the block of the hotel to walk a little bit because it was already a stressful situation and this guy was waiting for me and tracing me down."

Once he got a few blocks away from the hotel, our van picked him up without his "hawk" seeing us and we took him to a secluded park where he showed us part of what he had purchased. He didn't bring the body parts, but the two teeth were neatly stored in a small drawstring purse. A successful conclusion to the first part of the operation. But now Brooke faced another problem: How would she get the body parts back into Canada to have them tested against her DNA? She didn't trust the labs in Mexico, so she had to come up with a plan and she guessed she couldn't just waltz through Canada Customs and declare that she might have human remains in her bags.

Meanwhile, Ricardo didn't want to hang on to these parts. He was so disturbed by the experience in Mexico City that he wanted to get the parts out of there as quickly as possible. He couldn't just jump on a plane to Costa Rica with the jars and the teeth. If he was stopped, what could he say? So he called Jesus in Puerto Vallarta and asked him if he could come to Mexico City and take possession of the parts. Jesus didn't hesitate. He jumped on a plane and flew up to meet Ricardo. When they met, Ricardo divided up the parts, giving Jesus one tooth and the two jars. He took another tooth, the computer, and the documents. Jesus got on a bus for a 15-hour trip back to Puerto Vallarta – a journey he says he didn't look forward to. Not just because of the time involved but because he was worried about running into a checkpoint on the road back. Clearly, if they searched his bags, he'd have some awkward explaining to do. Ricardo flew back to Costa Rica. Jesus made it successfully back to Puerto Vallarta.

With the parts now safely stashed, Brooke had to try and plan how she was going to get them back to Canada for testing. She started with one of the teeth. Probably the easiest object to bring quietly back into the country.

One of her "good informants" was visiting Puerto Vallarta and planned to return to Canada in a few weeks. Brooke asked the woman if she would consider bringing back the tooth. She agreed. And so, on August 24, 2021, Brooke drove down and met the woman in a park near Pearson Airport. Brooke was handed the drawstring purse and had the unpleasant task of opening it up and looking at what very well could be one of her father's teeth. She says how those teeth were taken didn't bear thinking about – the pain her father might have endured or what might have led up to having them removed. It was all too macabre, and it didn't get any better when her informant told Brooke why she thought Marcela might have kept the teeth and body parts:

> *Informant*: "When they practice all that, *brujeria*."
> *Brooke*: "And what is it? Is it witchcraft?"
> *Informant*: "Yeah."
> *Brooke*: "Would she need something? Would they collect body parts?"
> *Informant*: "Even people collect hair or something from the person, even after the person's dead, if she practiced that much, people believe that maybe she have nightmare or something… something to protect themselves."

Brooke recalled that Marcela did seem superstitious and so it didn't seem out of the question to her that Marcela might have kept these tokens in order to ward off a malevolent spirit. Certainly, that theory was no more bizarre than many of the other surreal experiences she faced during this investigation. It took a little longer to get the other body parts back to Canada, so in the meantime Brooke decided to start the testing with the first tooth. "We're going to take them to get them tested for DNA, see if the DNA in the tooth matches my DNA." Brooke took the first tooth to Viaguard Accu-Metrics in Toronto. Dr. Harvey Tenenbaum was quite certain they could extract DNA from the degraded tooth. They took a swab from Brooke's cheek to create a comparison and told her it would probably be several weeks before they had any results. The other body parts didn't arrive back in Canada until the end of November 2021. They were brought back by Brooke when she returned from a filming trip. We took Brooke back down to Puerto Vallarta to have her show us around some of the key locations associated with the investigation. While she was there, she took swabs of the "body parts" in the jars (under instructions from a lab on how to do it properly). Ricardo met her there and gave her the second tooth. All of the swabs made it back to Canada.

In December 2021, she took in the rest of the samples to the lab. Once again, they warned her that they couldn't guarantee they would be able to extract DNA from all of the samples and that it would take quite some time to complete the testing. With time to wait, that left Brooke a chance to finally slow down and think about what had just transpired – a surreal series of events in which people had sold her body parts. "Sometimes you wonder if you've lost your stability and reality with the world because of the things you're seeing…You're being told about your dad's teeth and you're not even crying – there's another part of this horrible story. You just have to deal with it." What was even more surreal for Brooke was that she had just agreed to buy body parts, negotiated with a group of low-lifes, and the whole process unfolded as if she was buying a second-hand pair of shoes through Craigslist. Brooke wasn't oblivious to just how odd the whole situation was, nor was she oblivious to the possibility it could still all be a scam: "You know, I did go through those feelings and I thought about it, oh my god, what if they're not, they played me and got me, which is always their plan." Brooke ultimately decided that, regardless of whether the DNA matched, the money was worth paying just for her own peace of mind. And in the back of Brooke's mind was the possibility that if the

DNA matched, she would have a huge piece of evidence to hand to the Mexican prosecutors – one she was convinced they couldn't ignore. The test results would be ready sometime in February 2022.

CHAPTER THIRTEEN

THE PROSECUTION'S CASE

In the spring of 2021, the prosecutors began to file the evidence they had amassed so far in court. Some of it wasn't accessible to me. I had copies of the documents, but they were in Spanish. I would go through all the documents and selectively translate sections to help me understand what the document was about. Usually, the first couple of paragraphs would tell the story. If the document was just another step in the process (setting a date for a hearing, for example), then I would move on. If the document was about more than process, then I would translate the whole thing. That method was, to say the least, tedious. Cutting and pasting sections, translating them, and then building a new English version in Word took a lot of time. But there was no way around it since I didn't have the funds to hire a translator for all 5,000 pages. Yet I had to know what was in those police and court documents. Legally, I would be liable for any missed information. So I pushed ahead with my method of selective sampling, sending any documents I thought were critical out to a translator to have the whole thing worked on by a professional. After more than three years, I have quite an inventory of translated documents. Each time I would get a fully translated document back, it was like suddenly being handed another piece of a jigsaw puzzle – the overall picture became a little clearer and almost every time there were significant revelations.

By far the most interesting document was called the Acusacion, or Accusation. This document was a detailed summary of every piece of evidence the prosecutors felt was significant to the case: every photo, witness, expert's report, or testimony. They had amalgamated all of these items in the Acusacion. This was the overview that would be submitted to the judges – a kind of "this is what we've got" summary. Overall, what they had was impressive. But, as in most aspects of the Mexican justice system, it was both fastidiously detailed and yet had some key gaps. It began with a statement of the charges:

> Against MARCELA ACOSTA RAMOS, for the crime of DISAPPEARANCE COMMITTED BY INDIVIDUALS AGGRAVATED, foreseen in Article 34 in relation to Article 32 section VIII of the General Law on Forced Disappearance of Persons, Disappearance Committed by Individuals and the National System of Search for Persons, in aggravation of MALCOM ROBERT ANGUS MADSEN.

You'll note that the language is quite stilted. That's partly because the structure of Spanish is often quite different to English and the translation is literal so often the word order is somewhat scrambled. And occasionally the word choice is a little odd. On the whole, I think, it's possible to understand what's being stated. In this case, they're laying out the section of the law under which Marcela was being charged. This statement was taken from the Acusacion against Marcela. Similar documents were filed against Martín and Andrés. The language was virtually identical in all three cases. After the initial charge was laid out, the prosecutors summarize what they believe happened that night:

> The victim in the company of the defendant MARCELA ACOSTA RAMOS, were drinking alcoholic beverages, and during the course of the night the defendant painfully poured a substance into the drink that the victim MALCOM ROBERT ANGUS MADSEN was drinking, without him being aware of the situation, thus creating the conditions so that the victim was not aware of what was happening.

That was a very convoluted way of saying they believe Marcela drugged Malcom. They go on to make the connection to Marcela's co-conspirators:

> The accused, MARCELA ACOSTA RAMOS, had interaction with the co-defendants ANDRÉS JAVIER ROMERO ACOSTA and MARTÍN ALEJANDRO ACOSTA RAMOS, where she informed them of the transfer they will make from the bar "ANDALE" to a house located behind the nightclub bar called "MANDALA," which is located on Morelos Street in the Centro neighbourhood.

Again, a complex way of saying they all met near the bar called Mandala. And, finally, they laid out the trip the three accused made to the remote jungle area in Nayarit where they allegedly killed Malcom and disposed of his body. Note they re-emphasized that Malcom was drugged and incapacitated:

> ...later moved through different areas towards the locality of Valle del Dorado, in Bahía de Banderas in the state of Nayarit, being this place where the last location of the victim MALCOM ROBERT ANGUS MADSEN was found, and also emphasizing that at that time the victim no longer had autonomy in terms of his freedom of movement due to the ingestion that the defendant herself poured in his drink and therefore made him depend on the defendant MARCELA ACOSTA RAMOS. It was for this reason that the accused in the company of the co-defendants carried out a transfer totally different from the one she had stated in the complaint she filed, depriving the victim of his freedom, all with the purpose of hiding the victim, or his fate or whereabouts and that up to this moment the victim MALCOM ROBERT ANGUS MADSEN has not been located.

Summation: They took him to a remote jungle area and he's never been seen since. Now if you think that description of the events of the night of

October 27 and the morning of October 28 sounds a little familiar, then you'd be right. And that's because it's virtually the same theory Brooke presented to the police and prosecutors within a few weeks of her father disappearing. And, sure enough, when you look at the evidence in the Acusacion, other than some forensic evidence, most of the facts were provided by Brooke – starting, of course, with the video. They even acknowledge Brooke's role:

> She obtained some videos where you can see her father in the company of the accused inside and later leaving the bar called ANDALE… Likewise it will be noticed by means of the images, the behaviour of the accused MARCELA ACOSTA RAMOS, when she poured an unidentified substance in the drink that MALCOM ROBERT ANGUS MADSEN was ingesting, without being able to notice it, as well as her exit from the bar where they board the cab that would transfer them to a different place.

Another major plank in their case that Brooke provided early in the investigation was the fact that Marcela emptied Malcom's account in the days following his disappearance: "She became aware of the bank transactions in the victim's accounts made by the defendant in the days following the disappearance of the victim MALCOM ROBERT ANGUS MADSEN." The prosecutor now presented this as a motive for Marcela's actions against Malcom. You may recall that, initially, the police and investigating prosecutor, Ortega, were somewhat disinterested in these financial transactions. And, of course, Brooke's GPS evidence figures prominently as well:

> It was possible to obtain the locations of the routes or transfers of the Toyota vehicle, Avanza type, which the victim bought for the defendant MARCELA ACOSTA RAMOS, since the vehicle has GPS monitoring… information is obtained from the notifications

> of the Trackimo company that commercializes the tracking devices via satellite, of the Toyota vehicle type Avanza, with licence plates JPJ 3908, specifically of October 27 and 28, 2018.

Ironically, a piece of evidence that police and prosecutors had so easily dismissed, and that both Ricardo and Brooke had to fight tooth and nail for, now appeared as a critical piece of evidence. This evidence wasn't the only one that was initially dismissed and that now turned up as integral to the prosecutors' case. This may be the result of the case finally getting out of the hands of the local police and prosecutor and making its way up the food chain to prosecutors from Guadalajara. On the whole, they handled the material in a more professional manner. Certainly, by the time the evidence was being compiled, the head prosecutor in Guadalajara, Jaime Navarro, was watching the whole case carefully. That meant credible evidence couldn't be easily dismissed.

The prosecutors also leaned heavily on the correspondence Brooke provided: copies of the emails between Marcela and Malcom that strongly suggest her interest in the relationship was mostly financial. The prosecutors' statement begins by explaining which emails they will introduce in the case: "the messages via email sent by both the victim MALCOM ROBERT ANGUS MADSEN and the accused MARCELA ACOSTA RAMOS, where she repeatedly asked him for money under the pretext that she and her relatives were sick."

The prosecutors then connect these emails to Marcela's ongoing attempts to bleed money from Malcom: "Point of evidence: This will prove the existence of the messages sent by the victim MALCOM ROBERT ANGUS MADSEN to the defendant MARCELA ACOSTA RAMOS, where she mentioned the health problems of the defendant and her family in order to obtain money from the victim." Essentially, the prosecutors have accepted Brooke's contention that the relationship was purely financial for Marcela and that the motive for her and her family to get rid of him was the threat of losing that financial support. The prosecutors also believed Robb's statement that the kidnapping and killing were tied into Marcela's fear of losing the house: "what the victim told him about the plans to sell the house he had bought for MARCELA ACOSTA RAMOS, since he no longer wanted to continue in the relationship with her."

The prosecutors even brought up the text message exchange that Brooke had with Marco, Marcela's brother, in the days following her father disappearing. I didn't give it much weight because it's somewhat cryptic. Marco did say he had concerns about Andrés possibly being involved, but he also backtracked a little by the end of the exchange. The prosecutor didn't see it that way. He felt it was an important piece of evidence, one in which a family member was making an accusation that Andrés was involved in the kidnapping.

Jesus also appears in the document, corroborating Brooke's contention that her father would never take any other driver to get down to the ferry to Los Chonchos. In a statement to the police, Jesus claims, "MALCOM told him to contact him the next time he went to his cabin so he could pick him up and transport him." And they've included Jesus's account of his first visit to Marcela to ask about Malcom's disappearance:

> He will also state when Robb Stasyshyn contacted him to ask him about the victim, and how he went to the victim's home at Pavo Real 141, Colonia Las Aralias, municipality of Puerto Vallarta, Jalisco. Where the mother, the son and the accused MARCELA ACOSTA RAMOS told him that MALCOM had left on Sunday, and that the victim had gone to Los Chonchos Beach where he has his cabin.

The police corroborated what Jesus said by talking with the person who sold tickets for the water taxi, Gabriel García Plantillas, who not only said he never saw Malcom that day but added: "He will also point out the routine of the victim when he arrived at his place of work to be transported to his cabin in Los Chonchos, being that he was always taken by his cab driver Mr. Jesus." And, of course, they included the statement by the workers at Los Chonchos who again confirm they were expecting Malcom on the morning taxi, as usual, and were concerned when he didn't show up.

If I ever had any doubts about how much work Brooke put into her investigation, reading through the Acusacion soon dispelled them. She not only put in a huge amount of work, but her skills as an investigator improved with each passing month. The police did have a few compelling pieces of evidence of their own: the main one being the cell phone records they had obtained, analyzed, and tracked:

- Record of report of behaviour and locations dated November 04, 2019, relative to the telephone line 3221336740, belonging to the defendant MARCELA ACOSTA RAMOS, consisting of 26 sheets.
- Record of report of behaviour and locations dated November 05, 2019, relative to telephone line 3221296344, belonging to defendant MARTÍN ALEJANDRO ACOSTA RAMOS, consisting of 22 sheets.
- Record of report of behaviour and locations dated November 05, 2019, regarding telephone line 3223028008, belonging to ANDRÉS JAVIER ROMERO ACOSTA, consisting of 19 sheets.

Based on this evidence, their conclusion was that the three accused had lied to the police – they were not at home and they were not at some bar in Nayarit. They were in a remote jungle location near the same location as Malcom's car in the middle of the night:

> Point of evidence: 25, 26, 27, 28 and 29 with which the locations of the displacements that had both the victim MALCOM ROBERT ANGUS MADSEN, as well as the accused MARCELA ACOSTA

> RAMOS, in addition to her brother MARTÍN ALEJANDRO RAMOS ACOSTA and her son ANDRÉS JAVIER ROMERO ACOSTA will be accredited and corroborated, resulting of vital importance since in the testimonies of the referred ones they manifested to be in places totally different to the ones that are managed to be noticed, in addition to being in the same locations in which the last awareness of the victim MALCOM ROBERT ANGUS MADSEN was had, this on the day of the facts being October 27 and 28, 2018, same that will be incorporated by the investigating police officer FRANCISCO JAVIER MALDONADO LARA, according to the provisions of Article 383 of the National Code of Criminal Procedures.

You may recall that earlier I talked about the fact that being caught lying in a formal statement to the police, in and of itself, carries a pretty hefty prison sentence if you're convicted. Again, the police were well aware of this fact. It hangs over this part of the evidence like an unspoken threat. The police also incorporated the sale of the house into the case: Marcela sold it for 3.6 million pesos in September 2019. That's about USD 185,000, nearly CAD 250,000. Of course, the suggestion was that the sale would give Marcela a great deal of cash to play with if she needed to pay any "judicial costs," or leave town to avoid the police. And, in fact, they discovered she *had* used that money to avoid prosecution and arrest – she left town not long after the house sold: "Record of investigation report, dated January 31, 2020, in which upon conducting a field investigation with the neighbours of the property located at Pavo Real number 141, Colonia Las Aralias, in the municipality of Puerto Vallarta, Jalisco, where they had negative results in finding the accused MARCELA ACOSTA RAMOS, since she no longer lives in said property."

For good measure, the prosecutors added a statement that showed Marcela was mentally fit to stand trial:

> POINT OF EVIDENCE: Who will testify complying with the requirements indicated by articles 360, 368, 369, and 370 of the National Code of Criminal Procedures, in relation to the experience, methodology used, as well as the material, with which she determines the conclusions of the personality report dated October 13, 2020, in which semi-structured psychological interviews were conducted, open interview, review of the psychological file practiced to the accused MARCELA ACOSTA RAMOS, in which she is oriented in time, space and person, presents a coefficient equal to the average term in relation to people of her same age and schooling, in addition her state of consciousness is lucid, with adequate capacity of attention and concentration, does not present signs of organic brain damage, with conserved memory in short, medium and long-term.

To supplement the forensic data, the prosecutors added a slew of eyewitnesses – most of whom supported only trivial points but almost all of whom supported Brooke's narrative. The police spoke to several neighbours who had nothing to add other than that they liked Malcom and disliked Marcela: "Diego Richard Alves McGaughey… who is his neighbour, whom he describes as [Malcom was] a respectful and kind person with the neighbours. MARCELA ACOSTA RAMOS, was always very cold and distant with the victim, and in the same way he pointed out that MARCELA never had the intention of interacting with the neighbours."

Perhaps the key eyewitness they brought forward to discredit Marcela's official statements was the taxi driver who picked them up at Andales the night Malcom disappeared – José Guadalupe Ochoa García:

> He provided them with the transportation service starting his route from the bar "ANDALE" taking them to the bar "MANDALA," for such reason transit through Juarez Street, in the Centro

> neighbourhood, in the municipality of Puerto Vallarta, until reaching Morelos Street, and there leaving MALCOM ROBERT ANGUS MADSEN and the defendant MARCELA ACOSTA RAMOS, where he stated that both got off his unit by their own feet.

What I find interesting is that not only had Marcela lied about where they went, but she'd lied about what condition Malcom was in. She said he was so drunk he had to be carried into the house. The taxi driver said he got out of the cab on his own two feet. I'm not sure how to reconcile this statement with the events of the night. Clearly, it contradicts Marcela's narrative, but it also leaves me wondering why and how Malcom would be walking around on his own feet and still walk into some kind of a trap set up to kidnap him. Possibly it might be related to the kind of drug he was given. Some – like benzodiazepine, commonly known as "Roofies" – leave the person able to function with basic motor skills but retain no memory of what happened.

There were also a number of pieces of evidence that left me wondering why they were included at all. The prosecutors present, in detail, the two searches that were conducted of the car. All they seem to add is the colour and year of the model:

> Vehicle inspection record, dated December 05, 2018, related to the Toyota vehicle, type Avanza, champagne colour, model 2018, licence plates JPJ 3908 of the State of Jalisco, series MHKMF53F5JK021466, engine number 2NRF612457, property of the defendant MARCELA ACOSTA RAMOS.

And the search that was conducted of the house reveals nothing: "Photographic sequence record, consisting of 89 black and white digitized photographs, dated July 25, 2019, derived from the Search Warrant granted for the entry to the domicile located at Pavo Real street, number 141, Colonia Las Aralias, municipality of Puerto Vallarta Jalisco."

Remember, those searches were not conducted for weeks or even months after Malcom disappeared and all the while the car and the house were under Marcela's control. That means there was no clear chain of evidence. In Canada or the US, that would invalidate any evidence found in the searches. And what could they have reasonably found when blood evidence deteriorates within days? And yet the prosecutor felt he had to present this evidence as part of his case. I asked Juan José Mejía Gonzalez, the trial prosecutor, why they would do this. He explained that, similar to Canadian law, the prosecutor is bound to present everything they have as part of their investigation – similar to the process of discovery in Canadian court cases.

Regardless of the few weak spots, the case was solid. It would seem they had all three of them caught in multiple lies, they had a financial motive for the crime, and they had proven that the three of them had the means and opportunity to commit the crime. What they didn't have was a body, and that could prove to be a real problem. I was told that, under Mexican law, without the body, the case might very well still be an uphill battle. It's one of the reasons our fixer Gabriel suggested that cartel figures just "disappear" people. It's hard to convict them without the body. But then again, the three accused were not charged with murder. They were charged with making a body disappear. So they may have faced a different set of criteria.

And while the prosecutors prepared their case, Marcela, Martín, and Andrés prepared their defence. There's a glimpse of what they might have been planning in one document Martín's lawyer filed as part of an attempt to get his client's case dismissed early in the proceedings. It didn't work, but it provided a preview of where they were planning to go. For a start, as in his statement to police, Martín claimed he wasn't there. He and Andrés were at cockfights in Nayarit on the evening of the 27th, and then they went to a bar and drank until 4 a.m. on the 28th. Martín offered up three names that could corroborate this version of events. The problem with Martín's key witness, Rogelio Ruiz Rodriguez, was that he didn't actually support the full narrative. He only said he saw Martín at the cockfights on the 27th:

> He would have observed them leaving the cockfighting ring; and also contemporaneous, concomitant circumstances surrounding the facts that are the subject of the accusation; means of evidence that is relevant as useful and conducive to discredit the accusation that the aforementioned accused had been physically on Morelos Street, behind the bar Mandala.

That's a convoluted way of saying Martín couldn't have been at Mandala because he was in Nayarit at the time. But there was no sworn statement to accompany this so-called corroborating statement by his witness. In addition, Martín offered up several others who would attest to the fact that Marcela had no motive to kill Malcom – she and Malcom got along just fine:

> Evidence that is pertinent, useful and conducive to prove that the relationship that the co-defendant MARCELA ACOSTA RAMOS had with the offended party was a normal satisfactory relationship of a couple, contrary to what the prosecution would have us believe in its accusation, through its various witnesses, by indicating that they were on the verge of separating.

And, curiously, Martín's lawyer also presented a number of people who saw Malcom on the street waiting for his cab on the afternoon of the 28th.

> Witness who will tell us about the circumstances of time, manner and place in which MALCOM ROBERT ANGUS MADSEN was observed, approximately at 14 hours on October 28 twenty-eight, 2018, outside his home located at Calle Pavo Real number 141, in Colonia Las Aralias, along with some suitcases, when he together with his father, passed by that domicile.

What was particularly interesting about these "eyewitnesses" was that they lived (according to the information in Martín's defence statement) in neighbourhoods scattered across Puerto Vallarta, often some distance from where Marcela and Malcom lived. It was odd they all just happened to have been on the same street on that Sunday afternoon – a veritable convention of Martín's friends and acquaintances. Again, there is no suggestion that sworn statements had been made by these people – only the lawyer's submission that this was what they would say if they appeared in court. And, finally, Martín offered up a couple of "expert" witnesses to undermine the cell phone data:

> Criminal lawyer, expert in forensic sciences expert with specialty in criminalistics of field, authorized by the council of the judiciary of the State of Jalisco, with the experience for his professional knowledge in the matter of location and identification by means of satellite, of locations (co-ordinates) of objectives, who speaks to us regarding his professional quality, about the technical methodology, conclusions and other content referring to the report of behaviour and location of signals of the cell phones.

But I noted they were not offering up a forensic scientist to discredit the information. Rather they were offering up a lawyer who was an expert in the field. Once again, the statement by the lawyer was not included, only that they would present him as a witness at trial. So, all in all, Martín's case, and possibly by extension Marcela's and Andrés's cases, were based on some pretty insubstantial grounds – some questionable witnesses who would attest to the fact that Marcela and Malcom got along, a few more who say they saw Malcom the morning he disappeared, and a very shaky witness that puts Martín in Nayarit at the time the prosecution says his phone puts him in Puerto Vallarta.

One witness who came across as almost comical in Martín's case was his mother, Socorro Ramos Esparza. Martín said his mother saw Malcom the night of the 27th and the following morning on the 28th in the house they all shared. But in the prosecutors' case she gave a statement and refused to corroborate that, stating, "On October 28, 2018, in the early hours of the morning she observed together with the stairs some suitcases that belonged to MALCOM ROBERT ANGUS MADSEN, without being able to see *him.*" All she saw were his bags. Other family members didn't offer up much more in the way of support. Carlos Acosta Ramos (Marcela's brother) would only say that when he went over on the evening of the 27th to take care of his parents, "he did not observe that his sister MARCELA ACOSTA RAMOS was there and neither the victim MALCOM ROBERT ANGUS MADSEN, as well as no vehicle belonging to the accused, the Toyota Avanza or the Grand Cherokee of his nephew Andrés." In fact, Carlos undermined the alibi put forward by Martín and Marcela. About the only person who corroborated the family's narrative was Marcela's disabled son, Carlos Antonio Romero Acosta. He stated that "his mother the accused MARCELA ACOSTA RAMOS, woke him up by calling him on the phone, this with the intention that he would help her to get MALCOM ROBERT ANGUS MADSEN down since he was very drunk."

Given the preponderance of evidence the prosecutors had accumulated, it's little wonder they were asking the judge for the maximum sentence. In fact, they were asking to use a clause in the law that allowed penalties to be more severe when the victim was related to the accused:

> The law may be increased by up to one-half when: The perpetrator or perpetrators have ties of kinship, friendship, work relationship or trust with the victim. Which is fulfilled, since the accused MARCELA ACOSTA RAMOS, maintains a sentimental relationship and co-existence with the victim MALCOM ROBERT ANGUS MADSEN, therefore it is established that she took advantage of the bond of trust and sentimental relationship that existed.

Since Marcela was in a relationship with Malcom, and Brooke was

Malcom's daughter, that makes them related according to Mexican law. That meant Marcela was subject to a clause that increased penalties when the crime was against a relative – or so the prosecutors contended. The total prison time being suggested was between 20 and 50 years. On the few occasions when I exchanged messages with the prosecutor, he felt very bullish about his chances and was pushing hard to get the cases combined and to bring the case to trial. He said the defence was still stalling, but he believed the judge might soon reach the end of her patience with that tactic.

While these documents were being filed and the case was inching along in the courts, other "progress" was being made in the investigation. In March 2022, Juan Mejía contacted Brooke. He told her they were going to search five areas of Puerto Vallarta in the next 24 hours for Malcom's body. They were pulling out all the stops. The state police would be involved – local police, forensic specialists, body-searching dogs – even the military was going to be there. It was too late for Brooke to get to Puerto Vallarta and attend the search and she was somewhat upset by that. She said they knew how to reach her in minutes if they wanted to. Yet days had passed while the search was organized and they had not reached out. Brooke called Jesus and asked him to attend as her proxy. It was a somewhat unnerving proposal for Jesus – like many Mexicans, he likes to keep his distance from the police, the military, and any other quasi-judicial organization. For the most part, experiences with these groups don't go well for the average Mexican, and in this situation all the people of power who could destroy him on a whim would be gathered in one place. We asked him to take phone video and, showing great courage, he did so. The search didn't find Malcom, though as the prosecutors' press release indicated, several other bodies were found. But there was a problem with the search from the get-go: They were not searching in any area that was related to the key sites where Malcom might have been that night. The jungle area in Nayarit was completely ignored – though that was the place with the highest potential. Instead, they searched five unknown areas. One of them might have been close to where Malcom's phone last pinged a tower. Later I was told by Jorge that the search really had nothing to do with Malcom. It was related to some missing people who had powerful families in Guadalajara. They wanted some action and they got some. Jorge thinks Malcom's name was thrown in merely as a sop to Global Affairs, which had been asking for an update recently.

And while events continued to unfold in Mexico, Brooke continued to try and substantiate some information about the tissue samples she'd purchased and had taken to the lab in Toronto. Brooke was convinced the results might show the samples did belong to her father. Weeks later, Brooke finally got a report from the lab:

> Sample # 1 A large tooth.
> After a considerable amount of time, it was determined that the tooth was not human in origin but from some other species, such as a dog.
>
> Sample #2 A tooth which was the pendant portion of a necklace.
> The tooth was of human origin, and DNA was found and extracted. An evaluation of the DNA profile from the tooth indicated that the DNA had no genetic relationship to the DNA profile obtained from the oral swabs of Ms. Mullins.
>
> Sample #3 A sliver of ocular tissue, likely from the iris.
>
> Sample #4 A sliver of largely dermal tissue from the testicular area.
> The tissues were in separate containers immersed in some type of preservative solution. The issue however, in each case was that the biological samples had degraded substantially. The preservative solution also blocked PCR amplification of any genetic material that may have been present. The tissue samples were

> extracted and tested for the presence of any drugs with emphasis on Rohypnol, Ketamine, and Benzodiazepine derivatives. *Traces of Diazepam* were found in the testicular tissue sample. Diazepam can cause sleepiness, dizziness, and memory loss. Due to the uncertainty as to the source of the tissue, it is difficult to comment [emphasis mine].

The report was the worst of all possible outcomes. It could neither tell Brooke categorically that the samples did not belong to her father, nor could it tell her they did. What the report did say was that there was diazepam present in the samples but that they had degraded so much that they couldn't confirm a DNA match. Diazepam, sold under the brand name Valium among others, is available over the counter in Mexico. It might very well have been the drug Marcela used on Malcom. Quite conceivably the samples were from Malcom. But there was no way to prove it. The slam-dunk piece of evidence Brooke longed for was not to be. But the situation was not completely dire. As she prepared for trial, she could be content that the evidence she'd gathered to this point amounted to a compelling case against Marcela, Martín, and Andrés – one the prosecutors were excited to present in court.

CHAPTER FOURTEEN

MEXICAN JUSTICE

We take for granted in Canada that if we ever have an encounter with the law, we will face a relatively fair trial. I'm not suggesting our system is perfect – far from it. We've got built-in biases against people of colour and certain predispositions that allow anyone with sufficient economic means to get a much fairer shake from the system. But, all in all, we live in a judicial paradise compared to what people have to deal with in Mexico. I'm not going to try and sugar-coat this: Brooke's chances of success in a trial in this case were always minimal. I don't mean to undermine all the amazing work she's done in gathering together critical evidence and compelling the police to look at it and accept it as part of the case. In any normal judicial system, what Brooke had found by way of proof would be undeniable – the case would be pro forma and the verdict virtually certain. But Mexico has no ordinary justice system. In fact, by most standards, it has an extraordinary system – extraordinarily corrupt.

In order to delve a little deeper into this phenomenon, I did quite a bit of research and study after study said the same thing: Mexico's justice system is one of the most corrupt on Earth. I was struggling with why that was the case until I came across an article I thought put the whole system into a very understandable context. It is called "Corruption of Politicians, Law Enforcement, and the Judiciary in Mexico and Complicity across the Border," written by a law professor named Luz Nagle.[12] She's a fascinating person in her own right. After graduating with an advanced degree in law in her native Colombia, she began working as a judge during the height of the Pablo Escobar reign of terror. She took the honourable, but some would say foolish, position of refusing to accept bribes. After numerous death threats and a failed bomb explosion, she decided it was time to leave the country. She told her colleagues she was going on vacation to the United States and never went back. She set up in Los Angeles and went back to school for a couple of additional law degrees. She supported herself by working as a private investigator (that's another story). She's had a distinguished career fighting software pirates, human traffickers, and corruption in various countries around the world. She sits on legal committees for the United Nations, lectures at universities around the world, and is considered a leading expert on corruption.

What I found compelling about Nagle's 2010 article was that it suggested that corruption isn't just a casual affair in Mexico; it is part of an unspoken economic model. And what's more, when I talked to Nagle, she contended it was not getting any better:

> Nothing has changed. On the contrary. Corruption has increased and it has permeated to many other sectors of the Mexican society. I mean, when I did the article, I really focused on just a few aspects but if you look at 2009 to what we have today, 2022, is it has gotten worse. You have now a pretty much legalized corruption within the police forces. It's all over the place, to the point that a lot of Mexicans say that while on one side the police officers may try to help, then in the afternoon, they will try to rob everyone because of the corruption.

When Nagle told me about her research, I shared with her my story about the casual bribery I experienced with the police – being pulled over in Puerto Vallarta and having to hand over 800 pesos just to be sent on our way. Nagle shared a story of her own about a friend who was Mexican and wanted to take her children back for a visit. One of her main concerns was how much money she should take to pay bribes to the police. Her conclusion is chilling: "What type of system can we have when every citizen that is driving his or her car in the freeways in Mexico is thinking about whether or not they have enough money in their wallets if they get stopped by the police? I mean…that's not rule of law." In fact, Nagle reaffirmed her original theory to me – corruption is part of the economic game plan in Mexico: "Corruption has become a way to increase the salaries of a lot of people who work for the government. And it has gotten not only to the police officers, like I said, to the judiciary, it has permeated every single aspect of the Mexican government." According to Nagle, rather than pay more than the pittance that most Mexican police officers make every month, the government takes a laissez-faire position that in effect allows the police to supplement their incomes by shaking people down for bribes. And she contends the system works all the way up the line of authority, "and that has extended to other sectors of the society, so that they really don't have to pay people increased salaries in the judiciary, because through corruption, now the judges can make up for the difference." Nagle affirms that examples of this level of corruption are painfully easy to find: "I think it was in 2021, 25 judges were denounced for corruption and yet only one judge went to jail. And we're talking about the few judges that were exposed – what about the ones that have not been exposed?"

Nagle believes that not all the judges start off as corrupt. She says many will try to run an honest court, but it's an uphill battle for them:

> The problem is that the system as a whole, now, is so corrupted that it would be very difficult for one judge, or the very few judges who are not corrupt, to have the other parts of the system work with them without being tainted by the corruption that is embedded in the whole system. I mean, for the judges to do their job, they need the evidence to be clean, to be put forward to them so that they can objectively decide a case. Well, the problem is that then you have those who are supposed to be gathering the evidence that many of them, if not most of them, are corrupt.

> How do we trust that that evidence has not been tainted, how do we trust that someone hasn't been paid for that to be different from what the reality really reflects? So that's what I referred to when I said it's the whole system and one judge alone cannot operate within that system.

The whole system, according to Nagle, is becoming more corrupt despite the past president of Mexico's promise to clean up the judiciary. Andrés Manuel López Obrador ran on a platform of cleaning up the problem, but Nagle is not convinced:

> People are really upset, to the point that now there are concerns that a lot of the expansion of corruption with the other sectors of the society, it has come because the government has failed to act with regards to how the cartels are buying a lot of the public officials. So, no, [Obrador] hasn't done anything. If you look at the thermometer – because there is a thermometer for the countries when we talk about corruption – Mexico has declined in the last three years, it has declined two or three points, depending on which sector we are talking about. So, no, [he] hasn't done anything.

In fact, Nagle points to another alarming trend that's occurred during Obrador's tenure: "During his administration, what we have seen that is more concerning is the killing of a lot of reporters who dare to publicize anything with regards to corruption." That is the reason why Jorge keeps a very low profile. His life has been threatened more than once. During our conversation, Nagle mentioned several times the impact the cartels have on the justice system. Given her experience in Columbia, she is well aware of the obscene amounts of money these gangs can put on the table. When the average cop is making a few hundred dollars a month and the cartels are hauling in billions in profits, it doesn't take a math genius to understand that for them to offer double a cop's salary is a drop in the financial bucket – it wouldn't cover a single bottle of Dom Perignon at a cartel party. The cartels can buy who they want, when they want, and that undermines the entire government and legal system. But Nagle is quick to point out that blaming everything on the cartels is too simplistic:

> There's always been some type of organized crime, and they became stronger when they started a lot of the drug trafficking businesses, cocaine, being the middleman for Colombian cartels. But they became stronger when the Colombian cartels were attacked and the Mexican cartels became their own agents. The corruption prior to that in Mexico was manageable. When organized crime became so strong, the government couldn't offer the salaries that the cartel offered; they couldn't match it. And it's impossible to match it now. The amount of money that the cartels can put forward to all these people is just unbelievable. And it's not the money, it's the training that they get, the weapons that they get, the perks that they get. So it's competing economically in an impossible market. And to win this war against corruption, there has to be some ethics, some love for some standards, some love for the rule of law, and I just don't know if that is going to weigh more than the love that many have for money.

What Nagle is affirming is that the system is corrupt from top to bottom and there's little hope it will change – and little hope that a fair trial based on evidence can ever be achieved. Happily, Nagle says there is one exception to this rule: "If there's public pressure, if there is a report in the newspaper, if there is a report in Canada, if that report is sent through social media – and we have the public pressure because now we are requiring transparency. I'm sorry to say, but that will be the way to force the system to work with the evidence that they have in front of them. It's about transparency and pressure."

All this to say that while Brooke has had her share of dealing with corruption in the Mexican justice system – like when the Trackimo information she provided to the police was deleted – the work she did to put pressure on the Canadian government to get involved and inviting various media members in Mexico and Canada to get involved may have been the very action that would open up a faint possibility of a fair trial. Ironically, the Mexicans wouldn't want to be seen on the world stage as being totally corrupt.

The rub in the Mexican justice system is that there is always a possibility that a case will never get to trial. I'm not being facetious. There are multiple examples where accused have sat in jail for years without their cases being concluded, and Malcom's case was no exception. Consider the facts: Malcom disappeared in October 2018. The police and prosecutors had finished gathering evidence by the end of 2019. By the end of 2020, they'd managed to arrest all three suspects. They filed their cases at the start of 2021. And there's where the matter stayed for two years. Of course, there had been reams of filings on procedural matters, but nothing of any substance has occurred since then. Navarro, the head prosecutor, blamed the defence. Cases like Malcom's can stall for years. It's a case of Mexican judicial indifference versus Brooke's constant pressure.

If by some great stroke of luck a case is fortunate enough to be heard in front of a judge that isn't corrupt, it still has to wind its way through the Mexican court process, which is a very different system than American or Canadian courts. In order to get some facts about the system (there is a lot of misinformation out there), I called up an old friend, Luis Guillermo Cruz Rico. What makes Guillermo a valuable resource is that he is certified as a lawyer in both Mexico and Canada, so he understands the fundamentals of each system. I'd had contact with Guillermo on a couple of earlier cases in which Canadians had run afoul of the law in Mexico and he was hired by the families to help. My first question was based on a "fact" I'd been told in the past – that presumption of innocence is not the starting point for the accused in Mexico. Wrong, according to Guillermo: "The assumption of innocence is a principle of law," he says, "in both Mexico and Canada. So, in other words, it's up to the prosecutor to prove beyond a reasonable doubt that a case has grounds." In theory at least, Guillermo suggests, Mexico's system is not dissimilar to ours.

Now that's a very broad statement. What's more accurate would be that Mexico is trying to bring its system more in line with that of the US and Canada and has enacted some constitutional changes to reflect that process. But at its heart Mexico still relies on the Napoleonic Code not English common law, and that makes a huge difference to the role judges play in court proceedings and in the importance attached to case law for setting precedents. What this means is that, although Mexico's legal system is changing, Mexican judges still rely more on codes and statutes than case law, or precedents, to guide their decisions, the latter of which is the system in Canada and the US.[13]

Another piece of misinformation I was labouring under was that in Mexico there is no expectation that the accused is entitled to bail. I'd heard horror stories from reliable sources about people accused of crimes spending up to 18 years behind bars before they went to trial. In the Brenda Martin case, she spent a couple of years in prison without being convicted. But once again, in theory, that shouldn't be happening, according to Guillermo:

> The general rule is that a person who has been accused would be able to get bail, like in Canada, but also there will be exceptions to that rule, particularly when the person has been accused of a serious criminal offence. So, having said that, how would we determine if somebody would be under custody in a jail in Mexico, would be based upon the type of the criminal offence that this person has been accused. And number two, it would be if the conditions in order to grant bail have been fulfilled or not.

Once again, it sounds very much like our system of justice in Canada and in theory should provide for a solid system of justice – the presumption of innocence and the right to not be held in custody indefinitely.

There are, however, some marked differences. For a start, I noticed that when we talked Guillermo kept referring to the prosecutor as a "public servant." Eventually, I stopped the conversation and asked him about this distinction. His answer is important:

> They are public servants, they work for the government ... this agency that is part of the executive branch, of the administrative branch, mainly deals with what is the investigation, administration, and also the prosecution of possible criminal offences. This agency has a budget, has somebody who is the head of the agency, but at the end of the day, all of them work for the Mexican government.

In other words, in Canada the government employs prosecutors, but there is a clear line of separation between elected members of the government and the judiciary. The judicial branch is kept at arm's length from the political branch under the principal of judicial independence so judges are free to make decisions based on the law and evidence without fear of outside influence. In Mexico, the relationship between the two branches is less defined. You may recall that the Mexican ambassador to Canada wrote that letter to the attorney general of Jalisco State in which he expressed a great deal of dissatisfaction with how the case was being conducted. This letter didn't raise an eyebrow in Mexico. If that happened in Canada, there would be a huge hue and cry – in early 2023, when the premier of Alberta, Danielle Smith, was accused of having someone in her office contact the Crown prosecutor's office, there were calls for a full inquiry and for Smith's resignation.

Another key difference between the two systems, as I mentioned earlier, is that no one prosecutor in Mexico takes the case from inception to completion. Instead, a series of prosecutors are involved and, like in the American system, they're involved right from the start when the case is being investigated by the police. As Guillermo explains,

> In Canada, we are used to dealing with a criminal case and the prosecutor who is taking care of the case maybe will be the person who will be following up the case until the case is completed... In Mexico... it's unlikely there would be the same public servant from the beginning to the end. It's mainly each public servant would work a specific duty and would be part of a specific stage of the criminal process... the idea is that each public servant would be part of a specific desk and each desk would have a specific specialization. So the person who would be arguing the case won't be the person who was conducting the investigation or was leading the investigation.

That was absolutely true in the investigation and preparation of Malcom's case. I lost track of the number of prosecutors that handled the case – René Ortega led the investigation at the start and when I spoke to Guillermo, Juan Mejía was getting ready to argue the case in front of the judge. In between there had been as many as half a dozen names that cropped up on the files, and at times the head prosecutor Navarro stepped in and directed the case.

Another difference between our respective systems is that Mexico allows the defence to delay the case almost indefinitely. In December 2021, I spoke with Jaime Navarro, head of prosecutions for Jalisco State. I asked him why – at that time – it had been three years since the crime was committed and there was still not sign of a trial for the accused. He told me the defence kept asking for delays. I was initially suspicious of this reason and thought maybe it was an excuse to cover the prosecutors' indifference or general incompetence. But since then, a number of other people have mentioned the same issue. Guillermo says it's built right into the Mexican Constitution:

> It's a constitutional guarantee that has been in place for many years and the idea is to allow the defendant, in order to try to get as much evidence, as much information as possible, in order to fight the accusation. Please bear in mind... that somebody who has been accused of committing a criminal offence is fighting the whole system. It's somebody who is fighting the system because at the end of the day, the prosecutor's office is putting together all this information in order to try to prove the grounds of the accusation. For that reason, it was a constitutional reform of Article 20 of the Constitution and mainly, the defendant is allowed to ask for more time in order to make sure that he or she will be able to respond and address the accusation.

Guillermo also noted, "It's important to mention that the accused person, or the defendant, wouldn't be able to do that if that person is in custody... It would be in his or her best interest in order to ask for further time, in order to make sure that they would be able to have a proper defence." What that boils down to is the accused can ask for virtually limitless delays and if they're behind bars they get even more latitude from judges.

And if there are multiple accused, as there were in Malcom's case, they all have the final say on whether their cases are combined or not. If the prosecutor thinks the accused are stalling, he can take the complaint before a judge and ask that the case be moved ahead on a timely basis, but Guillermo says there's no guarantee the judge is going to rule in the prosecutor's favour: "the prosecutor would be able to ask, but it would be up to the judge to decide if it's time to have a date and time in order to hear all the evidence and make a final decision in the case." This gives the defendant a decided edge in the process. If the prosecutor has to bring his witnesses forward three times, as would happen in Malcom's case, then the chances of there being some kind of difference in the testimony goes way up. Any difference can be exploited on appeal. Like in the Canadian system, the Mexican system also has a rule that cases should be tried in a timely fashion. Guillermo notes that "the Constitution says that a criminal case shouldn't take more than a year, unless it has been requested by the accused, the defendant, in order to get more time in order to address the accusation."

These rules were applied liberally in Malcom's case. In late 2022, the current prosecutor, Mejía, took the case in front of a judge to ask that the three cases be combined and that a date finally be set for trial. The whole hearing got bogged down and nothing seemed to happen. I'm not quite sure why Marcela and her co-accused were stalling. After all, they'd been in jail for more than two years and counting. That couldn't have been fun. But possibly they just didn't see a way past the evidence. The case against them was pretty solid. Or possibly there was another reason. Guillermo suggests,

> If the evidence is so overwhelming, then maybe – and I'm saying maybe – the defence is trying to create some kind of fighting grounds in case a superior court would find that the procedure wasn't properly followed. Like in Canada, we have few mistrials … in Mexico, it happens that the defendant or the prosecutor would be able to appeal the decision in the criminal case and a superior court could be able to decide if the procedure was properly followed.

Possibly the only shot Marcela, Martín, and Andrés believe they had of ever seeing the light of day again was to take the conviction and then dissect the case looking for a flaw, for grounds for appeal. The longer they stalled, the more chance there was that some bureaucrat would make a mistake. Keeping their cases apart increases the odds that some witness would make a mistake. Perhaps they were just looking for any crack in the case they could exploit on appeal.

And speaking of appeals, another critical difference between Mexico's justice system and our own in Canada is the concept of *amparo* suits, which are "one of the most important type of cases the federal courts hear in Mexico [and] which have no exact equivalent in the common law tradition. Legally, the word encompasses elements of several legal actions in the common law tradition, specifically writ of habeas corpus, injunction, error, mandamus, and certiorari."[14] This form of appeal is open to anyone who believes their case has been mishandled and their rights have been violated according to Mexico's Constitution. It's a very broad legal concept and one that comes into play a great deal in criminal cases.

All in all, these days the system in Mexico, in theory at least, seems to be moving towards one that is similar to our own. In practice, the system is a whole other entity, one that is rife with corrupt judges, prosecutors, and police that distort the system beyond any recognition. Here's the stark reality of the Mexican justice system: 98 per cent of violent crimes in Mexico remain unsolved.[15] *The Washington Post* quotes various sources that say the 98 per cent figure has held steady for 15 years (as of 2019).[16] Additionally, 95 per cent of all crimes are unreported to, or uninvestigated by, the police.[17] And only about 56 per cent of all murders result in convictions.[18] Add to the corruption the fact that, as one article suggests,

> The weakness of institutions in Mexico is exacerbated by a shortage of justice officials. Mexico has 4.2 judges per 100,000 people, significantly below the global average of 16.23. This deficit of judges leads to slow trial times, contributing to the high number of prisoners held in pre-trial detention. The average level of prison overcrowding across the 31 states is 103% of capacity, which translates to 1,220 people per state. The worst state, Nayarit, has prisons filled to 223 percent of capacity, topping all others.[19]

Now cap this litany of judicial problems off with the fact that some judges are not only corrupt but also likely incompetent – appointed because of family connections, not qualifications.

> At least 51% of Mexico's judges and magistrates are related to someone else working in the judiciary, with that number as high as 80% in some states. (To take one particularly egregious but not totally anomalous example, in one judge's chambers, 17 employees were related to the judge.) This nepotism is not only corrupt in itself, but it also contributes to other forms of corruption. For one thing, corrupt judges can appoint those who will participate in, or at least be complicit in, corrupt practices – in some cases appointing individuals recommended by organized crime groups. But even when such deliberate wrongdoing is not the issue, untrained or unprofessional judicial bureaucrats and judges are more susceptible to corruption, and more likely to create the kinds of delays and inefficiencies in the system that both invite and obscure corrupt actions.[20]

Finally, if nepotism isn't enough to deal with, judges are routinely charged and investigated for taking bribes – mostly from narco-traffickers but not exclusively:

> The Federal Judiciary Council (CJF) and Attorney General's Office (FGR) have opened investigations into 12 Jalisco judges for corruption and ties to organized crime. The Financial Intelligence Unit (UIF) has already frozen the bank accounts of two of the suspects. Among the judges under investigation is one who in April ordered the release of one of the state's most wanted narco-traffickers. The released gangster is believed responsible for the murder of a police officer involved in his arrest.[21]

There have been several attempts to overhaul the system, none of them successful. It will be tough to change a system that has been entrenched for more than a hundred years. In 2024 a new president of Mexico, Claudia Sheinbaum, was elected. She has also pledged to clean up the judiciary.[22]

It was in this questionable environment that Marcela, Martín, and Andrés's trial got underway.

CHAPTER FIFTEEN

THE TRIAL

Frankly, the whole experience felt a little surreal. On a sunny spring morning in April 2023, Brooke, Zab, and I were boarding a plane to fly down to Puerto Vallarta. It was a moment I had been waiting for for nearly three years. Brooke and Zab had been waiting nearly five. There were many times during that long stretch that I believed this scenario would never play out. Many times, I had accepted that the corruption in the Mexican justice system meant that a trial was never going to be. Yet here we were, taking off from Toronto's Pearson Airport, heading for a trial that was to start the following morning. The lead-up to this moment had actually begun four months earlier: on December 10, 2022, Juan Mejía, the current prosecutor, told Brooke that a key hearing was to take place. He was going to ask to set a date for a trial to tell the judge that the prosecutor's office had had enough of the stalling tactics employed by Marcela and her lawyer. Brooke was invited to join the proceedings via an online link. But the whole affair turned into a bit of a clusterfuck. It took forever to get the link up and running, and then suddenly the judge announced that Brooke must have representation at the hearing. If she couldn't have her own representation, then she needed to sign a waiver that allowed the prosecutor to be her representative. That meant documents had to be written and signed and scanned and sent back and forth – all in real time. Ultimately, Brooke did what was asked, yet the whole hearing seemed to dissolve in confusion. At least that's what it looked like from our end. Apparently, though, it didn't. Unbeknownst to us, the hearing proceeded, because the next thing Brooke was being told was that another hearing was scheduled for February 14, 2023, to enter evidence. This was a crucial step in the process – a court hearing at which the prosecutor puts forward the evidence and witnesses he wishes to call and the defence has an opportunity to enter objections.

The day following the February court hearing I got a gleeful message from Juan. Everything they had submitted had been accepted. The defence didn't object to anything. I was frankly shocked by this. There were so many redundant witnesses in the lineup I felt sure Marcela's lawyers would want that pared down. But they had accepted every witness and every piece of physical evidence. Shortly after that, Brooke received another message from Juan: a trial date had finally been set – April 10. I didn't believe it. In fact, I contacted our fixer, Gabriel, and asked him to check the court system to make sure the trial was listed in the docket. I also connected with Jorge and asked him to check. Within a couple of days, they got back to me. The trial was on.

I booked a hotel and flight. I wanted to go down and cover this event, to see the story to the end. Brooke started to make travel plans. She also started wondering about whether the prosecutor was going to provide her with security and a translator – she was getting mixed signals. So, given that, she also approached Global Affairs to find out whether it could help. Worried that Marcela's family might try some act of vengeance, Brooke felt a representative from consular services in Puerto Vallarta might help. On March 31, she received this message from Alexandra Tardif at Global Affairs:

> Per consultation on the mentioned National code of criminal procedures, said articles refer to the responsibility of the Mexican courts to provide translation services when required. Mission is drafting a response reiterating the consular mandate and requesting that local authorities provide the corresponding services according to local procedures. However, should you wish to consider hiring a translator to be present if the authorities

> do not confirm one for the trial, you can find a list of professional translators attached. Your legal representative may confirm the assigned translator directly to the court at: Juzgado de Control Octavo Distrito Puerto Vallarta juzgadocontroldistrito8@cjj.gob.mx. Should your lawyer still not be responding, we can send the information on your behalf.

Bottom line: not our problem. If the Mexican prosecutors don't provide a translator, hire one yourself. No real surprise, given the approach by Global Affairs over the years.

On April 9, Brooke, Zab, and I flew down to Puerto Vallarta. The prosecutors had managed to pull their plans together between the end of March and mid-April. They had promised that a translator would be present; they had also assured Brooke she would have security the whole time she was there. They were as good as their word. As soon as Brooke arrived at the hotel, she met the two policewomen who would guard her. They were, Brooke says,

> heavily armed. We joked that they carried – they always had their handguns on them. Usually they had them concealed, but sometimes they'd also bring their rifles and we called it their banjo bag because it looked kind of like a big banjo. But yes, they were always very professional but fun as well, always checking in to see how I was feeling. They were constantly asking me if I was okay. They were really warm, wonderful people, very grateful that they were there.

The prosecutors also provided Brooke with a translator.

One notable absence at the trial was Ricardo. In February 2023, he disappeared. He did so while still owing Brooke a rather large amount of money from a real estate sale. It wasn't the entire amount, only what was held back to pay taxes, but it still amounted to thousands of dollars. Now

Brooke couldn't reach him. She called some of Ricardo's business friends – they said he also owed them money and they had not heard from him for months. I've reached out to him half a dozen times and have had no response.

Ricardo's absence didn't seem to faze Brooke. Her first job when she arrived in Puerto Vallarta was to spend an afternoon meeting with Juan and his team to make sure she understood their line of questioning. Zab and Robb were also talked through the questions they would face. I have to say the prosecutors had really pulled out all the stops for this case. There were no fewer than five lawyers who would be working the case the following day, including Juan's boss, the head of all prosecution for Jalisco State, Jaime Navarro. They had also brought along a young lawyer who was assigned to represent Brooke.

The team was excited about the case and feeling rather confident. I wasn't quite so bullish. I had spoken with Jorge Olmos earlier in the week and he felt all three accused could very possibly get off. As he said, "no body, no crime." I pointed out that the three accused were not accused of murder but of the crime "disappearing a body." He grudgingly thought that might make a difference.

DAY ONE

April 10 was a beautiful warm sunny day. I was staying at a different hotel than Brooke and Zab. We were all supposed to stay at my hotel, but the prosecutors mixed up the plans and moved Brooke and Zab at the last minute. I wasn't happy about that. I wanted to have access to Brooke during the trial and having her stay at another hotel impeded that plan. I did, however, have my own driver. I asked Jesus to pick me up at 9 a.m. The trial was supposed to start at ten.

I'm not sure what I was thinking. I guess I was basing my timing on dealing with Canadian and American courts and I wanted to get there ahead of the key players to film their arrivals. I also wanted to make sure there wouldn't be any problems with me getting inside to watch the trial. I should have known better. It's Mexico. People didn't even start straggling in until close to 10 a.m. The prosecution arrived around that time. There were more than two dozen witnesses to process and the armed court security people seemed a little overwhelmed. Long lineups formed. Some people were let in; others were told to wait. Some people went in and then came back out again. I was told they would get to me when there was time. Brooke was dealt with in a fairly respectful and efficient manner and soon disappeared inside, but I was clearly an afterthought. By the time I got through processing – with a short detour back to the car to get rid of everything except my notepad and pen – it was closer to 11:30. I sat down to wait for the opening arguments.

A brief aside. When Jesus and I arrived that morning, we noticed someone lurking around the grounds of the court. It was Carlito, Marcela's son. He paced back and forth until he noticed me taking video of him, then he left the grounds. But the incident really concerned Brooke and her security detail, and as she told me afterwards,

> I definitely had a couple of incidents where I was extremely nervous, to the point where I was shaking, especially when I found out when I got there, through one of my informants, that I was being threatened by a family member of Marcela's and the other accused. And then to show up at court and the first person I saw there was that person and to know that there are numerous days, that made me very [nervous]. I was scared at court more than anywhere else, to be honest.

Brooke's security was told about Carlito, and when Brooke arrived, they searched the whole area to make sure Carlito wasn't around. He showed up on at least one succeeding day.

The courthouse just outside Puerto Vallarta is a relatively new building – I heard it was built in 2015. Once you get inside, there is a long atrium with skylights running the full length of the corridor that connects all the courts, and a row of large palms grows along the corridor. Inside, the courtroom is also very modern and very spartan: plain bare white walls, white tiled floors, and the usual wooden judges' bench and wooden tables and chairs for the lawyers and accused. Over the whole room, just behind the judges' bench, there is a large crest of Mexico embossed in silver.

The prosecutors' bench looked a little overcrowded with five lawyers lined up. Over on the other side, there were two lawyers representing the accused. As soon as everyone was seated, security guards filled the room and a door to one side was opened. Behind it I could see barred doors. I heard some shuffling and the clank of a key turning before Marcela, Martín, and Andrés filed in, flanked by two more guards. They didn't look at anyone in the courtroom. They just shuffled over to their seats and sat down.

My first thought was that prison had not been kind to the three of them. Marcela and Martín had been behind bars for nearly three years; Andrés for two. Though Marcela had lost a little weight since the last pictures we'd received while she was in jail, she looked old and worn. Martín looked positively burned out. His eyes were bloodshot and his clothing somewhat dishevelled. Andrés had grown a goatee. He'd also packed on quite a bit of weight. His arrest photo showed a slender young man. Now he was thick and somewhat dull-looking. Brooke thought Marcela might react to her presence in the court.

> She looked kind of defeated; her clothes were a little tattered looking. She didn't look at me at first and I actually didn't think she would look at me. And I had turned to my interpreter and said I don't think she's ever going to look over here. And it's like she read my mind because at that point, when I glanced back

> over, she turned and looked at me and gave me a look that nobody's ever given me before. It was definitely a hard look to describe, but definitely a look of total hatred. But I wasn't scared of her at the moment when I saw her. Maybe a little more after the look because the look kind of gave me the feeling that, you know, that I should be worried while I'm there, that I'm on her turf kind of feeling.

Once everyone was seated, the three judges entered. The principal judge was Ana Rosa Carrillo Dueñas. She was supported by Samantha Sarahí Fierros Loza and Joaquín Torres Ángel. I asked Juan about the judges and whether there was any possibility they were corrupt. He said he knew them and had studied under one of them – he had absolutely no concerns about their integrity. Both women judges were quite young – in their early 40s at most, possibly their late 30s. They ran the court with an iron fist. Before the first witness was even called, the defence made an objection: The translator provided by the prosecutors was not court-certified. The defence made the point that they could not be certain when they were cross-examining a witness that what they were hearing was accurate. The judges huddled together and decided that while Brooke's translator could provide translation for Brooke, she could not do any legal work – the prosecution was given until the following day to find a court-certified translator and Brooke and Zab and Robb's testimony was delayed. A rocky start, I thought.

Following hard on that objection, the defence filed another one: All charges should be dropped immediately, they claimed, because the process to get this case to trial had infringed on their clients' constitutional rights to a speedy trial. This was a rich assertion. The constant delays to the case had been at the insistence of the defence: new lawyers had been hired, motions were filed that they were not ready to proceed, and there were requests for more time. The prosecution pointed out that the case had taken so long because Marcela and her co-accused had stalled it all along. The judges briefly conferred and then agreed with the prosecution and waved off the objection.

The defence was not quite done and raised yet another objection. They pointed out that if there was no body, there was no crime. Again, the judges conferred briefly and then they dismissed the objection. At that point, the defence declared they had no witnesses to call. The prosecution had 27, plus Brooke. With things progressing in this way, I started to think there was a vague possibility this trial might play out as Brooke had hoped.

It was time for the prosecution's opening statement. Juan gave the opening statement and it was clear from the start he had done his homework. He put together a seamless theory of how the crime had transpired, supported by multiple witnesses and massive amounts of physical evidence. Nonetheless, though Juan seemed confident in his presentation, he admitted to me afterwards that he had opening-day jitters:

> I was really nervous, and I must tell you not all the cases have three judges like in this one. Like, other cases have only one judge and you make the trial with one judge. So in this case there was three judges and that makes you nervous, that makes you have more pressure because there are three, three judges watching your job and you must do it correctly.

As Juan began to lay out his arguments, I was being helped by Brooke's friend Martina who was translating for me as the statement was being made (I was later given a written version to corroborate what Martina told me). Juan began with a dramatic opening:

> Honourable members of the trial court over the following days will hear a series of events that undoubtedly translate into one of the most serious crimes against humanity that the state of Jalisco has witnessed, and that the determination they make at the end

> of the trial, it will be worth remembering as a national and international reference in the face of the great crisis of disappearances of persons that the Mexican State is going through and that hurt our society and even the people who visit our beautiful country so much.

Juan wanted to make a couple of key points in his opening statement. He wanted to remind the judges that they were hearing about a crime that was part of Mexico's massive missing persons problem. He also wanted them to remember the world media was watching this case.

Having opened with those points, he then recapped Malcom's history of how he arrived in Puerto Vallarta and decided to settle down here for the winters. He recounted how Malcom met Marcela, started a relationship, and bought the house and put it in Marcela's name, but under the understanding the house still belonged to him. Juan also talked about how kind Malcom had been to Marcela's family. Juan then went on to set up the scenario that showed that once Marcela realized the relationship might be ending, she devised a nefarious plan that would enable her to keep all the money from the house and whatever money she could get from Malcom's bank accounts. Juan stated,

> It was for the end of the year 2017 and the beginning of the year 2018 that Malcom and Marcela began talks about their separation, due to the cold and distant attitude that Marcela always had towards Malcom and that she only used him for financial gain, agreeing between them that the house would be sold and the money would remain with Malcom. This in turn would give a part of the money to Marcela and that way they would conclude their relationship. However, Marcela, guided by her ambition and greed, chose to disappear him and thus keep the total amount that would be for the sale of the house in question.

Juan then painted a vivid picture of how Marcela, Andrés, and Martín conspired to drug Malcom, take him by taxi to a rendezvous point, and then make him disappear. He went on to state that the three believed they had just executed a flawless crime.

> The defendants mistakenly believing that they are executing an almost perfectly orchestrated plan – Marcela denounces the disappearance of Malcom, falsifying and omitting various information regarding what really happened and in tune with her, her son and brother [Andrés and Martín] they did the same, all evidently and without a doubt in order to hide the fate or whereabouts of Malcom, since then causing pain of inexplicable magnitudes to his daughter Brooke Sybelle Mullins, who had to go through, for the first time in her life, Christmas of that year without the company of [her] father. Marcela, in endless inconsistencies, after reporting Malcom's disappearance, withdrew money from his bank cards, and as if all this were not enough, sold the house that Malcom had bought and registered in her name, thus executing the last of [her] plans that led to the disappearance of Malcom.

By the time Juan sat down, he'd pretty much laid out all of the work accomplished by Brooke and the police during the past four years. He'd packaged together a neat narrative that explained all the events of the night Malcom went missing and the subsequent days when the accused covered up the crime.

Having found a bit of a stride, and unable to bring Brooke up as the first witness, the prosecution decided to play another trump card – the videotape. The defence immediately objected, stating they hadn't time to review it. Juan noted to the judges that the problem wasn't his concern. If the defence had not prepared properly, then that was their problem. To my shock (and Juan's, he later told me), the judges conferred briefly and decided to give the defence some time to review the tape. They recessed the trial for an hour. It was getting late, around 5 p.m., and the court had been running most of the day. We all hung around the hallway outside the court while the defence reviewed the tape. When everyone finally reconvened about an hour later, the defence said they wanted the whole tape to be played, not just the seconds the prosecution wanted. They claimed there was mitigating evidence earlier on the tape. That claim turned out to be utter bullshit. The full one-hour tape was played and nothing was pointed out by the defence to countermand the scene where Marcela spikes Malcom's drink. But the tactic had been somewhat successful. Playing the whole tape acted as a means of diluting the impact of the critical 15 seconds. I could see the judges were getting a little bored with the video. I'd seen the video, so while all this was playing out I spent time watching Marcela. I was more interested in how she would react to the video. She didn't. She showed no emotion.

The prosecution trotted out a number of witnesses during the rest of the first day. Some of them were downright lame – the cleaning lady across the street who saw nothing; the water taxi driver who couldn't remember Marcela; the guy who bought the house from Marcela. About the only person of interest, I thought, was the guy who drove the taxi from Andales to Mandala bar. He reiterated his story but couldn't really identify Marcela when he was asked to point her out in the court. This was partly because Marcela kept herself tucked in behind her lawyer and wasn't really visible from the witness stand. Nonetheless, I felt that was a blow for the prosecution.

The only really solid witness of the day was José Luis Del Real Arellano. I'd noticed his name cropped up on a lot of the documents when I was reading the police reports. He had been the key cop on most of the early stages of the investigation. When he hit the stand, he was excellent. He spoke slowly and clearly and over the course of about 45 minutes he eviscerated Marcela's statements to the police, showing clearly how many contradictions there were in the narrative she had created. Though the defence cross-examined Del Real, they only put forward a few questions and then they stopped. I'm not sure why. By the end of the first day, I would have to say it had been a mixed day for the prosecution. They'd started strong but had some real ups and downs. The trial dragged on until well past 9 p.m. Interestingly, the defence looked pretty happy by the time they left for the day.

DAY TWO

I was a little nervous as day two kicked off. The defence had revealed their strategy on day one. They were going to object to everything the prosecution presented. It wasn't a bad approach as they really had little to present by way of an alternative narrative, and even if most of their objections were shot down, they were still undermining the prosecution's case. The morning kicked off with a couple more semi-irrelevant witnesses – more water taxi drivers who had little to say. Finally, Jesus took the stand. He was much stronger and told his story about being called by Robb and setting off to speak with Marcela. He talked about her odd behaviour, but afterwards he told me that when he left the stand he felt as if the prosecution had not really asked the right questions.

In Jesus's pre-interview they'd talked about the irregularity of all the video cameras being broken simultaneously. During his court testimony they hadn't even bothered to query him about that information. Jesus wasn't the only one who felt that way. I spoke with Zab and Robb after they testified and they also felt the questions they'd been asked had been vague and didn't allow them to speak about what they knew best. In the afternoon, a certified translator finally turned up and Brooke started her testimony. Her recollections show clearly how she felt at the time:

> First of all, I should state I was incredibly nervous going into that. I sat outside by myself for a little while, my new translator stood

> a few feet away from me and I was incredibly emotional. I was crying. It was just so much. It's just so much energy balled up to know that I was going to go in and face them. I was scared of the defence because I didn't know what they were going to ask. I wanted to make sure I did my best but you know, it's hard on the spot, so I was worried that I'd forget things. I finally looked over at the translator and said to him, "Can you talk to me? Are you allowed to?" And he's like, yeah. I said, "Can you just talk to me?" So we just talked so I could clear my head.

Brooke was crying through much of the early stages of her testimony. When she walked to the stand, there was no reaction from Marcela, Martín, or Andrés. Once again, I felt the prosecutor's questions were a little vague and often confusing for Brooke. The translator had trouble getting the language right – at one point asking about Malcom's accounts he said, "Do you know where the money was allocated?" Brooke looked confused. So was I. Was he asking about who got the money? Was he asking about where the accounts were located? Was he asking how Malcom spent his money? He was, in fact, asking about where the accounts were physically located – in Canada. But getting to that answer took time and amid all of the confusion I felt, once again, the potential impact on the judges was being lost. When the questions did allow Brooke to speak, she spoke well and from the heart. "I was up there two and a half hours," she recalls,

> so after a while I started to realize, okay, they're not asking me the right questions, so I'm going to have to try and start adding more, which I've always been told don't. Don't over-share, don't say too much. But I was like, I have to start adding more or they're not going to get it because the questions were so vague.

The judges were clearly interested in what she was saying. At the end of her testimony, I believed her words had made a powerful difference. And when the defence tried to cross-examine her, the prosecution really showed their professional chops – Cynthia Bracamontes Rosales was the lawyer who had questioned Brooke and was responsible for defending her during cross-examination. She savaged the defence (legally speaking), shutting down all but three of their questions as being either off topic or too vague. The judges agreed with almost all of her objections. Finally, the defence gave up. Chalk up one for the prosecution.

Later that afternoon, a prosecutor named Yessica Guadalupe Alvarado Martínez questioned Zab. Either the translator just wasn't getting the questions right or her questions were vague and unfocused. Regardless, Zab's testimony was a bit of a train wreck. Zab looked confused most of the time. I was confused most of the time. The prosecutor spent more time asking him personal questions about Malcom rather than about what Malcom had said to him about his relationship with Marcela. The questions, according to Zab, in no way related to what they said they were going to talk about when he was pre-interviewed. As he left the stand, Zab looked crushed. Next up was Robb. He fared better than Zab but mostly because he ignored the questions he was asked and just related his narrative about how Malcom went missing and the steps he took in the aftermath of that event. He also managed to clearly state that Malcom was done with Marcela and that Malcom believed he still owned the house despite it being in Marcela's name. By the end of day two, it seemed the prosecutors were gaining a little momentum. The case was by no means a slam dunk, but they had made some progress.

DAY THREE

By the third day, the prosecution team seemed to have found its stride. The prosecutors brought forward a series of police experts, including Emmanuel Hernández Gómez. Juan mentioned him in his opening statement:

> Now, with regard to the witness Emmanuel Hernández Gómez, as an expert witness on that date, he will state on time how he extracted information from Brooke's cell phone from which a conversation emerged in which a relative of Marcela told the indirect victim herself that he mistrusted Marcela. He will also be clear in telling us everything related to the locations that the Avanza truck's GPS system showed, which were forwarded to him by Brooke to be analyzed later. Just as it will be clear in telling us the analysis he made regarding the video where Marcela and Malcom are observed inside the Andale Bar just at the moment in which Marcela would [slip] a substance in Malcom's drink.

Hernández was the prosecution's forensics guy. He was the one who examined the videotape, the Trackimo data, and the cell phone data. He also knew how to testify clearly and concisely. He was carefully led through the three main pieces of evidence and he validated and explained the relevance of each of them. He testified that he checked the video and it hadn't been tampered with, and he'd extracted some close-up shots that showed the action of Marcela spiking the drink very clearly. Though the technicians from the courthouse fumbled around trying to show his close-up shots, they did manage to get the job done eventually and the photos were crystal clear. There was no burying the evidence for the defence this time. Hernández also talked about validating the Trackimo GPS and plotting the points that showed the movement of Malcom's car throughout the night – movement Marcela and Andrés had said never occurred. Finally, he was questioned about tracking the cell phone data from Marcela's, Martín's, and Andrés's phones. This was the key data that tied Martín and Andrés to the conspiracy. Its importance was pre-eminent. He walked the judges very carefully through his work, and then the prosecution handed the witness over to the defence. They went after Hernández with some ferocity. They questioned his credentials and his methodology, but they made little headway. Hernández had been a forensic scientist for many years and a couple of questions undermining the software he used for pulling the frame grabs on the video made little impact on the judges.

One problem during the day for the prosecution was the ongoing incompetence of the technical staff at the courthouse. They were so inept at getting material played on their big screens that at one point Hernández asked the court if he could help. The judges were forced to call for recesses twice to allow the technicians to get material up. When they did get material on the screen, the resolution was poor – you couldn't really see what was going on. Juan claimed he was never nervous about this fiasco.

> That video was incorporated as a proof in the memory stick, we incorporated and we left it to the judges to watch them later. I mean, they must, in order to resolve, in order to make a fair judgment, they must see the video again, not only, not only in the time that we were seeing it at the trial.

Juan may not have been concerned, but I was. The judges may have had this evidence to review later, but the trial was where much of it was being explained and the dots connected. If the judges couldn't see the visual connection for the three key pieces of evidence, that might have created reasonable doubt. All in all, I would have to call day three a tie. The defence was doing a credible job of raising doubt.

DAY FOUR

For some reason I could not fathom, Juan dispatched Brooke up north to a city in the state of Nayarit to give a DNA sample on day four. He wanted her DNA on their database so that if any unknown bodies turned up, Nayarit police would have Brooke's DNA as a comparison. (You may recall that the evidence indicated Marcela et al. might have disposed of Malcom's body in a jungle area that was just across the border in the state of Nayarit.) But getting to the lab in Nayarit was a three-hour drive each way.

Brooke was supposed to give her victim impact statement on day four. It was a nail-biting situation. The judges decided to reconvene the trial earlier than expected, and Brooke was still hours away. While the prosecution stalled and tried to ask for another recess, Brooke and her security detail drove like mad buggers to try and reach the court in time. Navarro was forced to ask the defence if they minded a delay. They were indifferent and suggested Brooke's behaviour was disrespectful to the court. The judges were just starting to discuss whether they were going to allow the delay or insist that the prosecution begin their summary when one of the security guards indicated that Brooke had just walked into the building. When she finally took the stand, Brooke seemed a little scattered and her statement was inconsistent. She spent a lot of time thanking people rather than talking about what a massive emotional and financial burden this had been on her and her family. Nonetheless, the judges were interested in what she was saying, particularly when she read out a quote from her daughter:

> Marcela, the amount of pain that you have caused is unforgivable and unforgettable. My grandfather, Malcom, has done nothing but give to you. Your evilness destroyed all of that love and time that he was gonna continue giving us. I hope you realize that you have taken someone's life, a person who did nothing but love others and life. He didn't deserve your treatment or the end you gave him.

At the end of day four, the final activities were the closing statements. Juan took the lead and once again reviewed the narrative that built a case proving that, based on greed, Marcela and her son and brother had drugged and killed Malcom and then taken his money from his bank accounts and sold his house. As he went through the evidence, Juan cited legal precedents that supported using circumstantial evidence in this manner. It was a tight, comprehensive summary. The defence had little to say. They talked for some time when they made their summations, but all they could do was say that the evidence was fake and all the witnesses were coached. They did not offer any kind of alternative narrative that might explain the evening's events in another way. Juan remembered at one point they tried to suggest, "Well, the defence only said that, that Andrés is a young guy and he likes to party and he likes to go out and that is why the cell phone record was around Puerto Vallarta." He claimed the judges didn't buy the argument. The prosecution was allowed one final rebuttal of the defence's closing statements. Cynthia Bracamontes Rosales eviscerated the defence's complaints about the evidence and witnesses.

After that, Marcela, Martín, and Andrés were offered the chance to make a statement. They declined. The judges said they would have a verdict in 24 hours. Juan said that, despite his belief that they had presented a strong case, he was nonetheless nervous about the verdict:

> All the time, there is that kind of, of feeling that you don't know what their sentence will be because that is out of your hands. I mean, what is in my hands is all the job that has been done in the investigation and in the trial and the previous hearing that we had, but at that moment, there is nothing you can do.

I was also nervous about the verdict, as was Brooke.

We flew out of Puerto Vallarta the next morning. I was certain it would take the judges more than 24 hours to review the evidence and come to a decision. To our shock, the judges returned a verdict less than 24 hours after they'd recessed the court. We were still in the air on our way back to Canada – all three were guilty as charged. Brooke found out just as we touched down at Pearson Airport. "We all got on that plane not knowing what the verdict would be," she remembers. "We honestly had no idea. And when I landed, immediately, like I'm going to turn my phone on. And the first thing I saw pop up before I went in, obviously it just shows up on your phone, I could see all this confetti and thumbs up from the DA Juan and I was just like…" She gasps just remembering the emotion of the moment. "And I went in and he's like, 'Guilty, they're all guilty!'"

The judges reserved sentencing until Monday, April 17. When they handed the sentences down, it was crushing for Marcela, Martín, and Andrés: 56 years each. Juan said the sentences made a powerful statement:

> They got time in prison for 56 years and three months. That is a high, a high time in prison. It's actually one of the best sentences we have gotten. And then that is because we are argued and we explained the judges about the situation that this case of Malcom was going through in Mexico. I argued [to] the judges that Malcom did not have family or friends or close people in Mexico and his close people or his close circle was actually Marcela and the family, and he was betrayed by them. That is why the judges took this in consideration to give a high time in prison.

A 56-year sentence in Canada, if such a sentence were possible, would really only amount to about 18 years in prison before the person would be eligible for parole. Not so in Mexico. They will do the full 56 years unless they meet one of several conditions. They have to pay restitution to the state and to Brooke. "For doing that felony they have to pay their money for the state. As well, they were sentenced to pay money for Brooke," Juan told me when I asked him about it. "In this case we, we recognized Brooke as a victim, too. And they were sentenced to pay Brooke an amount of money that will be quantified later on in the process, as soon as Brooke has all the papers and documents that she can prove all the money that happen or she suffered for this, for what they did." If they pay restitution – whatever amount Brooke is asking for – they are eligible to serve only three-fifths of the sentence – around 43 years.

Brooke felt the sentence was harsh but ultimately for the good. "I'm not the person I was years ago," she said at the time.

> The anger's gone, even though I didn't see any remorse in the courtroom from any of them and they didn't take the opportunity to make a last-minute plea deal or speak on their own behalf. I don't have the anger and hatred towards them that I think a lot of people still do, maybe because I'm so worn out because it's been so long. Part of me is incredibly sad that three people's lives are probably gonna end in prison, that they'll never get a chance to go out and be decent members of society again, but that being said, I truly believe that they would have done something like this again. So they are where they have to be, but I'm not thrilled – like I'm not happy. I'm just happy that they're not going to hurt anyone else.

To be clear, Marcela and her family can file various appeals. They can file an *amparo* suit, claiming their rights have been violated, although Juan says he knew this could happen and the prosecution was extremely careful to run the case strictly according to legal procedures. Still, it's possible.

They can also ask an appeal judge for a review of the case. But they need a lawyer to do this, and they don't seem to have one at the moment. Given they were using a public defender for most of their case, and that public defenders don't usually appeal cases and that the three have little money, it's likely the three of them will spend the rest of their lives in jail.

For Brooke, what's more important about the decision was that the case she helped to create has now set a legal precedent in Mexico. According to Juan,

> Mexico is going through a huge problem in disappearance and all this kind of stuff. We are concerned and we are, we are aware about that problem. We are not trying to minimize it or we are

> not trying to make it like blind, we are concerned, we are aware what is happening, but this kind of felony is relatively new in the Mexican legislation, since 2017, or 18, there was this new felony, what it's called disappearance committed by particulars... that is the name of this felony. So there is not a lot of sentences in that felony. So, yes, this, I consider this makes a reference and sets a base line for future cases and we can even argue that a similar case was resolved in arguing those, arguing some, some things similarly, and that kind of stuff, like technical arguments and strategies for future cases.

Juan believes he still has work to do in this case. "I will be straight with you and with Brooke," he told me. "We are going to keep on working to find him. That cannot stop and that will never stop, that is something apart from the process of Marcela, Martín, and Andrés. We will keep on looking, on looking to find Malcom and looking all the places that he could possibly be."

Malcom's body has never been found.

EPILOGUE

There's an old saying that goes, "if you set out for revenge, first dig two graves." It's a saying that I think applies to Brooke's journey. I'm not saying she was motivated by revenge; rather I think she was motivated by a desire to do right by her father and to ensure that some kind of justice occurred. Nonetheless, this journey has cost Brooke a lot financially and emotionally, and in the massive amount of time she committed to seeing it through. Yet, oddly, when I asked Brooke about the impact this ordeal has had on her, she told me she believes it has been beneficial:

> I'd like to think I'm not so... what's the word I'm looking for? I'm not so reactive, I don't immediately fly off the handle if things aren't going my way or fall into a panic. Because I've so many times seen things... they were going well in the case and then they kind of crashed, and things that seemed they were playing out terribly and then suddenly they kind of ended up being a benefit or worked out to our advantage. So, I'm a lot calmer.

She acknowledges, however, that this transformation is not complete – there are still times when people just stay out of her way. Brooke admits that all they need to see is "that look" on her face and they know they should back off. She also acknowledges that during the course of this whole journey she's had numerous meltdowns. As Zab points out, "I remember her being in Mexico and she was just crying. She phoned me – it was two o'clock and she was just crying on the floor, yelling and screaming, 'Oh, I can't do this, I don't know why I'm here.'" Brooke also admits her behaviour has put stress on her whole family. "I know their patience with me has definitely changed over the last almost three years," she says. "There's not a lot of interest in talking about it anymore, or I can be cut off or the topic's changed."

Zab would have liked to see her drop the whole matter years ago. "I do wish she didn't do this," he says. "I think our family's suffered a bit; our relationship's suffered definitely." In the fall of 2021, Zab and Brooke separated, and since the trial Brooke has found a new person to share her life with. Despite the separation, Brooke believes Zab became reconciled to her determination to see this journey through. "He's made his peace with the whole thing and it's probably a little hard for him that I have not," she told me.

What's a bigger concern for Brooke is the impact this quest has had on her two daughters: "I think it's been really tough on my family." Brooke holds on to the hope that ultimately her two daughters will see some benefits from her fight for justice. "Like I hope that they will see this as a victory because they certainly had to lose a lot of their mother in the last almost three years…because I've been so focused on other things and that's been tough." Brooke is also saddened that her daughters will never really know Malcom. "They won't get to have him as they get older, because I think he's better with older children," she says. "I mean, he's very playful and little kids like him, but I think he's really better with teenagers and young adults. So I think it's, it's really sad they won't get to experience that."

Yet, despite the costs, for her family, her relationship, and her own emotional tranquility, none of that made her swerve from her course of action. As she says, "You gotta believe that good will triumph over evil. It's a very valuable thing to have, to have that belief, because it'll keep you going through the lower times too, right?"

On a personal note, I've spent a little time with Brooke's two daughters. I see them both as intelligent, charming, well-adjusted, kind, and considerate young women. They're a credit to Brooke as a mother. As for her relationship with Malcom, Brooke seems to have finally found some kind of peace. She seems to have forgiven her father for his early negligence and has only fond memories of their time together. And though it took many years, Brooke has also accepted that her father is dead, not just missing. She still remembers the exact moment this became a reality for her:

> We were pulling into the driveway and I got a call from one of my dad's close friends, April, and we were talking and she just said, "Brooke, he's dead, he's gone, we're not going to find him alive at this point, we have to realize that." And I think she said what was sitting there in the back of my mind but I was pushing that thought away. I had a massive angry breakdown in the car – everybody else got out; I did it by myself. So that was it, that was like when I made the switch to a different recovery. It started with finding him, he'll be okay, and then it became like "What state will his body be in?" and then it's like "Will there even be any body left?" And that's where we're at now.

Brooke had Malcom declared legally dead about a year and a half after he disappeared. "Either he's somewhere in the ocean and he's not coming back in any means there, or he's been buried or he's been burned or chopped up and buried. I like to imagine him in a jungle, a jungle that the GPS pinpoints, that we visited. I almost felt like he was there, and I'd like to think he's buried there and I think that that would be a beautiful place to have as your final resting place. I think that he would like that. I find it hard knowing he's so far away, but I think my father would think it's a wonderful thing to be buried in a jungle."

Brooke is starting to slowly move beyond this battle for justice. "I think I'm already starting to heal," she says. "Marcela, Martín, and Andrés are sitting in prison right now... I'm seeing my friends, I'm going out, I'm smiling. I'm not sitting in my bathtub every night [crying], so I'm already healing."

Brooke has also recently been more focused on helping others who have found themselves in the same position. The Mexican prosecutors asked her whether she would ever consider using her newly acquired investigative skills to help them liaise with other families from the United States and Canada. Brooke smiled when she told me that story, but I think that behind that smile there was a thought forming about what she could do to help others – what she might set out to do on her next crusade. "I am at peace," she says, "and I'm really happy and I'm trying to get to the point where I can say I'm proud of [what I did], that I contributed something good on this planet. I helped do something and I just have to work my mind around that still. I'm still, it's like such an easy cop-out to say it's surreal, I'm still in shock, but I think it'll take a bit longer to process everything that's happened."

Marcela, Andrés, and Martín are still in jail. They appealed their sentences in the fall of 2023 and lost. They will not be eligible for release until sometime after 2050. Brooke is still fighting to recover her father's money.

NOTES

1 "Gay Puerto Vallata," Gaytravel, August 28, 2024, https://www.gaytravel.com/gay-guides/puerto-vallarta.

2 "Number of Kidnapping Cases Reported in Mexico from 2015 to 2023," Statista Research Department, June 13, 2024, https://www.statista.com/statistics/979091/Mexico-number-kidnapping-cases/.

3 A note about Mexican names: Mexican names follow the Spanish naming custom, *doble apellido*, which is the tradition of using two surnames. A person has two surnames, first their father's paternal family name, then, second, their mother's paternal family name. When referring to someone by their last name only, it is common to just use their first surname.

4 "Jurisdictional Advance of Evidence," Criminal Court of the Second Judicial Circuit of San José, Mexico, July 30, 2004. Copy in author's possession.

5 Coralie Pring and Jon Vrushi, *Global Corruption Barometer Latin America & the Caribbean 2019: Citizens' Views and Experiences of Corruption* (Berlin, Germany: Transparency International, 2019), 18. https://images.transparencycdn.org/images/2019_GCB_LatinAmerica_Caribbean_Full_Report_200409_091428.pdf.

6 Centro de Justicia para la Paz y el Desarrollo (CEPAD), *Fiscalía a la deriva Informe a 5 ãnos de creación de la Fiscalía en Personas Desaparecidas de Jalisco* (Guadalajara, Jalisco, Mexico: CEPAD, 2022), 47, Fiscalia_a_la_deriva_Informe_a_5_anos_de.pdf.

7 "Observatory of Killed Journalists," UNESCO, October 3, 2024,

https://en.unesco.org/themes/safety-journalists/observatory/country/223773.

8 "Digital Security Risk Management," OECD, October 3, 2024, https://www.oecd.org/industry/tourism/MÉXICO%20TOURISM%20POLICY%20REVIEW_EXECUTIVE%20SUMMARY_ENG.pdf.

9 US Department of Justice, "Leader of $60 Million Internet Scam Pleads Guilty to Fraud and Money Laundering Charges," May 16, 2003, https://www.justice.gov/archive/criminal/cybercrime/press-releases/2003/waagePlea.htm.

10 Pring and Vrushi, *Global Corruption Barometer Latin America & the Caribbean*, 18.

11 Juan Camilo Jaramillo, "Entire Police Forces Continue to Be Arrested in Mexico," InSight Crime, August 21, 2019, https://insightcrime.org/news/brief/entire-police-forces-continue-arrested-México/.

12 Luz E. Nagle, "Corruption of Politicians, Law Enforcement, and the Judiciary in Mexico and Complicity across the Border," *Small Wars & Insurgencies* 21, no. 1 (2010): 95–122, doi:10.1080/09592310903561544.

13 "A Mexican Legal System Primer," Tecma, October 3, 2024, https://www.tecma.com/mexican-legal-system-primer/.

14 "General Structure of the Mexican Legal System," University of Arizona, James E. Rogers College of Law, Daniel F. Cracchiolo Law Library, https://law-arizona.libguides.com/c.php?g=1267358&p=9294226.

15 "Mexico, Events of 2019," World Report 2020, Human Rights Watch, October 3, 2020, https://www.hrw.org/world-report/2020/country-chapters/mexico.

16 "Justice for Victims of Violent Crime in Mexico Is Rare. Can Deaths of Nine Mormons Change That?" *The Washington Post*, November 8, 2019, https://www.washingtonpost.com/world/2019/11/08/justice-victims-violent-crime-mexico-is-rare-can-deaths-nine-mormons-change-that/.

17 "Mexican Unsolved Crime Rate Rockets," Deutsche Welle, September 29, 2016, https://www.dw.com/en/unsolved-crime-rate-in-mexico-climbs-to-93-percent/a-35919079.

18 "Failing Justice in Mexico: Institutional Weaknesses," Vision of Humanity, https://www.visionofhumanity.org/failing-justice-mexicos-institutional-weaknesses/.

19 "Failing Justice in Mexico: Institutional Weaknesses."

20 Jaylia Yan, "In Mexico, Justice Will Remain a Family Matter," GAB | *The Global Anticorruption Blog*, October 3, 2024, https://globalanticorruptionblog.com/2021/02/08/in-mexico-justice-will-remain-a-family-matter/.

21 Cody Copeland, "12 Judges in Jalisco under Investigation for Corruption," *Mexico News Daily*, November 15, 2019, https://mexiconewsdaily.com/news/12-judges-in-jalisco-under-investigation-for-corruption/.

22 "Mexico's Sheinbaum Sends Secondary Legislation on Judicial Reform Implementation," *Reuters*, October 7, 2024, https://www.reuters.com/world/americas/mexicos-sheinbaum-sends-secondary-bills-judicial-reform-implementation-congress-2024-10-07/.

ABOUT THE AUTHOR

Robert Osborne is an award-winning documentary filmmaker and investigative journalist. He's spent more than 25 years working for network television shows and developed a parallel career as a feature writer, providing articles for the *Toronto Star, The Globe and Mail,* and the *National Post.*

In 2012 he moved into the documentary field, first working as a script editor for the episode "The Beaver Whisperers" on CBC's *The Nature of Things*. During the past ten years, he researched, directed, wrote, and produced the documentaries *Unstoppable: The Fentanyl Epidemic, The Third Dive: The Death of Rob Stewart,* and *Malcom is Missing.*

He has won multiple Radio Television Digital News Association awards and a Canadian Association of Journalists award for investigative journalism. In 2009 he received a Citation of Merit from the Governor General's Michener Awards for a documentary on police accountability. In 2018 he won the Canadian Screen Award for Best Writing in a Documentary for *Unstoppable.*

He has published one previous book, also with RMB, *The Third Dive,* based on the documentary.